Santa Clara University

D0624907

08

COMPANY FARE

RONALD JOHNSON

SIMON & SCHUSTER

New York   London   Toronto   Sydney   Tokyo   Singapore

Simon & Schuster
Simon & Schuster Building
Rockefeller Center
1230 Avenue of the Americas
New York, New York 10020

Copyright © 1991 by Ronald Johnson

All rights reserved including the right of reproduction in whole
or in part in any form.
SIMON & SCHUSTER and colophon are registered trademarks
of Simon & Schuster Inc.

Designed by Deirdre C. Amthor

Manufactured in the United States of America

10   9   8   7   6   5   4   3   2   1

Library of Congress Cataloging in Publication Data

Johnson, Ronald, date.
    Company fare / Ronald Johnson.
        p.   cm.
    Includes index.
    1. Cookery.   I. Title.
    TX714.J63   1991
    641.5—dc20   90-26570
                                       CIP

ISBN 0-671-69510-X

For Dorothy
who taught me the virtues of the simple

Contents

Introduction

MOVIES HAVE PRESENTED US with raucous Roman banquets ad infinitum, and we've all read novels of the last century where so many are at table it was a rule to talk to neighbor on the right during soup, fish, and entree, and to neighbor on the left during roast, sweet and savory—a kind of culinary tennis match. Neither is today's idea of comfortable dining.

My theory is that conversation is always better than talk, and six is maximum, four better. I must admit to a group of eight friends who share roundabout, knowing each other so well we can nearly all talk at once and it would be understood. But to serve such you must own twice the service of silver and china if you don't want to wash up between courses, not to mention a large dining table. For this reason, except for desserts, I've geared the recipes here for four, though nearly all but roast chicken can be easily expanded for six or more.

To rethink how we dine has been a great preoccupation of the last decade, often with silly results. Great established cuisines have flooded young chefs with almost too many uprooted possibilities, new food products have preceded their known recipes, lust for the latest taste sensation has been the order of the day. Decreed, it seems, everything must be simultaneously hot, sweet, sour, rich, light, unusually placed on a plate, and garnished within an inch of its life. Surely we want fine food, but just as surely it should be simple and sensuous, and possible at home.

Much talk has been bandied about, too, as to whether the busy cook can turn out a meal in a half hour or less, and I say for family, yes, but these are exactly the minutes you need to welcome invited guests. So this is a book devoted to showing ways you can take little time and less rushed effort, even before company arrives, and still serve up a memorable affair. Frankly, I don't like to spend any more time in the kitchen than you, and practically none of it when dinner guests arrive. A dessert whipped up ahead, a main course and a side dish put together in a half hour, to be popped in the oven when guests arrive, is every host's prayer.

Of the many secrets I'd like to hand on is that guests really like to know what's going on in the kitchen, so unless yours is just a cubbyhole, it's fine to make that the heart of your hospitality. A bar can be dispensed there, while you stage-manage the first course, lay plates out, open wine, put a loaf of bread in a basket, and answer questions culinary or otherwise. It helps if you're practiced at any particular dish, in fact a rule of thumb is that experimenting on guests is not advisable.

The banner of the moment is for food without fats, and otherwise guilt free. However I think the signal remark of our time is Julia Child's "I don't think we should be afraid of our food" on a recent television interview. My personal belief is in the virtues of variety—to feel free to simply eat a salad one night, or a stir-fry of absolutely fresh vegetables, then settle in the next meal with a comfortable chop and buttery potato. I'm all for anything anyone wants to eat day-to-day, but I insist entertaining at home should be as expansive as at a restaurant—where, I notice, few count calories and most order dessert. So though there are dishes throughout this book any dieter would delight in, I haven't shied away from butter or cream when indispensable to a certain dish.

Sharing food, from first campfire to day after tomorrow, *is* civilization. Its secrets have been passed from no end of grandmothers and hunters, ancestors who have grown and caught and sowed and hooked ingredients, to those nowadays in a city apartment. But manners have not changed much in the way of simple hospitality. The very best you can summon from your larder in the way of salad, a little steak sauced to perfection, a sensuous dessert, a brave bottle of wine, should be presented with gusto, consumed and even commented on with gusto, everyone finding the world a little better place to be. What did Baucis and Philemon, welcoming visiting gods unaware to their hut's repast, do else?

IN THE
BEGINNING

Reconsidering the First Course

A SPRIGHTLY FIRST COURSE, like a concert overture, should just whet an appetite for major themes. Call it soup, salad, hors d'oeuvres, or just plain appetizers, it should be a plate to rouse one's palate yet reassure as to soundness of the meal to follow. In that light, and with belief in a new slimmed-down menu, let us begin, if not with a lengthily simmered soup, then at least to muster ourselves behind the inherited fish and/or cheese and/or salad courses, and come up with a flourish which will announce a fine dinner rather than punctuate it.

My prototype for this is Alice Waters's Hot Goat Cheese Salad, from Chez Panisse, in which slices of creamy goat cheese are marinated in fruity, green olive oil and fresh herbs, then drained and rolled in bread crumbs, and finally baked to set beside a salad of mixed baby greens. It quickly begot a lot of imitations and stood well to become a culinary cliché, but I argue this is a dish to be emulated like the classic Caesar salad. With one dish she propelled an industry to produce native rather than French goat's milk cheeses, brought freshest tiny *mesclun* lettuces to the supermarket, and sparked that array of virgin olive oils you see commonly everywhere.

I have stayed away here from real restaurant clichés, like Warm Duck Breast Salad, which can be both time consuming and pretentious, in favor of refreshing combinations you can put together in intervals while you vacuum the house, if necessary, or in the breeze of a last minute.

Stuffed Artichokes

4 medium-size artichokes
Lemon
1 cup fresh bread crumbs (see page 325)
1 cup coarsely grated Romano or Parmesan cheese
½ cup minced onion
1 clove garlic, minced
¼ cup minced parsley (preferably flat-leafed Italian)
Salt and freshly ground pepper
Olive oil

SERVES 4

THERE ARE *few things finer than artichokes simply boiled and served warm with a small bowl of melted butter and lemon to dip the leaves in as you eat, right down to the prize at bottom. But sometimes you want to honor company with a little more published effort, so stuffing is the way to go. A lot of artichoke recipes go overboard and what is essentially a delicate vegetable becomes both elaborate and leaden. I think this one is about right. Remember, artichokes can give wine a slight metallic aftertaste, so think twice about serving it with them. There's nothing wrong with a wineglass of water here, though I once heard a nationally famous writer embarrass himself and his hostess in such a situation by raising the glass as if in toast and remarking, "And I particularly admire this fine white wine."*

Trim stalks off artichokes, then cut about an inch off the tops (a serrated knife does this best). Remove tough outer leaves and discard. Snip off the ends of the leaves around the artichokes with scissors. With a spoon, remove and discard the flimsy inner leaves, then scoop out the chokes. Rub all cut surfaces with a little lemon to prevent discoloration, and place in a bowl of water.

In a large bowl combine bread crumbs, cheese, onion, garlic, parsley, and salt and pepper to taste. A food processor does all the chopping nicely, but add the cheese at the last or it will be ground too fine.

Drain the artichokes and pat dry with paper towels. Spread the leaves apart and tuck in a little of the stuffing, then fill the centers *loosely* with the mixture. Sprinkle the filling with a little oil. Place in a large kettle and fill with water about halfway up the artichokes. Add a good pinch of salt and a couple of tablespoons of oil to the water.

Bring to a boil, cover, turn down heat, and bring to a simmer. Cook 30 to 40 minutes, or until tender at the base when tested with a pointed knife. Remove from the pot and serve hot or at room temperature.

WINE SUGGESTION: water with a slice of lemon

Young Stewed Artichokes Provençale

12 small artichokes (before
    they develop a choke)
½ cup dry white wine
½ cup olive oil
Salt and freshly ground pep-
    per

SERVES 4

AT THE BEGINNING of artichoke season (or off and on throughout the year in California) you sometimes find artichokes so young as not to yet have a choke formed. This is a delicious way to serve them up, with, of course, French bread to sop up the oil.

Strip off any tough-looking extra leaves, trim the bottom stems, and cut artichokes in half vertically. Place in frying pan large enough to hold them all in one layer and add wine, oil, and water to cover.

Bring to a boil, lower heat to medium, cover, and simmer 20 to 30 minutes, or until tender. Uncover, raise the heat, and cook until all the liquid boils off and the artichokes are frying in the oil. Salt and pepper lightly and serve warm or at room temperature.

WINE SUGGESTION: a dry white

Asparagus with Two Cheeses

2 pounds asparagus
4 tablespoons butter
Salt and freshly ground pepper
Several drops lemon juice
⅓ cup freshly grated Parmesan cheese
⅓ cup freshly grated Gruyère cheese

SERVES 4

ASPARAGUS PARMESAN is a fine and lovely dish, but this goes it just that extra bit better.

Trim asparagus to about 6 inches. Simmer in enough lightly salted water to cover the bottom of a wide frying pan until just tender—don't overcook or you will have limp asparagus. Drain and return the spears to the pan with 2 tablespoons of butter, salt and pepper to taste, and some lemon juice. Toss just to coat and divide among individual ramekins. In a small bowl combine the cheeses. Sprinkle asparagus with the cheese and set aside. This can sit until you are ready to serve dinner.

Heat the broiler. Put the ramekins under the flame until the cheese just melts. Meanwhile, place the remaining 2 tablespoons butter in a small saucepan and cook over high heat just until it turns a light nut brown. Pour the sizzling butter over the asparagus and serve at once.

WINE SUGGESTION: a medium-bodied red

Asparagus and Prosciutto

1½ pounds asparagus
3 ounces thinly sliced prosciutto
3 tablespoons grated Parmesan cheese
6 tablespoons butter
Lemon wedges

SERVES 4

ONE OF THE BEST WAYS to set the tone of a fine dinner, these not only look great but also the contrast between the sweet asparagus and salty prosciutto is one you'll want to linger over with a glass of wine and some crusty bread.

Trim asparagus to about 6 inches. Place in a pot of boiling, salted water to cover and cook 5 minutes, or until they test done at the bottom of a stalk. Drain well. Divide into 4 bundles and wrap each with 2 slices of prosciutto. There should be an inch of asparagus showing at the tops and bottoms.

Butter a baking dish, lay the bundles in, and sprinkle with cheese. These may be prepared up to this point and set aside, covered with plastic wrap, until you are ready to bake them.

To do so, heat the oven to 400 degrees and bake about 3 minutes, or until the cheese melts. Meanwhile, place the butter in a small saucepan and cook over high heat until it sizzles. Place the bundles on warm serving plates and pour the sizzling butter over all. Serve at once with lemon wedges on the side.

WINE SUGGESTION: a medium-bodied red

Asparagus with Sun-Dried Tomatoes and Pine Nuts

1½ pounds asparagus
2 tablespoons olive oil
3 tablespoons sun-dried toma-
    toes in oil, slivered
1 tablespoon oil from the to-
    matoes
3 tablespoons pine nuts,
    lightly toasted
Salt

SERVES 4

I CALL THIS my Italian "stir fry," and, actually, with a mound of rice it could make a lovely lunch dish for two or a romantic, light late supper.

Snap off the tough asparagus stems—they will come apart where the tenderness begins. Slice diagonally in about 1-inch lengths, reserving the tips. Drop the sliced stems into boiling, salted water and cook 2 minutes, then add tips and cook another minute. Drain immediately and run cold water over them to stop the cooking. The asparagus can be prepared ahead.

Heat olive oil in a large frying pan, then add the asparagus and toss for 1 or 2 minutes over medium-high heat. Add tomatoes and their oil, toss a few times, then add nuts and toss again. Taste for crispness (the asparagus should still be firm) and seasoning. Salt lightly and serve at once on warm plates.

WINE SUGGESTION: a medium-bodied red

Avocados Vinaigrette

½ cup olive oil

1 teaspoon Dijon-style mustard

2 tablespoons lemon juice or wine vinegar

1 teaspoon minced parsley

Salt and freshly ground pepper

2 ripe avocados

2 Belgian endives, separated into leaves

SERVES 4

A CLASSIC: suave, rich avocado cradling a pool of sharp vinaigrette, perfect to be spooned up. These days, always on the supermarket shelf, no longer an exotic, we seem resigned to use the avocado as mere salad fodder instead of in its star role. From the days they were called "alligator pears," avocados have been served with a vinaigrette. I have a 1914 cookbook (not a good year for publication) that presents Avocados Vinaigrette so: "Make a hollow in a shallow square of ice with a hot iron; place the pears in this, evenly arranged with the stem end in center, and cover the edge of the ice with sprigs of pretty green." This, for a casual supper at home. . . . Easier by far, I like to ray endive leaves around them, the better to scoop out the avocado flesh—slightly bitter crisp against rich softness. And pass the vinaigrette. As host, take the first scoop yourself.

To make the vinaigrette, in a screw-top jar combine oil, mustard, lemon juice or wine vinegar, parsley, and salt and pepper to taste. Cover tightly and shake well. This can be prepared ahead and shaken again when ready to use.

Just before serving, halve and pit the avocados. Place avocados on 4 plates and arrange rays of about 6 or so endive leaves around them. Fill the avocado cavities with vinaigrette and pass the rest at table for guests to sprinkle.

WINE SUGGESTION: a dry white

Avocados with Consommé Madrilène

1 can Consommé Madrilène
2 ripe avocados
1 lemon, cut into wedges
½ pound cooked shrimp (optional)

SERVES 4

IF YOU USE a good brand of Consommé Madrilène, such as Crosse & Blackwell, this is a ravishing contrast of texture, flavor, and color. This used to be a staple of "ladies' luncheons" but has gone out of favor, for no particular reason I can fathom.

Melt the consommé in a saucepan set over medium-low heat, then place in the refrigerator until it gets syrupy, about 30 minutes.

Halve and pit avocados. Spoon the thickened consommé into their cavities, spreading it to cover all the flesh. If the consommé isn't quite of coating consistency, return it to the refrigerator along with the avocados. When slightly thicker, coat the avocados again. Refrigerate any remaining consommé. The avocados can be prepared hours ahead, covered loosely with plastic wrap, and refrigerated.

Serve with lemon wedges and the rest of the consommé (broken up into small pieces with a fork) placed at the base of the avocado. A sprinkling of small shrimp would not be gilding this particular lily.

WINE SUGGESTION: a medium-bodied red

Avocados with Pistachios

½ cup shelled pistachios
½ cup olive oil
2 to 3 tablespoons lime juice
1 tablespoon rum
1 clove garlic, slightly flat-
    tened and peeled
Salt and freshly ground pep-
    per
2 ripe avocados
4 Boston lettuce leaves

SERVES 4

A GREENY EXTRAVAGANZA from a friend in Los Angeles—home of the avocado.

Rub pistachios between paper towels to remove most of the outer papery coating, then chop coarsely. Set aside. This can be done ahead. To make the dressing, in a screw-top jar combine oil, lime, rum, garlic, and salt and pepper to taste. This also can be done well ahead.

To serve, halve, pit, and peel avocados. Cut each of the halves lengthwise into ½-inch-thick slices and lay them in a fan over the lettuce leaves. Sprinkle with the chopped nuts. Shake the dressing well, remove the garlic, and drizzle the dressing over the avocados.

WINE SUGGESTION: a medium-bodied red

Caponata in Red Pepper Shells

1 medium-size eggplant
(about 1½ pounds)
Salt
2 stalks celery (preferably inner stalks)
¼ cup plus 1 tablespoon olive oil
1 cup chopped onion
1 1-pound can Italian plum tomatoes
Freshly ground pepper
½ teaspoon dried basil
⅓ cup coarsely chopped black or green olives (preferably Italian)
1½ tablespoons capers
1 teaspoon anchovy paste (optional)
1 tablespoon sugar
2 teaspoons red wine vinegar
3 tablespoons minced parsley
2 to 3 large red bell peppers, roasted (see page 331)

SERVES 4 TO 6

CAPONATA IS DELICIOUS on its own, but makes a superb presentation stuffed into pepper shells. There are also fine bottled versions in good food shops that are just as good as home-made, so you only have to roast the pepper shells. The size of the peppers themselves will determine how many you buy. The very large peppers are fine for two servings, but smaller ones will serve only one—and if you can't purchase red peppers go ahead and use the ubiquitous green. The caponata here will probably even stretch to serve eight if you like, but whatever you have left over will make a fine lunch next day. For a less `formal meal, this dish makes a good companion with grilled meats at a barbecue.

Cut eggplant into 1-inch cubes—either peeled or unpeeled. Place in a colander and sprinkle liberally with salt. Drain cubes for 30 minutes or more.

Cut the celery into small dice. If using outer stalks, peel them with a vegetable peeler before cutting into dice (inner stalks need not be peeled). Drop celery into boiling water for a minute or so, then drain.

Heat 1 tablespoon of olive oil in a large saucepan and sauté onion and celery for several minutes, until the onion is translucent. Meanwhile, place tomatoes and their juice in a food processor and whirl until well chopped (or put through a food mill). Add the tomatoes, pepper, and basil to the onions and celery and cook over medium-low heat. Check the seasoning, but be sparing if you add salt, as there will be salt from the eggplant, capers, and olives added later. Cook until all the liquid has boiled away.

Run water over the eggplant to wash away some of the salt, then pat dry. Put remaining oil in a large frying pan set over high heat, add the eggplant, and toss until lightly browned. Combine with tomato mixture, olives, capers, anchovy paste (if desired), sugar, and vinegar. Let cool to room temperature and stir in parsley. Cover and refrigerate.

Clean roasted peppers. Fill each half with caponata and refrigerate until serving time.

WINE SUGGESTION: a medium-bodied red or dry white

Cauliflower Vinaigrette with Tapenade Croutons

1 large head cauliflower
½ cup vinaigrette made with
    2 tablespoons lemon juice
    and ½ cup olive oil
3 tablespoons minced parsley
2 red bell peppers, roasted
    (see page 331)
12 slices French bread, cut
    into ¼-inch slices
1 cup tapenade, homemade
    (see page 80) or store
    bought

SERVES 4

THIS SOUNDS LIKE *a lot of bother, but no step takes long in itself, and each can be done at any time. Besides, I think the result is worth it. In a rush, on the way home from work you can snatch bottled red peppers (or pimientos) and a jar of tapenade.*

Cut leaves and core from the cauliflower and separate into florets, each approximately the same size. Drop into boiling, salted water and cook about 5 minutes. The cauliflower is done when the tip of a small, sharp knife inserted into a stem goes in easily. Drain immediately and run under cold water. Place in a bowl while still warm and toss with vinaigrette and parsley. This can be kept several hours at room temperature or refrigerated, tossing now and again.

Clean roasted peppers, then cut into ½-inch strips. To make croutons, place bread in a hot oven and toast 10 minutes or so. Check now and again—the bread should be crisp, but not as dry as melba toast, which crumbles when you bite it. The croutons can also be made ahead. The tapenade should be at room temperature.

To serve, divide cauliflower among 4 plates, top with strips of pepper, then drizzle any vinaigrette left in the bowl over the top. Spread tapenade on the croutons and place 3 croutons around each serving of cauliflower.

WINE SUGGESTION: a medium-bodied red or dry white

Cauliflower, Watercress, Black Olives, and Blue Cheese

1 can large, pitted black olives
2 tablespoons plus dash of
    white wine vinegar
1 medium-size head cauli-
    flower
1 large bunch watercress
4 tablespoons crumbled blue
    cheese
¼ cup olive oil
2 tablespoons mayonnaise
Salt and freshly ground pep-
    per

SERVES 4

THIS IS a dish I picked up from the usually rather stuffy Picayune Original Creole Cookbook, *where it is titled "Choufleur à la Roquefort." There it is called "an opening course" with which "you will gain new renown with your family and friends." In my version, I nudge a little flavor with the olives, and prefer my cauliflower a trifle steamed rather than raw . . . and why not some of our native blue cheese?*

Drain olives and let marinate in a dash of vinegar for 30 minutes or so. Trim cauliflower into florets, drop into boiling, salted water, and cook just a minute. Drain and reserve. Remove any large stems from the watercress and separate into edible branches. If it seems limp, place in a bowl of water to crisp, then dry with paper towels. Drain the olives and stuff them with 2 tablespoons of crumbled cheese—fingers are just fine for this.

To make the dressing, in a small screw-top jar shake oil, 2 tablespoons vinegar, mayonnaise, remaining cheese, and salt and pepper to taste, just enough to incorporate the cheese. All of this can be done ahead.

To serve, cover 4 plates with a base of watercress and strew with cauliflower and stuffed olives. Sprinkle with the dressing and present at the table.

WINE SUGGESTION: a dry white

Oh, Caviar!

Once tasted, never enough. Twice in my life I've found almost surfeit, though beggar at the feast. The first was an invitation to accompany a fellow poet to the legendary haunts of his Aunt Honey, for Christmas, high up in a fashionable New York apartment. Just an undergraduate at Columbia, I had entered the lair of my first (but not last) dragon.

One whole chilled pound of beluga was set temptingly out, and to be enthralled, I thought, must be easy. The tree lifted gifts and more gifts to unwrap. It was signaled that perhaps after we knelt with each new surprise from her beloved accountants or relatives (more or less, we gathered, on-and-off in "the will"), we might help ourselves to a polite spoonful. Willingly we—the poet, the maid, and I—got right down again under that Tiffany-laden tree for more loot, obedient as trained lap dogs. It was not enough.

My second was a summons on the phone from one of Aspen, Colorado's, most endearing residents: "Do you know the So-and-sos? They're giving a hell of a Bash for their new house, all very Nouveau of course, and there'll be a line of footmen, *flambeaux* up the drive, and I know you wouldn't want to go but I hear there's to be a Mountain of Caviar." "Ah," I said, and we went.

Every word, true. All, along with the suckling pig centerpiece, I to this day can't take my eyes off. Nor can I the snapshot of us few anointed, poised with tiny silver spoons to dig in, around the base of a three-foot cone of chipped ice tiered with six tins of imported caviar, each round darkly sparkling. Quickly, blissfully, we tucked in. By the time the crowd elbowed in we'd retreated, polite before the much too much, smiling almost to satiety, past the remains of the pig still suckling its apple, down along the *flambeaux* and liveried footmen, to our Volkswagens and home.

Since . . . a spoon or two at best. Any lucky enough to buy or beg a spoonful of true caviar, though, should accompany it with brown bread sliced thin, and serve it in its own container set on crushed ice, with a few wedges of lemon beside, mainly for color rather than actual squeeze. And then the glass of just-popped champagne—leave to Russians their chilled, numbing vodka. A bite, then sip: The two bounce ghost bubbles off each other, dry champagne and caviar. Who would ask enough?

Celery, Mushroom, and Parmesan Salad

2 cups thinly sliced celery
2 cups thinly sliced mushrooms
¼ cup fruity olive oil
1 tablespoon lemon juice
Salt and freshly ground pepper
Wedge of Parmesan cheese

SERVES 4

THIS YEAR-ROUND Italian salad makes a fine first course with a good crusty bread and a glass of either red or white wine. Its simple combination of flavors and textures should not be tampered with much in the way of a fancier vinaigrette with herbs, mustard, onions, garlic, etc. Though the Italians sometimes add, when available, a few fresh porcini mushrooms— that is something else.

Toss celery, mushrooms, oil, lemon juice, and salt and pepper to taste in a bowl. This can be made an hour or so ahead—but don't let sit too long or the mushrooms will get too soft.

To serve, divide among serving plates. With a swivel vegetable peeler, slice off strips of the cheese over the salads. They will fall off in broad curls, and you will want 4 or 5 per serving.

WINE SUGGESTION: a dry white or medium-bodied red

Celery Root Rémoulade

1 pound celery root
Juice of ½ lemon
Salt
½ cup mayonnaise
1 tablespoon Dijon-style mustard
1 tablespoon red or white wine vinegar
1 tablespoon minced parsley
1 tablespoon minced fresh tarragon (optional)
4 tender lettuce leaves

SERVES 4

AFTER A TRIP eating and sight-seeing through France, I found Celery Root Rémoulade, with a poke at the pâté and a few crusts of bread, and a glass of straw-colored wine, just enough to see me through another night's five-course spread. This knobby, hairy root, celeriac, as the French name it, is now found in many supermarkets. If you haven't patience to cut the matchsticks you can grate it coarsely, but some of the magic is lost.

Peel celery root well and cut into julienne matchsticks. These should really be thin, or the result won't have the proper consistency. Place in a bowl and sprinkle with lemon juice and salt to taste. Toss well and let marinate for at least 30 minutes. Rinse in cold water, drain, and pat dry with paper towels.

Mix the rest of the ingredients well and toss with the celery root. This can be made in the morning and refrigerated until serving time. When ready, serve on lettuce leaves.

WINE SUGGESTION: a dry white

Simpson's Jellied Cheese

1 teaspoon unflavored gelatin
½ cup dry white wine
2 tablespoons each grated
  Parmesan, Gruyère, Stil-
  ton, and Cheddar cheese
1 teaspoon Dijon-style mus-
  tard
Salt
Cayenne pepper
½ cup heavy cream
Watercress and/or arugula
Olive oil
Vinegar
French bread

SERVES 4

INSTEAD OF mousse au frommage, London's famous Simpson's sticks to its English guns and calls this "jellied cheese." It is not a dish you would go out and buy cheese especially for, but one which can use up bits and pieces, if not dried out or otherwise beyond hope. Goat cheese is delightful and gives a mysterious tang, or you might simply try about one-third Parmesan to two-thirds blue or Roquefort cheese. In any case it never fails to delight even the more discriminating guest.

Stir gelatin and wine together in the top of a double boiler. After 5 minutes set over simmering water and stir until dissolved. Place in refrigerator until it becomes a mush.

In a small bowl combine cheeses, mustard, a pinch of salt, and a dash of cayenne. Whirl gelatin in a food processor until fluffy, then add the cheese mixture and process until smooth. Beat cream until stiff, then fold in the cheese mixture and taste for salt. Divide the mixture among 4 lightly greased ½-cup molds, cover with plastic wrap, and refrigerate until set.

To serve, preheat oven to 350 degrees. Meanwhile, wash greens well, spin dry or pat with paper towels, and divide among plates. Sprinkle with a little olive oil and vinegar. Slice bread diagonally in thin slices (3 or 4 per person), place on a baking sheet, and put in oven until dried out and lightly toasted. Unmold jellied cheese onto the plates by first dipping molds into a bowl of hot tap water then hitting them with a smart rap onto the plates. Place warm toasts around and serve at once.

WINE SUGGESTION: a dry white

Warm Roquefort Creams and Salad

⅔ cup crumbled Roquefort
  cheese
¼ cup heavy cream
2 egg yolks
¼ cup milk
Mixed lettuces or garden-fresh
  tomato slices and fresh basil
  leaves
Vinegar
Olive oil
Salt and freshly ground pepper
French or Italian bread

SERVES 4

THESE ARE purely wonderful spooned out and eaten with salad, or perhaps spread on bread as you eat. You may think while you're making the creams that they will need salt, but the cheese is salty enough, I think. Try them at first this way and see what you think.

Preheat oven to 325 degrees. Put cheese and cream in a food processor and whirl until well mixed (the cheese doesn't have to be completely pureed). Add yolks and milk and whirl just to combine. Butter 4 ½-cup ramekins and divide the mixture among them. Place in a baking dish and pour boiling water around until it comes two-thirds the way up the ramekins. Bake 30 minutes, or until set and a very pale gold on top. Remove and let sit until warm—or you can let these cool completely and reheat in the oven.

To serve, toss greens with a very little vinegar, oil, and salt and pepper. Or if you are serving tomatoes, salt and pepper them lightly and drizzle with vinegar and oil, then fan them out on plates with a basil leaf tucked beside each slice. Place the Roquefort cream on the side and serve with slices of French of Italian bread.

WINE SUGGESTION: a dry white

Salad
Perigordine

4 cups loosely packed mixed
  salad greens
1 cup walnuts
Goat cheese, such as Montrachet, sliced into 4 ½-inch
  rounds
Walnut oil
Wine vinegar
Salt and freshly ground pepper

SERVES 4

THIS IS kissing cousin to Alice Waters's Hot Goat Cheese Salad, Chez Panisse, and perhaps even better with all those crunchy walnuts.

Wash greens and either spin dry or pat gently with paper towels. Break walnuts up with your hands into large pieces and toast them lightly in the oven—don't brown them, just heat them up a bit, then cool them. Coat the cheese with walnut oil and place in a baking pan.

To serve, place greens on plates and lightly sprinkle first with walnut oil, then a tiny bit of vinegar and salt and pepper to taste. There's no need for a full-scale vinaigrette here, for you want most to taste the other ingredients. Sprinkle the cheese lightly with pepper and either place under a broiler until warmed through or bake several minutes at 450 degrees. Place cheese beside the greens, sprinkle with nuts, and serve.

WINE SUGGESTION: a dry white

Baked Feta Cheese with Red Peppers and Basil

4 ½-inch slices feta cheese
Fruity olive oil
3 large red bell peppers,
    roasted (see page 331)
Fresh basil leaves
Juice of ½ lemon
Salt and freshly ground pep-
    per
Freshly made bread crumbs
    for dredging (see page 325)
1 can flat anchovies (or black
    Greek or Italian olives)

SERVES 4

FETA BAKES as well as creamy goat cheese and may be easier to find. If you have a choice of different ones, try them all and choose which you like best. Some are a lot less salty and slightly more creamy. With all the color and flavor of the sunny Mediterranean this first course is every bit as good as the more refined versions.

Place cheese slices in a shallow dish and pour enough oil over them to cover. Marinate in the refrigerator for several hours. Clean roasted peppers, then cut vertically into 1½-inch strips. Lay out on a platter alternately with whole basil leaves. Pour over ¼ cup oil, lemon juice, and salt and pepper to taste. Let sit for an hour or so, spooning the dressing over them now and again.

To serve, preheat oven to 450 degrees. Drain the cheese, reserving the oil for other dressings, and roll in bread crumbs. Bake them 5 minutes. While they bake, arrange peppers alternately with basil leaves in a fan on 4 serving plates. Sprinkle the lemon dressing over, lay the hot cheese beside them, and decorate with a couple of anchovies or a small pile of olives. Serve at once while the cheese is hot.

WINE SUGGESTION: a dry white

Chicken Liver Pâté

1 pound chicken livers
¼ pound mushrooms
¼ cup parsley
¼ cup shallots or green on-
    ions
¾ pound butter
¼ teaspoon dried thyme
½ teaspoon salt
Pinch each of powdered
    cloves, ginger, and white
    pepper
1 bay leaf
2 tablespoons cognac
½ cup dry Madeira
8 to 10 Boston lettuce leaves
Cornichons
French bread or dry toast
    points

SERVES 8 TO 10

I HAVE a favorite coarse pâté made with five different meats in one form or another, either marinated in white wine or brandy, which takes a good two days to make and costs about thirty dollars. Needless to say, I only make it for Christmas and New Year's. This, however, is very easily put together and makes as fine a show as any but foie gras itself.

Rinse livers, pat dry with paper towels, and cut in half. Place mushrooms, parsley, and shallots in a food processor and finely mince. Melt ¼ pound (½ cup) of butter in a large frying pan set over medium-high heat. Add livers and toss to coat well, then add the minced ingredients along with thyme, salt, spices, and bay leaf. Cook, stirring often, until the livers firm up but are still a little pink inside. Warm the cognac in a small saucepan, set alight with a match, and pour over the livers. Stir until the flames die down, then add the Madeira. Heat to simmering, then turn off heat and let come to room temperature. Remove the bay leaf.

Scoop the mixture into a food processor and whirl until smooth. Divide the rest of the butter into pats and add 1 pat at a time. Process until smooth, then taste for salt. Pour into a 4- to 5-cup loaf pan, cover with plastic wrap pressed down on the top of the mixture, and chill overnight. The pâté will keep a week in the refrigerator, or it can be frozen for longer periods.

To serve, wash and dry a lettuce leaf for each person, top with a good slice of pâté, and make a little pile of cornichons at the side. Serve with bread or toast to spread the pâté on.

WINE SUGGESTION: a medium-bodied red or a dry white

Stuffed Clams

12 large clams (or 18
  medium-size)
4 tablespoons butter
2 shallots, minced
2 cloves garlic, minced
1 cup fresh bread crumbs (see
  page 325)
2 tablespoons minced parsley
¼ cup dry white wine
Salt and freshly ground pepper

SERVES 4

*I AM an advocate of the way shallots and garlic together make
something better than either alone. This is a prime example, to
serve with a full-bodied white wine and a good loaf of bread to
break.*

Wash and clean the clams. Place in a large saucepan
with ½ cup water, cover, and steam over high heat just
until they open. Pick out the meat and discard any tough
parts, then finely chop. Reserve half of the shells.

Preheat oven to 350 degrees. Heat 2 tablespoons of
butter in a small pan. When it sizzles, sauté shallots and
garlic over low heat. Remove from the flame and stir in
half of the bread crumbs, the parsley, and wine. Stir in
minced clams and season with salt and pepper to taste.
Divide stuffing among the clam shells.

Melt the remaining butter in a small pan set over medium heat. Stir in the other half of the bread crumbs and
keep stirring until they brown lightly. Sprinkle over the
clams and bake 15 minutes, or until hot and golden.
Serve at once.

WINE SUGGESTION: a full-bodied white

Corn on the Cob

The old saw goes that you should put the pot on to boil before picking the corn, though my method is to shuck it, rub off the silk, trim the ends with a knife, plunk the ears in a kettle of cold water, and turn on the heat. When the pot comes to a boil, the corn is done. The corn can sit in that turned-off pot and is better there than on the table for serving. Anyone will eat at least two. They should be hot so the butter slathers over, naturally.

I read recipes here and there attempting to make this exquisite simplicity into something for jaded palates: butter with chili powder, herbs, red pepper puree, and—unbelievably—peanut butter! I am even guilty of a recipe that places the ear of corn on top of a mild red chile sauce swirled with lime cream in my *Southwestern Cooking: New and Old*. That is a delicious bit of overkill, but it *is* overkill. In fact, I don't think this dish needs even bread or wine to get in the way.

Summers, when we can find corn picked that day in the city market, I can't think of a better way to commence a meal, especially for foreigners to our culinary shores. Nothing could be more democratic than the give-and-take with butter knives, rituals with salt and pepper, and general native know-how about how exactly to eat the object (no two people chomp the row a same way). People are always looking for something which is more American than apple pie, and this is it.

Crab
Bagnarotte

1 cup mayonnaise
2 teaspoons brandy
2 teaspoons lime juice
2 teaspoons tomato paste
   (preferably double concentrate from a tube)
1 teaspoon grated fresh ginger
4 Belgian endives
2 cups crabmeat
Lemon wedges

SERVES 4

THIS IS my version of Crab Louis, usually served on shredded iceberg lettuce with a drab pinkish sauce neither very good nor well suited to delicate crabmeat. Though I use lime rather than lemon, a good tomato paste instead of catsup, and have sneaked in fresh ginger for Worcestershire, I still call this after a sauce I learned from Alexander Watt's Simple French Cookery *published in 1960. It is also a superb dip for fresh vegetables or shrimp. A dab left makes a lovely addition to a simple vinaigrette. Actually, if some is in the refrigerator, I can't resist dipping a finger in.*

Mix together mayonnaise, brandy, lime juice, tomato paste, and ginger, cover with plastic wrap, and refrigerate an hour or more to mellow.

Discard any discolored leaves from the endives. Sever at the root end and place some of the largest leaves on 4 plates to make a star pattern. Cut the inner leaves into rings and scatter these at the center. Divide the crabmeat among the plates, placing over the cut endive, then top each with a spoonful of sauce.

Serve with lemon wedges and the remaining sauce in a small bowl for guests to add as they wish.

WINE SUGGESTION: a fruity white

Crab Cakes Maryland

3 slices white homestyle bread
⅓ cup olive oil
3 eggs, separated
½ teaspoon Dijon-style mustard
1 teaspoon Worcestershire sauce
Salt
¾ pound crabmeat
Paprika
2 tablespoons butter
Arugula leaves or tender lettuce
6 cherry tomatoes, halved
Lemon wedges

SERVES 4

MARYLAND CRAB CAKES are traditionally served with coleslaw, but they can have a more elegant presentation easily. I particularly like how the meaty taste of arugula contrasts with the sweet crab, with cherry tomatoes for color.

The traditional way to do the bread is to cut off the crusts, sprinkle with oil, and then, after it saturates completely, tear it into shreds with forks. Easier is to trim the bread, cut into thirds, and in a food processor with a metal blade process several turns or just until the bread is broken up. Pour the oil through the shoot with a few more turns and let sit until needed.

Beat the yolks lightly with mustard, Worcestershire, and a good pinch of salt. Mix with bread and crabmeat, then beat the egg whites stiff and fold them into the mixture. Shape into 8 oval cakes and dust lightly with paprika. Then sauté in bubbling butter just until golden on both sides. These can be made about 30 minutes before, set to dry on paper towels, and quickly reheated in the oven.

Wash and stem arugula and lay it out in a fan. Place the hot crab cakes over and decorate with cherry tomatoes and a lemon wedge.

WINE SUGGESTION: a dry white or dry rosé

Cracked Crab al Fresco (Local Delicacies)

Extracting the last moist sweet morsel from a local crab claw, I remember the late poet Robert Duncan evaluating, on the verge of a cross-country reading tour, each stop in terms of fresh fish, neighborhood cheeses, and stray ethnic noshes he might drum up along the way. "Mind, you have to know someone there," he cautioned. "You must make your way round hostesses who want to cook out of the newest gourmet magazine, and cross your fingers—but then!"

I was relieved he arrived back licking his chops, and glad to say pride still holds sway in the sticks. On foot over thirty years ago, hiking the Appalachian Trail from Georgia to New York with another poet, Jonathan Williams, we marveled as much at a sudden patch of wild garlic, added to spark the evening freeze-dried soup, as a drop into a Virginia town drugstore that served, as a listed specialty, grilled glazed doughnuts. They were so culinarily startling I still savor the effect, though I know even if I had at home one of those drugstore press grills for cheese sandwiches, I could never reproduce that first, starved for novelty effect.

Ever since that hike I've known, though, what real hunger meant, and that true refreshment was just sitting down with a cold tart lemonade offered off a mountain porch. It led me also to firmly believe that every household, with any connection to the past or the land, holds at least one culinary secret, and each hamlet, town, or city prides a different dish their own. But you must ask the way!

Fresh from army barracks, I remember visiting my great-uncle, at our farthest family outpost in balmy Los Angeles, to be served (snow falling elsewhere) half a ripe papaya with toast slices made from whole grains. We sat on that terrace, under the jacaranda tree, with petals falling in our coffee, and I began to understand the connections, vivid and vital, between food and travel.

So years later, living in San Francisco, when a friend or stranger turns up I step them out to the nearest sidewalk where we can sit and crack Dungeness crab just caught from the bay, with a warm sourdough loaf to break open, pats of sweet butter on ice, and a sun-shafted glass of white wine from vines just a few slopes away. And conversation. Certainly I could do this all at home, but in San Francisco, like Paris, often the truest is just off the streets.

Eggplant with Mint and Cherry Tomatoes

1 large eggplant (at least 1½
   pounds)
Salt
¼ cup olive oil
1 tablespoon white wine vinegar
1 teaspoon sugar
¼ cup chopped fresh mint,
   plus 4 sprigs for garnish
1 clove garlic, minced
2 cups cherry tomatoes,
   halved
French bread

SERVES 4

A SICILIAN dish that is—for those who admire eggplant—as refreshing as a summer breeze, particularly before lamb or veal chops.

Chop stem from the eggplant and, leaving the skin on, cut into ½-inch discs, then slice into ½-inch strips. Place in a colander set over a plate or bowl, sprinkle well with salt, toss, and let drain for an hour. Rinse eggplant with water to remove salt, then dry on paper towels.

Heat oil in a frying pan until hot but not smoking. Fry eggplant in batches, stirring just until lightly colored—2 or 3 minutes. Remove to a bowl as you cook them. If necessary, use more oil toward the end. When all cooked, add vinegar, sugar, ¼ cup mint, and garlic and toss well. Let sit at room temperature until needed. To serve, divide eggplant among 4 plates, place a ring of tomatoes around, and top with a sprig of mint. Serve with bread to break.

WINE SUGGESTION: a dry white

Endive with Boursin and Cherry Tomatoes

3 to 4 Belgian endives
1 cup cherry tomatoes (red or
    yellow)
1 tablespoon red wine vinegar
2 tablespoons olive oil
Salt and freshly ground pep-
    per
4 ounces Boursin or Rondele
    cheese

SERVES 4

BOURSIN (OR RONDELE) is a soft, spreadable cheese with garlic and herbs, and is a perfect foil for the crisp, slightly bitter taste of endive. It also makes a very pretty plate.

Discard any browned or wilted leaves from the endives. Separate the larger leaves, using the tiny inner ones for another salad. If necessary, put the leaves in a bowl of cold water to crisp. Wash and top tomatoes, cut in half, and put in a bowl with vinegar, oil, and salt and pepper to taste. Toss well and let sit at room temperature for at least 30 minutes.

To assemble the dish, pat endive dry with paper towels, spread a thin layer of cheese on the leaves, and arrange in a radial pattern on the plates. Divide the tomatoes in piles at the center of the leaves.

WINE SUGGESTION: a dry white

Green Bean, Red Pepper, and Gruyère Strips

1 pound green beans

2 medium-size red peppers, roasted (see page 331)

½ pound Gruyère (or Swiss) cheese

1 minced shallot or green onion

2 tablespoons red wine vinegar

¼ cup olive oil

Salt and freshly ground pepper

SERVES 4

A DELICIOUS tricolor salad—everything the same shape but with different taste and texture. It is a fine, light way to begin a meal, served with crusty bread.

Top green beans—if they're fresh you don't have to tail them. Drop into a large pot of boiling, salted water and cook until tender, about 4 to 5 minutes; they should still have a bit of crunch to them. Drain in a colander and refresh with cold water. Clean roasted peppers, then cut into strips about the width of the beans. Also cut the cheese into similar strips.

Anytime while preparing the ingredients, place shallots and vinegar in a bowl, stir, and let sit. Add green beans and toss, then toss with peppers. Add oil and salt and pepper to taste and toss well, then toss with the cheese. This can be made an hour or so ahead and tossed again before serving.

WINE SUGGESTION: a dry white

Greek Appetizer Plate

TARAMOSALATA

1 cup gently packed white bread cubes

¼ cup tarama or salmon roe caviar

½ cup olive oil

3 tablespoons lemon juice

1 tablespoon white wine vinegar

2 tablespoons finely grated onion, with juice

STUFFED CUCUMBER BOATS

2 medium-size cucumbers

Salt

3 tablespoons olive oil

1 tablespoon minced fresh basil (or ¼ teaspoon dried oregano)

Freshly ground pepper

¾ cup feta cheese, crumbled

1 large, ripe garden tomato, peeled, chopped, and drained

Kalamata olives

Sprigs of basil, mint, or parsley for garnish

French or Italian bread

SERVES 4

THIS SOUNDS rather a bother, but even if you can't locate Taramosalata already made in a Greek market, it really doesn't take much time to prepare yourself. And with typical Greek largesse it makes a very festive spread to put before a guest.

To make the Taramosalata: Put bread in a small bowl and sprinkle with water. Let soften several minutes, then squeeze out as much water as you can and place in a food processor. Soak tarama in warm water for several minutes to eliminate some of the saltiness, then drain it in a fine sieve. Add to the bread and process the mixture, adding ½ cup oil in a thin stream until you have a mixture like mayonnaise. Add lemon, vinegar, and onion and process briefly. Scoop into a bowl, cover with plastic wrap, and refrigerate. "Taramosalata" can be made a day or more ahead. (It can also be bought in Greek markets ready-made.)

To make the cucumber boats: The cucumbers should be peeled and sliced lengthwise, then the seeds scooped out with a small spoon. Salt them well and lay cut side down on a plate for an hour to drain. Mix oil in a small bowl with the basil or oregano and add salt and pepper to taste (not too much salt because of the cheese). When it is smooth, stir in the feta.

To serve, wash cucumbers off and pat dry. Mix tomato into cheese mixture and stuff into cucumber boats. Place a heap of Taramosalata beside (top, if you have some extra, with tarama or salmon roe), surround it with olives, and garnish with a sprig of basil, mint, or parsley. Serve with slices of bread to spread the Taramosalata on.

WINE SUGGESTION: a dry white

Leeks in Red Wine

8 medium-size leeks
4 tablespoons olive oil
Salt
½ cup dry red wine
¼ cup canned beef bouillon

SERVES 4

ONE OF *my favorite dishes of all time, not only for flavor but the surprising purplish color which everyone remarks. They can be garnished with hard-boiled egg quarters or a sprig of watercress, or both. And of course you'll want a fine crusty bread.*

For this dish choose leeks all the same size. If you are lucky enough to find smallish leeks you'll need a dozen. Cut the tops off almost down to the white and trim off the roots. Rinse with water to clean out dirt or sand, and check to see if any lies under the white flesh. If so, make a small slit with a knife and place in a bowl of water for several minutes to leach it out.

Drain leeks and pat dry. Heat olive oil in a large frying pan. Fry leeks over medium heat until they start to take color, then turn and cook the other side. Season with a sprinkle of salt as they cook. Pour wine over them and let it sputter up. Then add the bouillon, cover the pan, and let cook 10 to 15 minutes, turning once during the process. They are done when a small knife pierces the root end easily.

Lift the leeks out onto a dish. Turn heat high and cook the liquid down until it makes a slightly thickened sauce. Pour over the leeks and serve warm or cold.

WINE SUGGESTION: a medium-bodied red

Leeks Vinaigrette

8 medium-size leeks
1 tablespoon white wine vine-
    gar
¼ cup fruity olive oil
1 teaspoon Dijon-style mus-
    tard
Salt and freshly ground pep-
    per
2 tablespoons minced parsley
1 hard-boiled egg yolk

SERVES 4

ONCE IN *a farmer's market I found a large bunch of young leeks about ½ inch in size, and these made the best of a fine thing. But if you can get medium ones, all the same size, they do beautifully. Serve with French bread.*

Trim green tops off leeks and cut away most of the roots (you want the leeks to hold together in the cooking). Clean as in the preceding recipe.

Place them in a large frying pan and cover with boiling, salted water. Cover the pan and simmer over medium-low heat until soft—about 15 to 18 minutes. Drain well, cut vertically in half, and lay them in a shallow casserole. Whisk vinegar, oil, mustard, and salt and pepper to taste, then pour over leeks while still warm. Cover and refrigerate for an hour or more to marinate.

To serve, lift out onto plates. Mix parsley with the marinade left in the pan and pour over the leeks. Push the egg yolk through a sieve to sprinkle over the leeks. Serve at room temperature.

WINE SUGGESTION: a dry white

Braised Lettuce with Roquefort

2 large heads Boston lettuce
Salt
6 tablespoons butter
2 tablespoons Roquefort cheese
Freshly ground pepper

SERVES 4

A VERY lovely dish, and even better for those who grow their own garden lettuce and may be able to use a head of limestone lettuce for each serving! I'm not much a one for braised Belgian endive—a favorite of the French—since it seems to lose all its flavor, but in this the lettuce loses only its crispness—none of the savor. Serve with sliced French bread.

Choose fairly compact heads of lettuce for this dish. Trim their stems a little, but not so much as to detach the leaves. Slice in half vertically. Bring about 2 inches water to a boil in a large pot, put in the lettuce stem end down, cover the pot, lower heat, and let steam 5 minutes. Drain in a colander. When cool enough to handle, squeeze them gently with your hands to extract as much water as possible, then pat dry with paper towels. They can be prepared well ahead to this point.

To serve, reheat—preferably by laying the lettuce packets in a steamer over simmering water. Salt them very lightly as they heat. Melt butter in a small saucepan, crumble in the cheese, and add a generous amount of pepper. Lay the lettuce on warm plates and pour the Roquefort butter over them. Serve at once.

WINE SUGGESTION: a dry white

Mushroom and Shrimp Salad

1 pound mushrooms
½ cup olive oil
4 tablespoons lemon juice
1 small clove garlic, minced
Freshly ground pepper
1 pound shrimp, cooked and
   peeled
Salt
4 leaves butter lettuce
2 tablespoons minced parsley

SERVES 4

A LIGHT and remarkably tasty beginning for any meal. You could save work and use small "shrimp meat" here, but the slightly larger ones you boil and peel yourself are just that bit better.

Wipe mushrooms clean, cut off stems flush with the caps, and thinly slice. Place in a bowl with oil, lemon juice, garlic, and several grinds of pepper. Cover with plastic wrap and refrigerate 2 hours or more.

Thirty minutes before serving, stir in shrimp and salt to taste and let sit at room temperature. To serve, place a lettuce leaf on each of 4 plates, divide the salad mixture among them, and sprinkle with parsley.

WINE SUGGESTION: a fruity white

Lettuces with Walnuts

1 pint assorted baby salad
    greens (or 1 head Boston
    lettuce)
3 slices homestyle bread
1 clove garlic (optional)
⅔ cup walnuts
2 tablespoons wine vinegar
¼ teaspoon Dijon-style mus-
    tard
6 tablespoons walnut oil
Salt and freshly ground pep-
    per

SERVES 4

A CLASSIC salad from the Loire region of France, and difficult to improve upon, particularly if you use the assorted tiny lettuces available these days, what the French call mesclun. *Walnut oil is expensive, but you'll see its worth here. It is available in gourmet and other markets. (I have a friend who pops popcorn with walnut oil and says nothing can beat it, but it's not an oil you want to cook with ordinarily.)*

Preheat oven to 275 degrees. Wash lettuces (or if you are using Boston lettuce, separate the leaves, tearing the larger into halves or thirds) and dry well. Trim the bread of crusts, and if you wish, flatten the garlic clove pretty well, peel it, and rub over the bread. Cut into dice and place on a baking pan. Heat in the oven 15 minutes or so, or until lightly browned. At the same time place the walnuts in the oven and heat for 5 minutes or so. Remove and chop the nuts coarsely. This may all be done ahead.

To serve, place the greens in a bowl. Mix vinegar, mustard, oil, and salt and pepper to taste and toss the greens well. Sprinkle the croutons and walnuts over the salad and serve at once.

WINE SUGGESTION: a dry white

Mussels
Marinière

2 pounds mussels
4 tablespoons butter
2 shallots, minced
1 cup dry white wine
Pinch of dried thyme
½ bay leaf
Salt and freshly ground pep-
    per
¼ cup minced parsley

SERVES 4

THIS IS at once the simplest, most usual, and still about the best way to serve mussels. Saffron and curry do bring out the sweetness of these bivalves, but this is still hard to beat. Serve with French bread to sop up the juices.

Pull beards from the mussels and scrub with a stiff brush. These days cultured mussels need very little cleaning. Place in a bowl of cold, salted water, discarding any that seem unduly heavy or light or that do not close their shells at a tap. Keep in water 30 minutes or more—this helps them disgorge any sand.

Put butter and shallots in a deep kettle and stir a minute or so. Add wine and let cook another minute, then add thyme, bay leaf, and only a little salt (mussels are salty, remember) and quite a few grinds of pepper. Add mussels, cover tightly, and let steam over high heat about 5 minutes. Shake the kettle well a couple of times to make sure they cook evenly. Remove mussels with a skimmer, returning any that haven't opened for a minute or more cooking. Discard those that still won't open.

Place mussels in wide soup plates. Let the liquid settle a minute so any sand sinks to the bottom, then ladle over the mussels and sprinkle with parsley. Serve at once.

WINE SUGGESTION: a dry white

Mussels in Saffron Cream

2 pounds mussels
3 tablespoons butter
2 chopped shallots or green
    onions
1 bay leaf
¾ cup dry white wine
Salt and freshly ground pep-
    per
¼ teaspoon saffron threads
½ cup crème fraîche (see page
    327) or heavy cream
Minced parsley

SERVES 4

THESE DAYS we are blessed with fresh mussels grown in underwater farms with no noticeable loss in taste, and best of all, clean shelled and already flushed of sand. The simplest, Mussels Marinière (see page 51), are cooked just like this, but without the cream and saffron. Delicious as those are, saffron has a kind of affinity with these bivalves, and the smoothness of cream (especially the slight tang of crème fraîche) brings the dish to the point of perfection. Serve them with a crusty baguette.

If necessary, scrub and pull beards from mussels and let sit in water as in the preceding recipe. Melt butter in a large saucepan set over medium heat and sauté shallots a few minutes. Add bay leaf, wine, salt and pepper to taste, and saffron. Let it bubble a few minutes more. Add mussels, cover the pot, and let steam until mussels open and release their juices—a matter of minutes, 10 at the most.

Remove open mussels with tongs, discard their tops, and place on warm serving plates. Remove the un-opened shells from the pot. If the mussels were aqua-cultured there is no need to fuss with the sauce, but with shore-gathered mussels, at this point you must make sure to put it through a fine mesh to remove any sand. Then add the cream, raise heat to high, and cook, stirring, until you have a smooth, slightly thickened sauce. Pour over the mussels and serve, sprinkled with a little parsley for color.

WINE SUGGESTION: a full-bodied white

Onions and Zucchini à la Grecque

3 small zucchini
16 small white "boiling" onions
½ cup olive oil
½ cup dry white wine
1 clove garlic, peeled
2 sprigs fresh tarragon and/or
  rosemary (or dried herbs)
1 teaspoon salt
1 teaspoon freshly ground
  pepper
1 teaspoon dry mustard
1 teaspoon mustard seeds
2 whole cloves
2 tablespoons white wine vinegar
1 tablespoon tomato paste
1 teaspoon sugar
½ cup golden raisins
Lettuce leaves
Minced parsley
Greek or Italian olives

SERVES 4

COOKING VEGETABLES in this manner originated in Greece, but is now common in many countries, using what is at hand. I like always to use onions, but also fine are knobs of cauliflower, sliced green beans or batons of carrot, okra pods, leeks, cherry tomatoes, mushrooms, or snowpeas. Each vegetable should be cooked separately and until just barely tender. It is a loose and easy dish, and other seasonings to be considered are dill, fennel, bay leaf, mint, savory, marjoram, basil, thyme, cinnamon, or saffron. (Curiously, even the Greeks don't seem to use their ubiquitous oregano.) Raisins can be omitted, if you wish, but to me they add a particularly Greek touch to a mixture which ought to be ever so slightly sweet and sour. For parties, it's great to cook up a larger batch with a whole mélange of vegetables for guests to spoon onto their plates.

Wash zucchini well. Trim tops and bottoms, cut them in half vertically, then slice each half into 4 sticks. Drop onions into 2 cups boiling water for a couple of minutes, then drain and slip off skins. Trim tops and bottoms.

Put the rest of the ingredients up to the raisins in a good-size saucepan and bring to a boil. Drop in zucchini and cook 3 to 4 minutes, or until barely tender. Remove with a slotted spoon. Add onions to the pan and simmer 15 minutes, or until tender when tested with a small knife. Turn off heat, add the raisins, and let cool to room temperature. Add zucchini, then let the dish marinate either refrigerated or not for several hours. If refrigerated, bring to room temperature before serving.

To serve, place a lettuce leaf on each plate and divide vegetables among them. Sprinkle with some of the marinating liquid and parsley. Add about 4 olives to each plate. Serve with French bread to sop up juices from the plate.

WINE SUGGESTION: a fruity white

Orange and Olive Salad with Red Onion Rings

4 large navel oranges
4 tablespoons fruity olive oil
1 tablespoon lemon juice
Salt
2 thin slices red onion
Curly endive
Greek or Italian oil-cured
    black olives

SERVES 4

A TONIC SALAD from Sicily, where blood oranges are used. It may sound curious, but both salt and olive oil bring out the best in any orange, and the contrasts in both taste and color make a lively plate, very good before some rich dishes, such as roast duckling or goose or pork.

Peel oranges, removing as much of the white pith as possible. Slice in rounds (over a bowl to catch the juice) and place in a shallow, wide dish—a pie plate is fine—then sprinkle with orange juice, olive oil, lemon juice, and salt to taste. Separate the onion into rings and place in a bowl of cold, salted water. Let both these sit at room temperature at least 30 minutes before serving.

To serve, place a ruffle of endive on serving plates, make a fan of orange slices, top with a few drained onion rings, then place a small pile of olives at the side. Sprinkle with the marinating juices from the oranges and serve.

WINE SUGGESTION: a fruity white

Oysters on the Half Shell

If I had to call up a last meal it would begin with a dozen or more oysters on the half shell. I'd summon along a few lemon wedges to squeeze or a small pot of Sauce Mignonnette (see below) to dip the oysters in if I wished, a loaf of light yet flavorful country bread, and a glass of the sommelier's choice. When I started a restaurant over a decade ago in San Francisco, there was no reliable supply for oysters. Now I live around the corner from a restaurant you can go to for all the above, plus the choice of six or more oysters from around the wide world. Each with a different flavor, tang, texture, even.

This is the celebrated Zuni, and they open oysters there like this: First you scrub the shells clean with a stiff brush. Then you fold a towel in several layers so it fits your palm, place an oyster on it with the cupped shell down and the hinged edge facing away from your body. Keep the oyster balanced so its liquor doesn't run off once opened. Take an oyster knife with a broad pointed blade and gently force it into the shell at the hinge (just to one side), working it in and twisting slightly back and forth to penetrate by about half an inch. The top shell should spring open. Then you pivot the knife blade against the upper shell and cut the muscle where it attaches to the top shell. Finally, you ease the knife under the oyster to cut the muscle that attaches it to the bottom shell and lay it proudly out on a bed of ice.

Easy does it. Have you ever noticed how scarred the hands of professional oyster shuckers are? I'd open an oyster with an axe if need be, though with a proper oyster knife and padded gloves I've risked a few dozen, to pry for a guest, and lay out on a plate of hand-crushed ice. But mostly I'd rather have them at whim, around the corner over a sidewalk overlooking the city's main boulevard.

One thing I've learned is never to put the first example of an oyster in a sauce when sampling a new and unknown breed. To compare, you want it in all its brininess *sans* Mignonnette. This sauce is made with a good slosh of mild white wine vinegar, a shallot minced almost to a paste, and a few generous grinds of fragrant white or "mignonnette" peppercorns. You don't need more than a thimble of it, either, with any oyster worth the while.

Oysters Fried with Crab

12 to 16 fresh oysters
1 cup freshly made bread
  crumbs (see page 325)
½ cup flaked crabmeat
Salt and freshly ground pepper
Ground mace
Cayenne pepper (optional)
Flour
2 eggs
Oil for frying
1 bunch watercress
1 lemon, cut into wedges

SERVES 4

THIS IS really a smash to serve if you have fresh oysters at hand, East or West Coast. And though I always use fresh Pacific crab, I don't think you'd lose much with a small can of crabmeat here. It is surely a dish to flourish forth at New Year's or some more private festival. And in its way it also deserves champagne.

I use large Pacific oysters for this—the ones good only for cooking, anyway. Three apiece are enough, but if you use smaller oysters, better count on 4 a serving.

Combine bread crumbs, crab, salt and pepper to taste, and a dash of mace (a little cayenne, if you like). Place flour on a small plate, whisk eggs in a bowl, and lay a sheet of wax paper out on a baking sheet.

Dip oysters in flour, then in eggs, then roll to coat completely in the bread crumb mixture. Lay out on the wax paper as you go. Refrigerate for an hour or more before frying.

To prepare the dish, discard the tougher stems from washed watercress and divide among 4 plates. Heat oil to shimmering and fry oysters in batches until golden brown all over. Lay them out on paper towels. Place while still hot over the watercress, decorate with lemon wedges, and serve.

WINE SUGGESTION: a dry white

Fresh Peas with Prosciutto

3 pounds fresh green peas
4 tablespoons butter
¼ cup finely chopped onion
Salt and freshly ground pepper
Pinch of sugar (optional)
3 ounces thin prosciutto, cut into tiny strips
4 croûtes, cut into 4 triangles (see page 328)

SERVES 4

MAKE THIS only when you have access to tiny garden peas in season—not big mealy ones here, much less frozen—it is then a sublime dish to set forth, with the peas properly on their own without being drowned in the usual carrots and gravy.

Shell the peas. Melt butter in a saucepan set over medium-low heat. Add onion and cook until transparent, then add peas and season to taste with salt and pepper. Add ½ cup of water, cover the pan, and simmer 10 to 15 minutes, or until the peas are just tender. If the peas are not straight from the garden, you might add a pinch of sugar. A couple of minutes before peas are done stir in prosciutto.

Divide the mixture among 4 plates and tuck the croûtes around the edges. Serve immediately.

WINE SUGGESTION: a dry white or medium-bodied red

Prosciutto and Melon (or Figs)

When one tastes for the first time the contrast between paper-thin salty ham and sweet, cool fruit, it is easy to understand why this is one of the most popular of all first courses. As far back as Apicius we find Romans dressing melon for a salad, even if they hadn't invented prosciutto yet. It does what all good starters do: arouses the appetite without surfeit.

We are particularly lucky these days to have had the ban on genuine Italian prosciutto lifted, for it is much less salty than domestic imitations, and strikes a delicate harmony with cantaloupe or honeydew or crenshaw. If you get fresh figs in season, either black or white, you'll find this rarer combination perhaps even better. Some peel the figs, but this seems rather finicky to me. I just stem them and cut into quarters—not quite through—so they lay like flowers on the plate. You only need a couple. Some wrap the peeled and sliced melon in the prosciutto, and some just lay them attractively side by side, but however presented it is really the forkful of one and then the other, with a sip of perfect wine between that counts.

WINE SUGGESTION: a fruity white

Salad with Croûtes Vaudoise

8 slices French bread, cut on
    the bias
⅓ cup dry white wine
6 tablespoons butter, melted
2 tablespoons flour
¼ cup milk
¼ cup cream
¼ cup grated Gruyère cheese
1 egg yolk, beaten
Salt and freshly ground pep-
    per
Freshly grated nutmeg
Assorted baby salad greens
Olive oil
Wine vinegar

SERVES 4

I LIKE TO USE *the newly available tiny mixed greens called* mesclun *for this, but if your market doesn't yet have this delicacy, shoot for things like watercress, endive, or butter lettuce.*

To make the croûtes, place bread slices in a large buttered baking pan and sprinkle with wine. Drizzle with 2 tablespoons of butter.

Put 1 tablespoon of butter in a small saucepan set over medium-low heat. Stir in flour and cook a few minutes, then add milk and cream. Stir until smooth and thickened. Add cheese and then egg yolk and stir another few minutes. Season to taste with salt, pepper, and a wisp of nutmeg. Spread this over the bread slices and drizzle with another 2 tablespoons butter. This can be made well ahead and covered with foil until needed.

To continue, preheat oven to 375 degrees and bake 20 to 25 minutes, or until golden and bubbly. While they cook, wash and dry salad greens, arrange on 4 plates, and drizzle with a little olive oil, a bit of wine vinegar, and salt and pepper. Toss a bit, then place 2 hot croûtes at the side of each plate. Serve immediately.

WINE SUGGESTION: a dry white

Salad with Sautéed Shiitake Mushrooms

4 cups assorted baby salad
   greens or stemmed watercress
¾ pound fresh shiitake mushrooms
¼ cup parsley
1 clove garlic, slightly flattened and peeled
Grated peel of ½ lemon
¼ cup olive oil
Salt and freshly ground pepper
Red wine vinegar
Wedge of Parmesan or Ro-
   mano cheese

SERVES 4

NOW THAT we can find fresh field mushrooms regularly, this is one of my favorite first courses, for it shows the shiitake off to perfection. Just remember to have a light hand with the vinegar, for you don't need a hefty vinaigrette here, only a whisper of acidity.

If necessary, wash and dry greens. Cut stems off mushrooms and slice the caps into ¼-inch strips. Very finely mince parsley with garlic and combine with lemon peel. This can all be done ahead.

To serve, divide greens among 4 salad plates. Heat oil in a frying pan set over medium-high heat. Add mushrooms and toss 2 to 3 minutes, sprinkling with salt and pepper to taste. Add parsley mixture, toss, and cook another minute. Sprinkle the greens very lightly with vinegar and mound the hot mushrooms on top. With a swivel vegetable peeler, shave several thin strips of cheese over the salad and serve immediately.

WINE SUGGESTION: a dry white

Salad of Watercress, Grapefruit, and Hazelnuts

1 large bunch watercress
2 grapefruits
4 tablespoons olive oil
Salt and freshly ground pepper
½ cup hazelnuts
Gruyère cheese (optional)

SERVES 4

A FIRST COURSE that is splendid for any rich meal to follow. I don't know where I picked it up, but I've been using it for some years to precede my once-a-year Cassoulet made from the Christmas goose.

Everything can be done ahead. Crop watercress of its largest stems, breaking into bite-size branches. Place in a bowl of water. Peel grapefruits, cutting as much of the white pith away as possible. Separate into sections, saving the most perfect for the salad—about 4 a person. Slice the sections down the middle and carefully peel off the outside skin. Lay them on a plate, cover with plastic wrap, and refrigerate. (If this sounds a bother, just cut in half and spoon out the grapefruit—as you would to eat it—and cut into large pieces.)

To make the dressing, squeeze the unused grapefruit and measure out ½ cup of juice. Stir with oil and season lightly with salt and pepper. This is to be a very sprightly, light dressing!

Preheat oven to 300 degrees and bake nuts in a pan 10 minutes, then cool to room temperature and chop coarsely. A food processor is too ungainly for this.

To serve, drain and pat the watercress dry with paper towels. Spread out the cut grapefruit in a fan, side it with a mound of watercress, sprinkle with nuts, then drizzle the stirred dressing over. To make the salad more substantial, shave curls of cheese over, adding yet another compatible texture and flavor.

WINE SUGGESTION: a good brut champagne

Smoked Salmon Pâté with Radishes

2 tablespoons chopped green
   onion
2 tablespoons fresh dill
¼ cup sour cream plus extra
   for coating pâté
12 ounces sliced smoked
   salmon, cut in sections
1 bunch radishes
Fresh golden whitefish caviar
   (if possible)
Dill sprigs

SERVES 4

THIS IS suggested by lovely, lively food writer Flo Braker as "California Caviar." She means in part the wonder of having local fresh golden caviar at a fraction of the cost of beluga. I find it remarkable even with bottled red caviar, and in fact it really doesn't need any at all if pure taste were the object. Of course you would not use prime Nova Scotia or Scotch salmon here, which can cost an arm and a leg and surely needs only the classic accompaniments of lemon wedge, a caper scattering, and hot buttered toast to hand with a good pepper mill.

Whirl onion and dill with ¼ cup sour cream in a food processor until fine. Add salmon and process with an on/off motion until chopped fine, but do not puree. Scoop out, place in a bowl, cover with plastic wrap, and refrigerate until needed. The radishes can just be washed and set aside or, if you feel ambitious, trimmed and cut into "roses" with a small knife, then dropped into a bowl of cold water to separate. Silly, but pretty.

To serve, round a mound of pâté on 4 plates, smooth over with more sour cream, and sprinkle with caviar. Tuck in a dill sprig, distribute radishes around, and serve.

WINE SUGGESTION: a full-bodied white

Braised Scallions with Chèvre Toasts

4 bunches green onions
3 tablespoons butter
Salt and freshly ground pepper
⅓ cup chicken stock
⅓ cup dry white wine or vermouth
3 tablespoons minced parsley
4 slices bread, trimmed, toasted, and cut into triangles
3 ounces chèvre

SERVES 4

THIS GOES as quickly, almost, as tossing a salad, and even in the winter smacks of springtime. You want to pick out bunches of onions all more or less the same size, if you can. If they look scrawny add another bunch. If you don't like, or can't get, goat cheese, try a good cream cheese or just plain slices of crusty French bread.

Remove any tired leaves from the onions, cut off the roots, then cut off tops leaving about 3 inches of green. Put butter in a large frying pan set over medium heat. When it sputters, add onions, cooking them about a minute a side. Sprinkle with salt and pepper to taste as you turn them, then add stock and wine, cover the pan, and cook 3 to 4 minutes, or until they test tender when pierced with a sharp knife. Remove onions with a slotted spatula to warm plates.

Turn up heat under the pan to high and let the juices cook down until they thicken to a buttery glaze. Pour over the onions, sprinkle with parsley, and surround by toasts spread with cheese. Serve immediately.

WINE SUGGESTION: a dry white

Shrimp Crostini

4 slices white homestyle bread
¼ cup grated Parmesan cheese
Pinch of ground mace
½ pound cooked shrimp,
    finely chopped
2 tablespoons minced parsley
1 tablespoon capers
1 tablespoon lemon juice
4 tablespoons melted butter
Watercress sprigs

SERVES 4

AT FIRST you're going to think at least three of these per serving, but they are so rich and tasty only a gargantuan eater would want more for a first course. And a glass of fine white wine, certainly.

Trim bread of crusts and toast it. Cut each slice diagonally in half and place on a buttered baking dish. Sprinkle with half the cheese. Mix a dash of mace into the shrimp (because of the cheese I don't think you need any salt here, but you might like a whisper). Spread the shrimp on toast, sprinkle with parsley and capers, and squeeze a few drops of lemon juice over. Drizzle butter over the toasts. The dish can be made ahead up to this point, if necessary—but not much more than an hour.

To continue, preheat oven to 400 degrees. Pop the crostini in and bake 10 minutes. Serve hot, with a mound of watercress.

WINE SUGGESTION: a fruity white

Shrimp and Artichokes

1 pound shrimp, peeled and
    deveined (or precooked tiny
    shrimp)
4 to 6 artichokes (or 2 10-
    ounce packages frozen)
1 lemon, cut into slices
⅔ cup mayonnaise
1 tablespoon lemon juice
4 green onions, minced
2 tablespoons chopped fresh
    basil
2 tablespoons capers
1 or 2 drops Angostura bitters
    (optional)
Freshly ground pepper
4 tender lettuce leaves

SERVES 4

EITHER WITH the full-scale production or with precooked shrimp and frozen artichoke hearts, this is something to sing about—and eat with gusto, a glass of wine, and friends.

Cook shrimp in boiling, salted water until just pink. Drain and reserve. Precooked shrimp are fine just as is. Cut stems off the artichokes and simmer in salted water with lemon slices 20 to 30 minutes, or until they test tender when pierced with a small, sharp knife inserted at the base. Drain and let cool. If using frozen artichokes, cook as the package directs. When cool, cut into halves. Shuck the leaves off the whole artichokes (scraping the flesh of the meatiest into the mayonnaise, if you like), then cut out the chokes and slice into quarters or sixths, depending on their size. Cover with plastic wrap and reserve.

Combine mayonnaise, lemon juice, green onions, basil, capers, and bitters, if you use it. Add pepper to taste. It is preferable to let this sit an hour or so to gather flavor, either at room temperature or refrigerated. To serve, mix shrimp and artichokes with the mayonnaise dressing. Spoon onto serving plates lined with a lettuce leaf.

WINE SUGGESTION: a dry white or dry rosé

Wilted Spinach and Bacon Salad

1 pound spinach
¼ pound bacon (preferably thickly sliced)
1 egg
1 cup light cream
¼ cup wine vinegar
1 tablespoon sugar
Salt and freshly ground pepper
¼ teaspoon dry mustard
¼ teaspoon dried tarragon (optional)
6 green onions, minced
8 radishes, sliced

SERVES 4

THE FRENCH *often spark their salads with* lardons *made with salt pork or crackling of chicken or duck skin. They can be very fine indeed, but I really prefer bacon-topped, old-fashioned American wilted salad.*

Remove stems from the spinach and wash the leaves through several waters to remove any dirt and sand. Drain in a colander and dry on paper towels (or, better yet, in a salad spinner). Cut bacon into small strips and fry over medium-low heat until crisp. Remove bacon and discard all but 2 tablespoons bacon fat. Beat egg with cream in a small bowl, then beat in vinegar, sugar, salt and pepper to taste, mustard, and tarragon, if desired. Add to the bacon fat and stir over low heat until it thickens—do not let it come to a boil. These steps can be done ahead.

To serve, place spinach on salad plates and heat up the sauce and pour over. Sprinkle with onion, radish slices, and bacon strips. Serve immediately.

WINE SUGGESTION: a dry white

Tomatoes Baked with Gorgonzola

4 medium-size garden tomatoes
2 tablespoons olive oil
Salt and freshly ground pepper
½ cup crumbled Gorgonzola
cheese
Mixed lettuces or watercress
Red wine vinegar

SERVES 4

I GOT this recipe from a Swiss cook who uses thinly sliced Camembert on hers—they are fine, though I prefer a cheese such as Gorgonzola, since something odd seems to happen to cooked Camembert to my mind. Any blue-veined cheese could be used, and the whole dish is deliciously open to experiment when you have a crop of tomatoes on the vine (ones that aren't vine-ripened aren't good enough for this dish).

Remove stems from tomatoes and cut horizontally in half. In a frying pan large enough to hold all the tomato halves, heat oil over medium-high heat. Put tomatoes in cut side down and cook 3 minutes, then turn and cook another 3 minutes or so. Salt and pepper as they cook. The tomatoes should be heated through, but don't cook them so much that they start to fall apart. Dead-ripe tomatoes will take less time to cook, of course. Sprinkle the tops with cheese and place in an oiled baking dish. These can be made ahead and kept covered at room temperature.

To continue, preheat oven to 325 degrees and bake tomatoes until they are heated through and the cheese is melted. Place on plates and surround with greens, then sprinkle a few drops of vinegar over the plate and serve.

WINE SUGGESTION: a dry white

Smoked Trout

4 smoked trout
½ cup mayonnaise
1 tablespoon prepared horseradish
1 tablespoon capers
Watercress

SERVES 4

THOSE LUCKY ENOUGH to have smoked trout available will find them one of the most delicious ways to commence a meal (and certainly one of the easiest). Though I have never had a smoker, I'm told by those who do that one of the best things you can produce with them is smoked trout—of course the farmed kind, not those you catch out of a stream. Quite a few can be done at a time, and laid up in the freezer like good deeds in heaven.

Lay trout on serving plates. Mix mayonnaise, horseradish, and capers and put a dollop beside each trout, then tuck in a few branches of watercress.

WINE SUGGESTION: a medium-bodied red or dry white

QUICK AND COMFORTABLE MAIN DISHES

Fish and Shellfish

THE LAST DECADE has brought a bounty of fresh fish to market, and many breeds once unavailable are now often flown in fresh daily. Even in the Midwest, Americans have taken to seafood as never before—most on their doctor's advice that the old ideal of a hefty, fat-marbled T-bone will lead them to the Pearly Gates before their time. I grew up in a large family of lake and stream fishers, so was always blessed even in landlocked Kansas. But many neighbors there were set in stolid habits of beef, pork, and chicken, with perhaps a holiday turkey: no lamb, no veal, no game, even, and certainly no fish or shellfish of any stripe. I believe, as my mother before me, that we all thrive on variety. That a sirloin or rib roast once in a blue moon, even, is a necessity of the spirit as well as body. I also admire salmon, trout, and exotic mahi-mahi, as well as shrimp, scallops, and oysters, for themselves and not because they are good for the arteries.

Another boon is that both trout and catfish (as well as oysters and mussels) are farmed these days, which makes them not only available but also inexpensive. Fishermen are right to claim brook trout need only a toss in the pan. But while some of the flavor of the wild has been bred out of farmed trout, they are fine candidates for other methods than exquisite simplicity and a squeeze of lemon. Farmed catfish, on the other hand, are actually finer than fresh caught, since they are fed rather better than they could scrounge in the wild from muddy river bottoms.

Remember always, when choosing, that fresh are preferable to any frozen, for thawing breaks down the flesh and may mask the delicate quality of some fish. Always look for the glistening scale or bright eye, and try to get close enough to sniff, if possible. Smell, in fact, is all: Fish fit to eat has no strong odor. Properly cooked, in just a flush of sustained heat, both fish or shellfish will do you proud at table, from daily family to the grandest of guests. And perhaps best of all, except for a whole salmon or other large catch, they also take little more time for the cook to turn out than that flash-in-the-pan ideal of the trout fisher.

"Fisherman's" Fillets

4 tablespoons butter

1 tablespoon Dijon-style mustard

2 shallots, minced

2 tablespoons minced parsley

1 cup dry white wine

4 serving portions fish fillets
  (sole, trout, or salmon)

1 tablespoon lemon juice

SERVES 4

A DISH of the late great chef Fernand Point, which he made with fresh fillets of merlan. In this country that translates to frozen whiting, certainly unavailable de pêcheur (straight off the hook) as Point had them. But this still remains a masterly way to treat fine fish in the home kitchen—and a plus being that it calls for neither salt nor pepper. Point, shining through even a long line of illustrious restaurateurs, is well known in these abstemious times as the author of "Butter. More butter. Always butter." As this dish shows, I believe he should be remembered more for his remark, "Success is the sum of a lot of small things done right."

Preheat oven to 300 degrees. Spread 1 tablespoon of butter in a baking dish wide enough to hold all the fish in one layer. Whisk mustard, shallots, and parsley in a bowl, then whisk in wine bit by bit. Pour into baking dish, add fish, and dot with 2 tablespoons of butter.

Bake 15 to 20 minutes, or until the fish flakes gently with a fork. Remove with a slotted spoon to a shallow ovenproof casserole or individual ramekins. This can be covered and kept until serving time.

To serve, pour the cooking juices into a saucepan. Heat to boiling and cook until reduced by half—only a matter of minutes. Whisk the remaining butter into the sauce. Then whisk in the lemon juice and strain over fish. You can either brown this in a 500 degree oven until bubbling or more briefly under the broiler.

SERVE WITH Green Beans Parmesan (page 169) and/or Mashed Potatoes with Green Onions (page 218) or *Sformato* with Peas and Lettuce (page 251)

WINE SUGGESTION: a dry white, a full-bodied white (with salmon), or a good brut champagne

Fish Fillets or Steaks with Sauce Chinoise

4 serving portions fish fillets
  or steaks
Salt (optional)
1 shallot
1 clove garlic
¼-inch slice fresh ginger
½ cup rice wine vinegar (or
  white wine vinegar with a
  pinch of sugar)
Parsley sprigs or fresh coriander

SERVES 4

I CALL this Sauce Chinoise because it is based on a simple Chinese condiment using green onion, garlic, and ginger. One day I had only shallots and this ingredient made all the difference in the world. It may be used with any fish or shellfish to take the place of Sauce Mignonnette with fresh oysters, or as a lively dollop for sautéed chicken or even a steak.

The fish here can be prepared any way you wish: poached, grilled, pan-fried—so long as it is not overcooked. It may also be left unsalted, for those on sodium-free diets. The sauce is so tasty as to preclude either salt or fat, if you wish.

Combine the shallot, garlic, and fresh ginger in a food processor or, better yet, simply mince the shallot, garlic, and ginger separately, then stir them into the vinegar. Kept separate, the three different flavors make tiny, glorious explosions on the tastebuds.

Serve the fish hot with a sprinkle of the sauce and a tuft of parsley or coriander.

SERVE WITH Rice with Pine Nuts (page 207) and/or Asparagus with Walnut or Hazelnut Oil (page 168) or any of the green bean or broccoli dishes.

WINE SUGGESTION: a dry or fruity white

Fish Fillets with Pistachio "Stuffing"

3 tablespoons butter
2 shallots, minced
⅔ cup shelled pistachios,
   coarsely chopped
1½ cups fresh bread crumbs
   (see page 325)
4 serving portions fish fillets
   (trout, salmon, or sole)
Juice of ½ lemon
1 bay leaf
Salt

SERVES 4

NOT ONLY is this stuffing delicious, it stays crisp rather than going soggy, as stuffings that are actually inside the fish tend to do. It also needs no salt, remember, because of the saltiness of the nuts. Feel free to garnish with lemon slices or wedges, and a tuft of parsley for color, though I don't think the fish really needs a squirt of lemon for taste.

Melt butter in a frying pan set over medium heat. Add shallots and cook a few minutes, then add pistachios and cook another minute. Stir in bread crumbs until they absorb the butter, then cook a few minutes more until the crumbs start to turn golden. This can be made ahead an hour or so and reheated.

Poach fillets in a little water seasoned with lemon juice, bay leaf, and a pinch of salt. Very thin delicate fillets will take only a minute or so. Remember James Beard's timing for fish: 10 minutes cooking time for each inch of thickness and you can't go wrong.

While the fish cooks, reheat the stuffing. Lift the fillets onto warm plates with a slotted spoon. Sprinkle the stuffing on top and serve immediately.

SERVE WITH Carrots with Cognac (page 184) or Green Beans with Shallots and Balsamic Vinegar (page 170).

WINE SUGGESTION: a full-bodied white

Fish Fillets Ubriacati

4 serving portions fish fillets
  (or steaks)
2 shallots, chopped
1 bay leaf
4 peppercorns
Pinch of salt
1½ cups dry white wine
1 cup fresh oysters and their
  juices
2 tablespoons butter
2 tablespoons capers
3 tablespoons chopped cornichons (or any tart pickle)
3 tablespoons minced parsley
2 tablespoons lightly toasted
  pine nuts

SERVES 4

*A WONDERFUL DISH from poet and writer of musical com-
edies, Bill Benton. It can be adapted for practically any catch of
the day and for either East or West Coast–bottled tiny oysters.*

Pat fish dry with paper towels. Put shallots, bay leaf,
peppercorns, salt, and wine in a large frying pan. Bring
to a boil over medium heat and simmer 5 minutes. Add
fish and poach just until it flakes. With a slotted spoon,
remove to plates and keep warm.

Add oyster juices to the pan and simmer another 5
minutes. Strain liquid and return it to the pan. You
should have a cup of stock. Add butter, capers, cornichons, parsley, pine nuts, and oysters and cook just
until the edges of the oysters curl. Pour over the fish
fillets and serve at once.

SERVE WITH *Sformato* with Green Beans (page 249), Broccoli Puree with Gruyère and Madeira (page 180),
Zucchini-Stuffed Baked Potatoes (page 232), or Cauliflower and Arugula Gratin (page 243).

WINE SUGGESTION: a dry white

Fish Steaks Côte d'Azur

4 serving portions steaks
   (swordfish, tuna, or
   salmon)
2 tablespoons olive oil
1½ cups canned tomatoes,
   drained and roughly
   chopped
¼ teaspoon dried thyme
Pinch of fennel seeds
½ bay leaf
1 clove garlic, slightly flattened and peeled
1 strip orange peel
¼ teaspoon saffron threads
4 peppercorns
Salt
1 cup dry white wine
1 lemon, thinly sliced

SERVES 4

A DELICIOUS DISH for a summer's day.

Pat fish dry with paper towels. Swirl oil in a large frying pan, then add tomatoes, herbs, garlic, orange peel, saffron, peppercorns, and salt to taste. Heat over medium-high flame and add the wine. Cook a minute, then snuggle the fish steaks down into the sauce. Cover, turn down heat, and simmer 8 to 10 minutes, depending on the thickness of the fish. They should be springy to the touch. Turn off heat and let the fish cool in the sauce. Cover and place in the refrigerator.

Serve the fish cold, with some of the sauce strained and poured over. Garnish with lemon slices.

SERVE WITH *Sformato* with Green Beans (page 249), *Sformato* of Artichokes (page 253), or Gratin of Fennel (page 246)

WINE SUGGESTION: a dry white or rosé of cabernet sauvignon

Romesco Sauce for Fish

¼ cup sliced, blanched almonds
1½ teaspoons tomato paste
½ cup mayonnaise
1 clove minced garlic
¼ cup garden or canned tomatoes, peeled, seeded, and chopped
1 tablespoon red wine vinegar
¼ teaspoon cayenne pepper (or to taste)
Salt and freshly ground pepper

SERVES 4

AN EASY, vibrant sauce for any fish, hot or cold, prepared in any simple manner. I particularly like it over poached trout with their skins peeled off.

Heat oven to 350 degrees. Scatter almonds on a pie plate or cake pan and bake 5 to 7 minutes, or until lightly browned. Cool to room temperature.

Put tomato paste in a small bowl with 1½ teaspoons water and stir until smooth. Stir in mayonnaise, then all the other ingredients. Stir in almonds just before serving.

IF HOT, serve with Baltimore Fries (page 220) and/or Broccoli with Buttered Crumbs (page 176). If cold, with Green Beans with Sesame and Pimiento (page 173) and/or Rice Pilaf (page 208).

Watercress and Caviar Sauce for Fish

⅓ cup sour cream
⅓ cup mayonnaise
⅔ cup chopped watercress
  leaves
1 teaspoon grated onion pulp
1 teaspoon lemon juice
4 drops Angostura bitters (optional)
Freshly ground pepper
2 ounces red lumpfish caviar
Salt

SERVES 4

THIS IS excellent and attractive with any simply prepared fish, hot or cold. It is pretty to save four fine sprigs of watercress out of the bunch to garnish the fish. Salmon roe also may be used, though the smaller lumpfish roe is really better—and if you can get the new fresh "golden" caviar from California you have a sumptuous sauce indeed. The sauce can be made several hours in advance, though on hot nights it should be refrigerated.

Simply stir ingredients together except salt. Let the mixture sit for 15 minutes or more, then taste for salt—the caviar should add almost enough.

IF HOT, serve with Fried Potatoes with Shallot-Parsley Butter (page 222) and/or Spinach "en Branche" (page 211). If cold, serve Sformato of Artichokes (page 253).

Fresh Tuna with Tapenade

1 cup pitted Italian or Greek brine-cured black olives
6 anchovy fillets
2 cloves garlic, peeled
2 tablespoons capers
2 tablespoons lemon juice
1 4-ounce can tuna packed in oil
¼ cup olive oil, plus extra for coating steaks
1 tablespoon brandy (optional)
2 tablespoons minced fresh basil (optional)
4 fresh tuna steaks
Basil or parsley sprigs for garnish

SERVES 4

TAPENADE HOLDS all the pungent tastes of Provence in a spoon. You will end up with much more than you need here, but it is a fine thing to have on hand in the refrigerator, and you'll find many uses for it. It's delicious spread on toast, in place of butter, to accompany a simple tomato soup or scrambled eggs. Robust fish like tuna (or most of the larger fish cut into steaks) hold up well to it, though it can also be stirred into mayonnaise and spread over delicate chilled fillets of fish.

To make the tapenade, pit and measure the olives. You don't want oil-cured wrinkled olives here because they are too salty. Toward this I can only advise you to choose your olives well and wash the anchovy fillets under water to rid them of as much salt as possible.

Place olives, anchovies, garlic, capers, and lemon juice in a food processor and use short pulses of power to chop them up. Drain tuna and add it, using a few more pulses to mix. Then add olive oil, as you run the machine, in a fine stream. Some cooks in Provence puree this to an almost mayonnaise-like smoothness, but I like a bit of texture left.

Remove to a bowl and stir in the brandy and basil, if desired. Cover with plastic wrap and let sit at room temperature several hours or keep overnight in the refrigerator and bring to room temperature before serving. Tapenade mellows after 24 hours.

Wipe tuna dry with paper towels and brush well with olive oil. Either grill or broil 3 to 4 minutes a side, depending on the thickness of the fish. Test to make sure the steaks are cooked through, then place on warm plates. Spread about a tablespoon of tapenade over each and serve immediately, garnished with a sprig of basil or parsley.

SERVE WITH Red Pepper Gratin (page 242) and a loaf of French bread.

WINE SUGGESTION: a full-bodied white

Salmon with Beurre Blanc

3 tablespoons minced shallots
3 tablespoons white wine vinegar
3 tablespoons dry white wine
7 ounces (1¾ sticks) unsalted butter, chilled
Salt
White pepper
4 salmon steaks or fillets
2 tablespoons vegetable oil
Parsley sprigs

SERVES 4

A BEURRE BLANC is a fine sauce to master and can be used for any simple fish. I especially like it with delicate, rosy salmon, since with white fish you can end up with everything pale on the plate if you aren't careful with the garnish. You may also put it with grilled or poached salmon, though grilling can dry out fish if you aren't practiced, and poaching doesn't give the hint of crispness and color that sautéing does.

One of the secrets of a beurre blanc is to mince the shallots almost to a puree, so don't shirk this. Place in a small saucepan with vinegar and wine and cook over medium-low heat until the shallots are soft and the liquid has almost disappeared. Turn off the fire and let the pan cool for a couple of minutes. Then whisk in all but 2 tablespoons butter, a tablespoon at a time, adding a new pat immediately after the previous one has been incorporated. The whole process should be warm rather than hot, and only takes a minute or so. The sauce will have the consistency of thick cream. Add salt to taste and a dash of white pepper. Place in a warm spot to keep the butter from congealing, careful not to really heat it, or the butter will separate. If necessary, put the pan in a small bowl with warm tap water. The sauce can be made an hour in advance.

To cook the salmon, wipe dry with paper towels and sprinkle lightly with salt. Melt remaining 2 tablespoons of butter with oil in a large frying pan set over medium-high heat. Sauté the salmon 2 to 3 minutes a side, or until the outside is a soft gold and the flesh flakes. Remove to warm plates and pour the sauce over. Nestle a parsley bouquet for color at the side. Serve at once.

SERVE WITH steamed asparagus with some of the beurre blanc poured over it or with Broccoli with Buttered Crumbs (page 176).

WINE SUGGESTION: a full-bodied white or a good brut champagne

Swordfish with Cassis Onions

Olive oil
4 medium-size onions, peeled
    and thinly sliced
2 tablespoons crème de Cassis
Salt
4 swordfish steaks (or other
    fish steaks)
2 limes, cut into wedges

SERVES 4

ANOTHER DISH *from Bill Benton who seems to serve a lot of fish between composing his Cole Porter-esque songs high above Central Park West. The contrast between the slightly sweet onions, tart lime, and swordfish is exquisite.*

Heat 2 tablespoons of oil in a large frying pan. Add onions and lower heat so they just sweat. First they will separate into rings, then soften, then start to turn gold. To encourage this, you should turn them every few minutes. If the telephone rings, turn the heat off. When golden, add the Cassis, toss several times, and continue as before—always over lowest heat—until the onions are well glazed. Salt to taste toward the end. From start to finish this process should take at least 20 minutes. The onions can be held at room temperature.

To serve the dish, brush olive oil over the steaks and grill them or panfry in a dab of oil. Either way, cook the steaks 3 to 4 minutes a side, depending on their thickness. Salt as you like during cooking. When the steaks flake at the bone, transfer to plates and garnish with the onion *confit* and lime wedges to squeeze as you savor.

SERVE WITH Potato-Shell Fries (page 221) or Potatoes Maxime (page 224).

WINE SUGGESTION: a full-bodied white

Salmon Steaks with Sorrel Sauce

½ cup dry white wine
¼ cup dry vermouth
1 cup fish stock or bottled
   clam juice
2 shallots, minced
1 sprig fresh tarragon
   (optional)
¼ cup heavy cream
4 salmon steaks
8 tablespoons butter
2 tablespoons vegetable oil
¼ cup fresh sorrel
Salt and freshly ground
   pepper

SERVES 4

EVEN IN San Francisco I seldom see sorrel for sale, but when I do I remember how well it goes with salmon. Hiking in England someone pointed out sorrel growing wild, and once I knew what it was I saw it everywhere. It took little time to pick enough for a tart addition to many a meal, and I found it more versatile than its rare appearance in cookbooks would suggest. It is particularly fine as a greeny sauce for chicken or veal, though it even works with scrambled eggs.

Put wine, vermouth, stock, shallots, and tarragon, if desired, in a small saucepan. Simmer over low heat until reduced by half, then add cream and reduce until very slightly thickened. This can be made ahead and left to sit in the pan.

To prepare the dish, wipe the fish, then heat 2 tablespoons of butter along with oil in a large frying pan. Cook the steaks about 4 minutes a side over medium-high heat. They are done when they flake easily with a small, sharp knife and seem cooked inside at the bone. Don't overcook.

While the fish sautés, bring sauce to a bubble. Remove stems from the sorrel, cut into thin strips, and add it to the sauce, cooking until just wilted. Remove from the fire and whisk in the rest of the butter, a tablespoon at a time, until you have a smooth, glossy sauce. Season to taste with salt and pepper. Remove the tarragon if you used it. Place fish steaks on warm plates and glaze with the sauce. Serve at once.

SERVE WITH Mashed Potatoes (page 218), with a knob of butter on top, or *Sformato* Bianco (page 254).

WINE SUGGESTION: a dry or full-bodied white

Lemon-Soy Mahi-Mahi with Avocado Butter

4 mahi-mahi fillets (about ½ pound each)
3 tablespoons soy sauce
4 tablespoons lemon juice
½ teaspoon grated lemon peel
1 clove garlic, flattened and peeled
1 teaspoon Dijon-style mustard
¼ cup vegetable oil
¼ cup butter, at room temperature
¼ cup avocado
Salt and freshly ground white pepper
Sugar

SERVES 4

THOUGH THIS MARINADE complements mahi-mahi excellently, I don't see why it wouldn't work with swordfish, too. You could also use lime instead of the lemon. It makes a superb forkful as the avocado butter melts into the fish.

Wipe fish and lay in a glass dish. Combine soy sauce, 2 tablespoons of lemon juice, lemon peel, garlic, mustard, and oil and pour over the fish. Marinate at least 1 hour. Combine butter, avocado, and the rest of the lemon juice and mash well with a fork. Add salt and pepper to taste, along with a pinch of sugar. Cover with plastic wrap and keep at room temperature.

To serve, either grill or broil the fish, brushing with the marinade as it cooks. Time the fish according to 10 minutes total cooking time for each inch of thickness. It will be done when it flakes lightly and shows no pink inside. Don't overcook. Serve on warm plates with the avocado butter on top.

SERVE WITH Rice with Pine Nuts or Sesame seeds (page 207).

WINE SUGGESTION: a dry white

Halibut with Fried Capers

4 6-ounce halibut steaks
Salt and freshly ground pep-
    per
2 tablespoons grated lemon
    peel
3 tablespoons minced chives
5 tablespoons butter (or olive
    oil)
Vegetable oil
2 tablespoons capers

SERVES 4

*I FIRST had this sauce with halibut at a friend's house, but it
is good for any favored catch that is not too delicate—like fillets
of sole. At first you will think there is too much lemon peel, but
try it this way first and see.*

Preheat oven to 350 degrees. Pat fish dry with paper
towels, sprinkle with salt and pepper, and place in a
baking dish wide enough to hold all in a single layer.
Sprinkle with lemon peel and chives and dot with butter
(or pour olive oil over). Bake 10 to 12 minutes, depending on the thickness of the fish, basting now and then
with the pan juices. The fish is done when it is white at
the center.

While the fish bakes, put about ½ inch oil in a small
saucepan set over high heat. Pat capers dry with paper
towels. Test oil with one of the capers—it is hot enough
if the caper immediately sizzles on contact. Add them all
and cook 1 or 2 minutes, or until the capers are crisp and
starting to brown. Immediately remove with a slotted
spoon to paper towels.

Place fish on warm plates, divide the cooking juices
among them, and sprinkle with the capers. Serve at
once.

SERVE WITH Gratin Dauphinois (page 239) and/or Green
Beans with Shallots and Balsamic Vinegar (page 170).

WINE SUGGESTION: a dry white

Catfish with Coarse-grained Mustard Sauce

4 medium-size catfish
Ingredients for poaching (see
  below)
½ cup dry white wine
¼ cup white wine vinegar
2 shallots, minced
1 bay leaf
1 sprig fresh tarragon (or ¼
  teaspoon dried)
1 cup sweet butter
1 tablespoon heavy cream
2 tablespoons coarse-grained
  mustard
2 tablespoons minced parsley
Lemon juice

SERVES 4

THIS IS an example of how basic beurre blanc (see Salmon with Beurre Blanc, page 8) can be augmented for other, less subtle uses. Catfish—especially the farm raised—can be rather bland, but never particularly delicate, so it stands up to this perky sauce very well.

Poach fish in water with any of the following: white wine, bay leaf, a slice of onion, peppercorns, parsley. The time will vary according to the size of the fish. Remember James Beard's rule of 10 minutes per inch of thickness. When no longer pink at the bone, remove the fish and skin and cut the fillets off the bone. Place these on plates and keep warm in a low-temperature oven.

Add wine, vinegar, shallots, bay leaf, and tarragon to a small saucepan. Boil over high heat until reduced to almost a syrup. While this is going on, remove butter from the refrigerator and cut into tablespoon-size slices. Remove the saucepan from the heat and stir in cream. Reduce the heat to very low and whisk in butter, a piece at a time. If the sauce starts to break down at any time, remove the pan from the heat and whisk in the next 2 pieces of butter away from the stove. When all the butter is incorporated, strain the sauce into a bowl and whisk in mustard, parsley, and a few drops lemon juice to taste. (I don't think this sauce needs salt, but you might.)

Remove fish from the oven and coat each fillet with sauce. Serve immediately.

SERVE WITH Dandelion Greens Provençale (page 192), Broccoli with Bacon Maxime (page 177), or Mushrooms Bordelaise (page 195).

WINE SUGGESTION: a dry or full-bodied white

Trout Amandine
Brennan's

8 trout fillets (or 4 whole
    trout)
1 egg
1 cup milk
Flour
Salt and freshly ground pep-
    per
½ cup butter
⅓ cup blanched almonds, sliv-
    ered
2 tablespoons lemon juice
2 tablespoons Worcestershire
    sauce
2 tablespoons minced parsley

SERVES 4

MOST TROUT *amandine is done with whole fish, which looks fine, but none of the sauce or nuts get near the flesh—where it counts. This recipe, from the redoubtable New Orleans restaurant, does it just right, I think, with its unexpected perky Worcestershire (the real secret). I like to use the new White Wine Worcestershire now in every market, making the sauce just a shade more subtle.*

If you are unable to purchase fillets and must use the whole fish, it makes a very pretty presentation to "butterfly" them. Take a small, sharp-pointed knife and cut the belly side from head to tail. Cut through the backbone just down to the top skin and gently lift out the bones. Wash well and pat dry with paper towels.

Whisk egg with milk. Dip in the fish, let excess drip off, and dredge in flour seasoned with salt and pepper. Shake off excess flour and place on wax paper. These can be done an hour or so beforehand if you like.

Heat the butter in a large frying pan set over medium-high heat. When foam subsides cook the trout in batches 3 to 4 minutes a side. They should just flake when tested with a knife. Lift the trout out and keep warm in a low-temperature oven.

The butter shouldn't have burned, but if it has, dump it out and put in fresh. Add the almonds to the pan and stir for a minute, or until pale gold. Add lemon juice, Worcestershire, and parsley and stir just until bubbly. Pour over the trout and serve immediately.

SERVE WITH Mashed Potatoes (page 218) and/or Green Beans with Tomatoes (page 172), or perhaps with Potatoes Maxime (page 224), to bring two great restaurant dishes together.

WINE SUGGESTION: a dry white

Trout with Red Wine

4 tablespoons butter
2 minced shallots or green
onions
2 tablespoons minced parsley
1 cup thinly sliced mushrooms
1 small bay leaf
⅛ teaspoon dried thyme
½ cup dry red wine
¼ cup water
Salt and freshly ground
pepper
4 medium-size trout

SERVES 4

EVERY RULE, they say, is made to be broken, and white wine only with fish is one of them. Even the French, every once and a while, surprise with a light red (you don't want a deep, subtle wine here).

Put 3 tablespoons of butter in a saucepan set over medium-high heat. When sizzling, add shallots and stir a minute, then add parsley and mushrooms. Stir another couple of minutes, or until the mushrooms start to exude juice. Add bay leaf, thyme, wine, water, and salt and pepper to taste. Turn heat to low and simmer 5 minutes.

Wipe trout and sprinkle lightly with salt and pepper inside and out. Pour a little of the sauce in a baking dish large enough to hold the trout in a single layer. Lay trout in and pour the rest of the sauce over. Dot with remaining butter. The dish may be prepared ahead to this point and kept covered at room temperature.

To cook, preheat oven to 375 degrees. Bake fish uncovered for 20 minutes, or until the flesh tests flaky and white with the poke of a sharp knife. Serve hot on warm plates with the sauce poured around.

SERVE WITH new potatoes tossed with butter and parsley, Potatoes Maxime (page 224), or Leek and Zucchini Gratin (page 244).
WINE SUGGESTION: a medium-bodied red or good rosé

Trout in Cream

4 medium-size trout

2 minced shallots or green
   onions

1 sprig thyme (or ¼ teaspoon
   dried)

1 sprig tarragon (or ¼ teaspoon dried)

1 bay leaf

1 cup dry white wine

1 cup water

8 peppercorns

Salt

1 cup cream, heated

1 teaspoon white wine vinegar
   (or to taste)

Parsley or tarragon sprigs for
   garnish

SERVES 4

A FINE SAUCE that lets the trout shine through.

Place trout in a large frying pan with shallots, herbs, wine, water, and peppercorns and a pinch of salt. Bring to a boil, lower heat, cover the pan, and simmer 6 to 8 minutes, turning once. Test the fish with a small, sharp knife to see if it flakes at the bone. Remove to a platter and keep warm in a low-temperature oven.

Raise heat under the pan and reduce the liquid by about half. Add cream and let it reduce until slightly thickened, then stir in vinegar to taste—it should be very subtle.

Remove top skin from the trout, leaving the heads and tails intact. Place on warm plates. Strain the sauce over and garnish with parsley or fresh tarragon. Serve immediately.

SERVE WITH Rice with Pine Nuts (page 207), or if you want more color to the plate, with any of the green bean or broccoli dishes.

WINE SUGGESTION: a dry white

Trout with Tarragon and Mushrooms

4 medium-size trout
Salt and freshly ground pepper
Flour
4 tablespoons butter
1 minced shallot or green onion
½ pound mushrooms, thinly sliced
½ lemon
1 teaspoon fresh tarragon (or ½ teaspoon dried)
2 tablespoons minced parsley

SERVES 4

THIS IS one of the best balanced sauces for trout there is—everything seems to complement everything else.

Wipe trout and sprinkle inside and out with salt and pepper. Dust lightly with flour. Place 2 tablespoons of butter in a large frying pan set over medium-high heat. Sauté the trout about 4 minutes a side, making sure the butter doesn't burn. Remove to a plate and keep warm.

Add shallot to the pan and stir a few minutes, then add mushrooms and a little more salt and pepper. Toss and cook over medium heat about 2 minutes, or until mushrooms start to exude juice. Squeeze in lemon juice to taste—starting with just a little and sampling. Immediately stir in tarragon and parsley and cook another couple of minutes.

Place trout on warm plates. Remove the top skin and divide mushroom mixture over trout, covering all but the heads and tails.

FOR SOME reason I like these with Classic French Fries (page 219), but you might pair them with Potatoes Maxime (page 224), or even Gratin Dauphinois (page 239).

WINE SUGGESTION: a dry white

Scallops with Saffron and Chives

1½ pounds scallops
½ cup dry vermouth
2 shallots, minced
¾ cup heavy cream
Pinch of saffron
2 tablespoons minced chives
12 tablespoons butter
Salt
White pepper
Cooked rice or angel hair
   pasta
Golden caviar (optional)

SERVES 4

AS EXTRAVAGANZAS go, this is a very simple one—and all that wonderful butter! If you can't get California fresh golden caviar, don't mess around with anything else, and it really is so good you won't miss it.

Wash scallops and pat dry. If they are large sea scallops, cut off the small ligament where they were attached and cut into halves or quarters—bay scallops are fine as is. Bring vermouth to boil in a saucepan set over medium heat. Drop in scallops and cook 2 to 3 minutes, or until just opaque. Remove with a slotted spoon to a bowl.

Add shallots to the pan and cook until most of the liquid has vanished and shallots are soft and glazed. Lower heat, add cream and saffron, and simmer until the sauce has thickened slightly. Stir in chives, then butter—tablespoon by tablespoon. Add salt and pepper to taste, then add scallops and cook just enough to heat them through.

Serve over rice or angel hair pasta, with a dollop of caviar on top, if you like.

WITH RICE or pasta you won't need much but some snow-peas to give color.

WINE SUGGESTION: a full-bodied white

Scalloped Scallops

2 pounds scallops
6 tablespoons butter
1 minced shallot or green on-
    ion
¾ cup dry white wine
1 tablespoon white wine vine-
    gar (preferably tarragon)
10 peppercorns
1 teaspoon dried tarragon
2 tablespoons flour
1¼ cups milk, heated
¼ cup heavy cream
1 tablespoon Dijon-style mus-
    tard
Salt and freshly ground pep-
    per
¼ cup freshly made bread
    crumbs (see page 325)
¼ cup grated Gruyère or
    Parmesan cheese
Lemon quarters

SERVES 4

THIS IS BETTER, I think, than the usual Coquilles Saint-Jacques the French serve as a first course. I wish we could get scallops as they do in England or the Continent, still in the shell with the delicate red coral attached, but here I suppose they go into cat food and no amount of pleading will ever obtain this sweet lovely morsel for the table.

Wash scallops and pat dry. If they are large sea scallops, cut off the small ligament where they were attached and cut into halves or quarters—bay scallops are fine as is. Put 2 tablespoons of butter in a frying pan set over medium-high heat and sauté the scallops only about 2 minutes. Remove from the heat. Put shallot, white wine, vinegar, peppercorns, and tarragon in a small saucepan set over heat. Boil down until reduced by half. Put 2 tablespoons butter in another saucepan set over medium heat and stir in flour. Cook, stirring, several minutes. Add the hot milk all at once and stir until you have a smooth sauce. Strain in the reduction, add cream, then stir in mustard and salt and pepper to taste. If the scallops have released any liquid, add that as well.

Use a little of the sauce to coat the bottoms of 4 scallop shells or ramekins, divide the scallops among them, and top with remaining sauce. Melt remaining butter in a saucepan. Mix bread crumbs and cheese and sprinkle over, then drizzle with melted butter. These may be prepared ahead and kept covered.

To serve, heat a broiler and place the scallops about 4 good inches under the flame. Broil until hot and bubbly and just starting to brown. Serve with lemon quarters.

SERVE WITH Asparagus with Walnut or Hazelnut Oil (page 168) or Green Beans with Shallots and Balsamic Vinegar (page 170).

WINE SUGGESTION: a full-bodied white

Lemon Scallops with Crispy Potatoes

1 pound baking potatoes
⅓ cup vegetable oil
Salt and freshly ground pepper
1 pound bay scallops
2 tablespoons olive oil
1 tablespoon butter
2 shallots, minced
½ clove garlic, minced
Juice of 1 lemon
¼ cup minced parsley

SERVES 4

THIS IS an odd-sounding combination, but really quite delicious. Be sure to have everything at hand—it should go like a breeze so the scallops don't overcook. Overcooked scallops might as well be rubber bands.

Peel potatoes, cut into tiny cubes—they should be less than ¼ inch—and rinse. If you're not going to cook them right away, put into a bowl and cover with cold water.

When ready to cook, drain and pat dry with paper towels. Heat vegetable oil in a large frying pan. When very hot, add potatoes and cook, stirring frequently, until they are golden and crisp—about 10 minutes. Scoop out with a slotted spoon onto paper towels to drain. Salt and pepper lightly.

Wash scallops and pat dry with paper towels. Discard the vegetable oil in the frying pan and put olive oil in. Heat over medium-high flame, then add scallops and salt and pepper to taste. Cook 1 minute, stirring well. Add butter, shallots, and garlic. Stir and cook another minute. Stir in potatoes, add lemon juice and parsley, and stir again. Serve on warm plates.

SERVE WITH Broccoli with Ripe Olive Sauce (page 179) or Green Beans Parmesan (page 169).

WINE SUGGESTION: a full-bodied white

Scallops with Cucumber

1 cucumber
2 tablespoons butter, plus extra melted butter to coat bread
1 shallot, minced
1½ pounds scallops (cleaned and cut as in preceding recipes)
Salt and freshly ground pepper
2 tablespoons tomato paste
¾ cup heavy cream
2 teaspoons lemon juice
1 tablespoon minced fresh tarragon (or 1 teaspoon dried)
4 slices white bread, crusts trimmed

SERVES 4

I GUESS because the French usually only serve scallops as a first course, and then only in variations on the same recipe, good recipes are hard to come by. But this is a very fine one indeed.

Peel cucumber, slice in half lengthwise, and scoop out seeds with a small spoon. Slice into ¼-inch half-moons and drop into boiling salted water. Cook 1 minute, then drain.

Heat butter in a large frying pan set over medium-high heat. Stir in shallot and cook a minute. Add scallops and salt and pepper to taste. Stir briefly, then add cucumber and stir again. Add tomato paste and cream and stir another couple of minutes.

Lift scallops out with a spoon and place in a small bowl. Add lemon juice and tarragon and reduce liquid to slightly thicken it. Taste for salt. This can be done ahead and kept covered.

To serve, brush bread with melted butter and fry over medium-low heat until crisp and browned. Add scallops to sauce just to warm through. Serve over the bread slices.

WITH THE cucumber and the croûtes, I don't think this needs any accompaniment except, perhaps, a fine rose of parsley.

WINE SUGGESTION: a full-bodied white

Scallops and Shrimp with Pesto

1 pound shrimp
1 pound bay scallops
3 tablespoons butter
3 tablespoons olive oil
Juice of 1 lemon
Salt and freshly ground pepper
1/4 cup pesto
Cooked rice or angel hair pasta

SERVES 4

THIS IS simple but absolutely, indescribably delicious. It can be done with either shrimp or scallops alone, but I like the fine contrast. If you can't buy pesto, it's easy to make. In a food processor, process 2 cups fresh basil, 1/2 cup olive oil, 3 tablespoons pine nuts, 2 cloves garlic, and 1 teaspoon salt until fine. Stir in 1/2 cup Parmesan or Romano cheese, and 3 tablespoons butter at room temperature.

Shell and devein shrimp. Wash scallops and pat dry with paper towels. Melt butter and oil in a large frying pan set over medium-high heat. When the butter sizzles, add shrimp and scallops. Cook, turning constantly until the shrimp turn pink. Add lemon juice and salt and pepper to taste—use only half the lemon before you taste. Add pesto and toss and cook another minute or so. The scallops will exude some juice, and if it looks too much, simply scoop out the shellfish with a slotted spoon and reduce over high heat until syrupy. Return shellfish to the pan and reheat. Serve over the rice or pasta.

SERVE WITH Green Beans with Shallots and Balsamic Vinegar (page 170) or with steamed and buttered snowpeas.

WINE SUGGESTION: a full-bodied white

Shrimps Waldorf

1½ pounds shrimp, peeled
   and deveined
¾ cup sweet vermouth
½ cup olive oil
Salt
Paprika (sweet Hungarian, if
   possible)
¼ cup butter
1 clove garlic, slightly flattened and peeled
Cooked rice

SERVES 4

THE WALDORF'S secret was the sweet vermouth rather than the expected dry. And what a fine and tasty difference it makes—and how simple.

Place shrimp in a glass bowl with the vermouth and let marinate 1 or 2 hours.

To cook, preheat the broiler. Drain shrimp and place in a baking dish large enough to hold them in a single layer. Add oil, salt to taste, and a blush of paprika. Broil about 7 minutes, or until pink and sizzling—they should be turned once. As they cook, melt butter with garlic until it begins to color, then discard the garlic.

Scatter shrimp over rice and top with garlic butter. Serve at once.

SERVE WITH steamed snow peas or Peas Braised with Cucumbers (page 201).

WINE SUGGESTION: a fruity white

Shrimp in Tarragon Cream

1½ pounds shrimp, peeled and deveined
3 tablespoons butter
2 shallots, minced
1 tablespoon minced fresh tarragon (or 2 tablespoons chives)
Salt and freshly ground pepper
1 teaspoon lemon juice
3 tablespoons brandy
¾ cup heavy cream
1 tablespoon flour mixed with 1 tablespoon softened butter
8 slices toasted bread, cut into triangles (buttered or not, as you please)
Tarragon or parsley sprigs for garnish

SERVES 4

A SMALL masterpiece that can be put together in moments.

Prepare shrimp ahead, and just before serving, have all your ingredients handy and the toast points crisping on warm plates in the oven.

Melt butter in a large frying pan set over medium-high heat. Add shallots and toss a minute, then add shrimp. Toss and turn just until they are an even pink—a matter of 3 to 4 minutes.

Toss with tarragon and salt and pepper to taste. Then toss with lemon juice. Pour brandy over and set aflame with a match. Toss while this burns, to help the flames. When it dies out, add cream and let bubble up. Add the flour and butter mixture in small pieces, stirring all the while, but don't add any more than will make a silky sauce. Pour over toast and serve with a fresh sprig of tarragon or parsley.

SERVE WITH Peas Braised with Cucumbers (page 201).

WINE SUGGESTION: a dry white

Shrimp with Capers

8 slices white homestyle
  bread, crusts trimmed
Olive oil
1 clove garlic, slightly flattened and peeled
1½ pounds shrimp, peeled
  and deveined
1 tablespoon capers
2 tablespoons minced parsley
3 tablespoons lemon juice
Tabasco sauce
Salt

SERVES 4

SWEET SHRIMP take kindly to a hint of tartness, and this is just about right. The dish can also be elevated with the addition of sliced, cooked artichoke hearts.

Cut bread diagonally in half. Brush with olive oil and toast in a large frying pan over medium heat until crisp and golden on both sides. These can be prepared ahead, but should be waiting on warm plates in a low-temperature oven when you go about the shrimping.

Heat 3 tablespoons olive oil in a large frying pan set over medium heat and add garlic. When golden, discard it and add shrimp. Toss until they turn pink. Add capers, parsley, lemon juice, a dash of hot Tabasco, and salt to taste. Toss a couple of minutes more and serve over the toast.

SERVE WITH Broccoli with Ripe Olive Sauce (page 179).

WINE SUGGESTION: a dry white

Shrimp with Sherry and Saffron

2 tablespoons olive oil
1½ cups chopped onion
2 cloves garlic, minced
1½ pounds shrimp, peeled
   and deveined
Salt and freshly ground pepper
⅛ teaspoon saffron threads
½ cup dry sherry
Cooked rice

SERVES 4

I LIKE to use a very good sherry like Tío Pepe here, rather than an ordinary "cooking" sherry—it's worth the bit extra in the way it balances with the saffron.

Heat olive oil in a large frying pan set over medium heat and sauté onion and garlic until soft. Add shrimp, salt and pepper to taste, and saffron. Toss over medium-high heat 4 to 5 minutes, then add sherry and simmer another few minutes.

Serve over hot, fluffy rice (for a nice, colorful addition, toss the rice with cooked tiny peas).

IF YOU'VE found garden peas to toss with the rice, this needs no accompaniment but crusty bread. If not, serve perhaps with Broccoli with Ripe Olive Sauce (page 179).

WINE SUGGESTION: a dry white

Greek Shrimp with Feta and Pine Nuts

¼ cup butter (or olive oil)
1 medium-size onion, chopped
2 cloves garlic (1 clove minced, 1 clove slightly flattened and peeled)
¼ cup minced parsley
1 teaspoon dried oregano
2 cups Italian plum tomatoes, drained from the can and coarsely chopped (reserve the juice)
Salt and freshly ground pepper
½ cup dry white wine
½ cup pine nuts
1½ pounds shrimp, peeled and deveined
1 cup feta cheese, crumbled
Cooked rice

SERVES 4

I THINK this dish holds its own with our famous, long-cooked, complex gumbos in the South. It is much easier to construct, too, and will delight any guest with its crisp nuts and melting sharp cheese.

Put half the butter (or oil) in a saucepan set over medium heat. Add onion and minced garlic and cook several minutes, then add parsley and oregano. Stir in tomatoes and enough of the juice to moisten the sauce well. Add salt and pepper to taste (salt only lightly due to the feta) and turn heat down to medium-low. Cook, uncovered, 20 minutes. If necessary, add a little tomato juice from time to time, but after 20 minutes it should be cooked down almost dry. Add wine, turn heat up high, and cook 2 minutes. The sauce can be made well ahead.

To finish the dish, put the rest of the butter or oil in a frying pan set over medium heat. Add the clove of garlic and cook until it turns golden, then remove it. Add pine nuts and toss a minute, then add shrimp and toss just until they turn pink. Heat up the tomato sauce and add to the shrimp. Toss well and add ⅔ cup of cheese. Cook just until heated through. Serve over rice, sprinkled with the rest of the cheese.

I DON'T think this dish needs any accompaniment except some French bread.

WINE SUGGESTION: a dry white or medium-bodied red

Steaks, Chops, and Scallops

FOR GOOD REASON these are staples of restaurant cooking, where each dish must be turned out quickly to order. The basic grilled or pan-fried steak or chop can be seared and sauced with little more than the flick of a wrist, and needs only a side dish of note for full effect. I do not mean to slight the sirloins of yesteryear, done to a turn on the barbecue grill, baked potatoes and all the trimmings, sliced beefsteak tomatoes, corn on the cob, and chocolate layer cake with homemade vanilla ice cream. But we can eat lighter, and love it just as much.

The steaks here need not be filet mignon, but they should be ones you would be happy eating without any sauce at all. Veal too should be top quality, cut by the very best butcher you can find. Recipes here assume you can get thick veal sirloins, or at least decent, thick chops (the best, if you like, with a cut of kidney curled into the tip). I also call for thinly cut slices of loin for scallops or scallopini—recipes you can literally whistle through. My ideal way to eat or treat lamb is to spend the time roasting a leg just studded with garlic slivers and needles of rosemary. But for those in a rush, good, meaty, thick chops are easy to get comfortable with as any steak.

Instead of shying away totally from red meats, I don't see why we can't occasionally splurge with a tender small steak or lamb chop, or with a creamy-sauced veal scallop, for sustenance and company?

Steaks with Red Wine Sauce

4 1-inch-thick steaks (any tender boneless cut—about 1½ pounds total)
Salt and freshly ground pepper
2 tablespoons vegetable oil
2 tablespoons butter
2 minced shallots or green onions
⅔ cup dry red wine

SERVES 4

A QUICK French classic, usually served in bistros with pommes frites (french fries) and requiring only a sound wine and tender meat. It is an example of a dish where the wine you cook with should be the wine you are going to drink with the meat, rather than the ends of any jug or bottle at hand.

Pat steaks dry with paper towels and sprinkle with salt and pepper. Heat oil in a large frying pan set over high heat. When hot (but not smoking), sauté steaks until browned—about a minute per side. Then lower heat to medium and cook about 4 more minutes, turning once. This should be fine for medium-rare. Remove from the pan, keep warm, and discard oil from the pan.

Add 1 tablespoon of butter and over medium heat sauté shallots a minute. Add wine, stirring to deglaze the pan. Bring to a boil and reduce the wine over high heat until almost syrupy. Remove from heat and stir in remaining butter. Pour over the steaks and serve immediately.

SERVE WITH Classic French Fries (page 219) and a sprig of watercress, or to be fancy, with Gratin Dauphinois (page 239) and/or Mushrooms Stuffed with Pine Nuts (page 196).

WINE SUGGESTION: a full-bodied red

Steak au Poivre

4 1-inch-thick steaks (any
   boneless cut—about 1½
   pounds total)
Coarsely cracked pepper
3 tablespoons vegetable oil
⅓ cup dry white wine
⅓ cup brandy
3 tablespoons butter
Salt (optional)

SERVES 4

AFTER SEVERAL dismal experiences with Steak au Poivre in France, where I had to scrape the pepper off before I could eat a rather lackluster steak, I dropped this from my repertoire. But a friend, John Hartman, suggested that it didn't need a huge crust of pepper, and that a fine glaze of wine and brandy and butter would make it even finer, and he was right.

Pat steaks dry with paper towels and trim any extra fat, if necessary. The secret of these steaks is the fragrance of the pepper. I use a small mortar and pestle to crack them, though you can also use a pepper mill turned to the widest setting. The amount of pepper is one of taste, but the steaks should be at least evenly coated. Press the pepper firmly into both sides of the steaks with your hands, then let sit at room temperature at least an hour to gather flavor.

To cook, heat oil in a frying pan set over high heat. When hot (but not smoking), sauté steaks until browned—about a minute a side, then lower heat to medium and cook about 4 more minutes, turning once. At this point they will be medium-rare. Remove the steaks from the pan and keep warm. Discard the fat from the pan and add wine and brandy. Cook over medium-high heat until reduced by half, then remove from heat and whisk in butter, a tablespoon at a time. Taste the sauce—it shouldn't need salt, unless you have used unsalted butter. It's up to you. Glaze the steaks and serve immediately.

FOR AN exceptional presentation, serve these with Polenta Cups with Chèvre and Sun-Dried Tomatoes (page 204) and Mushrooms Stuffed with Pine Nuts (page 196), but they would be just as good served with Gratin Dauphinois (page 239).

WINE SUGGESTION: a full-bodied red

Steaks
Bordelaise

4 1-inch-thick steaks (any ten-
    der boneless cut—about 1½
    pounds total)
Freshly ground pepper
12 round-cut slices marrow
    bone
Salt
3 tablespoons butter
¼ cup minced shallot
¼ cup minced parsley
2 tablespoons vegetable oil

SERVES 4

THIS IS a variation on a dish Elizabeth David describes. Hers is grilled, which is fine, but the shallots and parsley are raw, which is not. Also, taking a tip from the wonderful Mildred Knopf, I think it's easier to bake the marrow, rather than poach, for if you're not careful the marrow can just dissolve in the poaching liquid. It makes a great dish.

Preheat oven to 350 degrees. Pat steaks dry with paper towels and lightly pepper both sides. Lay marrow bones in a baking dish and cook 15 minutes, then remove. When they are cool enough to handle, remove the slices of marrow with a small knife, lay them on a plate, and salt lightly.

While the marrow bones are baking, melt butter in a small saucepan set over medium heat. When it sputters, add shallots and parsley and cook about a minute. Put oil in a large frying pan over high heat. When hot (but not smoking), sauté steaks until browned—about a minute per side. Lower heat to medium and cook about 4 minutes, turning once. This should be fine for medium-rare.

Place steaks on warm plates, top each with 3 marrow slices, and sprinkle the shallot-parsley mixture over the top. Salt lightly and serve.

SERVE WITH Mushrooms Stuffed with Pine Nuts (page 196) and Potatoes in Red Pepper Butter (page 228).

WINE SUGGESTION: a full-bodied red

Three Simple Sauces for Steaks

Brandy Cream Sauce

Prepare steaks as in Steak with Red Wine Sauce (page 102). At the point you put butter in the pan, add ½ cup dry vermouth. Bring to a boil and scrape up any browned bits. Add ¼ cup whipping cream and reduce sauce by half over high heat. Warm ¼ cup brandy in a small saucepan, ignite with a match, and pour into sauce. Roll pan until the flames die out, then pour over warm steaks.
SERVES 4

Marchand de Vin Sauce

Put ⅓ cup minced shallots in a small saucepan with 1 cup good red wine. Cook over medium-high heat until the wine is reduced by half. Add ¼ cup strong beef stock and cook several more minutes. Strain, pressing down on the shallots to release liquid. Return to the saucepan. Mix 6 tablespoons butter with 2 teaspoons flour until thoroughly blended. Bring liquid in the saucepan just to a boil, remove from heat, and beat in butter and flour mixture bit by bit, stirring well each time until it dissolves. At the end you should have a thick, glossy emulsion. Add a few drops lemon juice and 2 tablespoons finely minced parsley at the end. Serve over warm steaks of any kind.
SERVES 4

Shallot and Balsamic Vinegar Sauce

Simply combine ⅓ cup finely minced shallots with enough balsamic vinegar to cover well. Let sit at least 30 minutes to mellow before using. This is a recipe invented by San Francisco food writer Jim Wood, and is not only delicious with steaks or other meats but also has no fat and very few calories.
SERVES 4

Original Stroganoff

1 pound fillet of beef
½ cup plus 1 tablespoon flour
2 tablespoons freshly ground
  pepper
4 tablespoons butter
2 tablespoons vegetable oil
1 onion, very thinly sliced
Salt
1 cup chicken stock
2 tablespoons Dijon-style
  mustard
2 tablespoons sour cream

SERVES 4

THE TALE comes down that the Princess Alexandra Kropot-kin took it upon herself to descend to the palace kitchens to discover the exact secrets of a Stroganoff. If her investigations were correct, what we think of as Stroganoff is a dish as far from its native shore as Chop Suey. It has quite a lot of pepper, first off, and is not swimming in sour cream and sherry, and it is delicious—not just culinary archaeology. A friend tells me she had it once in Paris very much like this, but with crème fraîche and homemade noodles—surely a presentation to emulate.

Thinly slice meat. If your knife isn't quite sharp, freeze the fillet 30 minutes before. Shake the pieces well in a bag with ½ cup flour and all the pepper. Lift out, making sure all are coated, and place on wax paper. If necessary, use more flour. Let sit at room temperature until all evidence of the flour has disappeared—it will soak into the meat.

Heat 2 tablespoons of butter and oil in a large frying pan. Sauté beef in batches over medium-high heat until just seared. Remove from the pan as they cook and place on a plate. Add remaining butter and onion to the pan and cook over low heat until it separates into soft, golden rings. Salt them a little as they cook (the original recipe has *no* salt, but I think it needs a little at this point). Stir in 1 tablespoon of flour and stir several minutes. Add stock and stir into a sauce. Return beef to the pan and turn up heat. Toss with mustard and then sour cream. Cover, remove from heat, and let sit 20 minutes before serving.

SERVE WITH buttered noodles and perhaps Broccoli with Buttered Crumbs (page 176).

WINE SUGGESTION: a full-bodied red or white

Flank Steak with Herb Butter

1 whole flank steak (1½ to 2 pounds)
1 cup dry red wine
¼ cup olive oil
1 clove garlic, slightly flattened and peeled
Freshly ground pepper
4 tablespoons butter
2 tablespoons minced herbs (tarragon, parsley, thyme, basil, chives, rosemary—or a mixture)
½ teaspoon lemon juice
½ teaspoon Worcestershire sauce
Salt

SERVES 4

TRY A FLANK STEAK next time you are grilling meat, rather than the same old T-bones—with some marination they are quite delectable. Also, compound butters can be made with other than just herbs. A very fine one, rather like a beurre blanc, is to reduce chopped shallot and white wine to a glaze before incorporating it into the butter. I've seen a recipe that does this with a good red wine and dried herbes de Provence, and another that uses an admirable Stilton and a few drops of port! I use compound butters often with steaks of one kind or another, as they make the simplest possible sauce.

Cut steak in half lengthwise down the middle and place in a large, flat, nonreactive dish. Add wine, oil, garlic, and several generous grinds of the pepper mill. Let marinate for several hours.

Combine butter, herbs, lemon juice, and Worcestershire in a small bowl with a fork (frankly, I use my hands) until well mixed. The butter will probably not quite absorb all the moisture, but it doesn't matter. This can be made well ahead and refrigerated.

To cook the steak, preheat the broiler (or a charcoal grill) and cook steaks 3 to 4 minutes a side. They should be seared brown on the outside and pink in the middle. Remove and salt lightly. Cut into strips at a sharp slant across the grain and fan them out on warm plates. Divide the butter among them while quite hot so it will melt into the slices.

SERVE WITH any of the potato dishes, but if you are cooking outside, a good choice would be My Mother's Creamed Parmesan Potatoes (page 235), which can be prepared in advance and reheated on the grill. Or perhaps Red Pepper Gratin (page 242).

WINE SUGGESTION: a full-bodied red

Flank Steak Teriyaki-Style

1 whole flank steak (1½ to 2
    pounds)
1 cup soy sauce
¾ cup sugar
¼ cup dry white wine
2 cloves garlic, slightly flat-
    tened and peeled
4 slices fresh gingerroot
Vegetable oil

SERVES 4

THIS MAKES a simple, tasty family dish as well as a company one.

Cut steak in half lengthwise down the middle and place in a large, flat, nonreactive dish. Place all the ingredients except the oil in a small saucepan and bring to a boil, making sure the sugar dissolves. Let cool a little, then pour over the steak and let marinate several hours, turning now and again.

To cook, preheat a broiler or start a charcoal grill. Remove steak from the marinade and brush well with oil on both sides. Broil or grill fairly close to a flame about 3 to 4 minutes a side. You want a well-seared outside and a pink inside.

Cut into strips at a sharp slant across the grain and fan out on warm plates.

I LIKE to serve this with rice, strewing both meat and rice with lightly toasted sesame seeds and chopped green onions. And I usually accompany it with beer rather than wine.

WINE SUGGESTION: a good imported beer

Veal Steaks with Green Peppercorns

4 veal loin steaks, about 1
inch thick (or 8 chops)
Salt and freshly ground pepper
2 tablespoons butter
1 tablespoon vegetable oil
2 shallots, minced
¼ cup brandy
2 tablespoons lemon juice
½ cup heavy cream
1 tablespoon green peppercorns
1 teaspoon minced fresh tarragon or parsley

SERVES 4

GREEN PEPPERCORNS *are somewhat of an acquired taste, but in the few years they've been available I've certainly acquired it, and always keep some in the refrigerator.*

Wipe veal dry and lightly salt and pepper. Heat butter and oil in a frying pan large enough to hold the steaks (chops might have to be fried in batches with a little more butter and oil) and sauté them over medium-high heat about 4 minutes a side. They should be seared brown on the outside and still pink inside. Remove and keep warm in the oven.

Add shallots to the pan and cook over medium heat a minute or so, then add brandy and lemon juice. Reduce by half over low heat, then stir in cream and turn up the heat. Mash half the peppercorns and add along with the whole ones and tarragon. When the sauce is almost syrupy, add salt and pepper to taste. Glaze the meat with the sauce and serve immediately.

I LIKE these with simple mashed potatoes, but practically any of the potato recipes here will do, or any of the gratins or *sformati*.

WINE SUGGESTION: a medium-bodied red

Veal Steaks with Gorgonzola Butter

3 tablespoons unsalted butter
¼ cup Gorgonzola cheese
Freshly ground pepper
4 veal loin steaks, about 1
   inch thick (or 8 chops)
Salt
¼ cup olive oil

SERVES 4

THIS IS a signature dish from a neighborhood San Francisco restaurant—though theirs are the largest sirloin chops I've ever seen and are done over a mesquite grill. Even without that extra zing, though, these are simply delicious at home.

Put butter and cheese in a small bowl and mash with a fork. You don't want to do this in a food processor, as there ought to be little lumps of cheese through the mixture rather than all whipped up. Grind rather a lot of pepper into the butter and mix well. This can be prepared well ahead and refrigerated or not.

Wipe steaks dry with paper towels and salt them on each side. Heat oil in a large frying pan and sauté them over high heat 3 to 4 minutes a side. They ought to be well seared outside and still pink in the middle. It is best to do this in batches so each one sears quickly. Place on warm serving plates and divide the Gorgonzola butter over the tops.

SERVE THESE with Classic French Fries (page 219) or perhaps Baltimore Fries (page 220), and tuck in a large sprig of watercress for greenery. Or for something really special, Pumpkin Gnocchi with Sage Butter (page 205).

WINE SUGGESTION: a medium-bodied red

Veal Chops with Anchovy Sauce

8 veal chops, about 1 inch
  thick
Salt and freshly ground pepper
4 tablespoons butter
2 tablespoons olive oil
2 teaspoons anchovy paste (or
  2 flat anchovies, minced)
1 clove garlic, minced
2 tablespoons minced parsley
½ cup dry white wine

SERVES 4

YOU MIGHT *think anchovies odd with veal in this admirable Italian dish, but they give pizzaz rather than fishiness to the finished product.*

Wipe chops dry and sprinkle with salt and pepper to taste. Put butter and oil in a frying pan large enough to cook chops in 2 batches. Turn heat to medium-high. When the butter sizzles, add the chops. Cook 3 to 4 minutes a side, or until golden outside and still pink in the middle. Keep warm in the oven.

Add anchovy paste and garlic to the pan. Stir a minute, then add parsley and wine. Turn heat up high and reduce the sauce slightly. Pour over the chops, garnish with a tuft of parsley, and serve immediately.

FOR AN ideal pairing serve these with *Sformato* with Green Beans (page 249).

WINE SUGGESTION: a medium or full-bodied red

Veal Chops with Rosemary Sauce

2 tablespoons butter
1 minced shallot or green on-
    ion
1½ teaspoons minced fresh
    rosemary
2 tablespoons dry white wine
½ cup beef stock
½ cup heavy cream
Salt and freshly ground pep-
    per
8 1-inch-thick veal chops
Olive oil
Rosemary sprigs for garnish

SERVES 4

A REMARKABLE DISH, and one you could substitute dried rosemary in, though fresh is best. Bland veal needs something always to perk it up, and rosemary is one of the best ways of all.

Melt butter in a small saucepan set over medium heat. Stir in shallot and cook 2 minutes. Add rosemary and wine and reduce over high heat until only a little liquid remains. Add stock and let it reduce by half. Add cream and boil down until it thickens slightly. Strain the sauce and keep warm. Season with salt and pepper to taste. This can be made ahead and then reheated.

Pat chops dry and either panfry in a little olive oil or brush with oil and broil or grill them. This will take only 3 to 4 minutes a side for medium-rare. Place on warm serving plates, spoon sauce over, and put a sprig of rosemary at the side.

CELERY ROOT PUREE (page 190) would be admirable here and/or Peas Braised with Cucumbers (page 201) and/or Carrots with Cognac (page 184).

WINE SUGGESTION: a medium-bodied red or full-bodied white

Veal Scallops with Prosciutto

8 medium-size veal scallops
Salt and freshly ground pep-
    per
Flour
4 tablespoons butter
3 tablespoons vegetable oil
8 thin slices prosciutto
Juice of ½ lemon
2 tablespoons minced parsley

SERVES 4

THIS IS a dish they used to serve at the Waldorf-Astoria, easy to turn out both from a restaurant or home kitchen. It is a genial, simple yet spectacular dish which takes less actual working time than reading the recipe.

Preheat oven to 350 degrees. Place veal scallops between wax paper and pound lightly to about a ¼-inch thickness—they should be as thin as scallopini. Season lightly with salt and pepper, then dredge in flour.

Heat 2 tablespoons of butter with oil in a large, ovenproof frying pan and in batches sauté the veal over medium-high heat 3 to 4 minutes a side, or until golden. When all are cooked, pour off about half the cooking fat and return veal to the pan. Place in the oven and bake 10 minutes.

Turn oven off. Arrange 2 veal scallops, alternating with 2 slices prosciutto, on each dinner plate. Return to the oven to keep warm. Heat remaining butter in a small saucepan. When it sizzles, add lemon juice and cook a minute or so until it becomes lightly golden. Add parsley and immediately pour over the meat.

SERVE WITH Potato-Shell Fries (page 221) or Gratin of Fennel (page 246).

WINE SUGGESTION: a medium-bodied red

Veal Scallops with Marsala and Mushrooms

8 medium-size veal scallops
Flour
Olive oil
¼ pound sliced prosciutto, cut
   into ¼-inch strips
½ pound button mushrooms,
   stemmed (or 1-inch mushrooms, quartered)
¼ cup unsalted butter
½ cup dry Marsala

SERVES 4

AN ABSOLUTELY *delicious dish, and at first you will think I left out the salt and pepper. Neither are needed because of the prosciutto. Also, don't skimp on the quality of Marsala in this—get a good one and keep it on hand.*

Put veal scallops between sheets of wax paper and pound lightly until they are thin and almost double in size (I use a rolling pin for this, but an empty wine bottle will do). Dredge lightly in flour.

Heat a couple of tablespoons oil in a large frying pan set over medium-high heat and in batches sauté the veal about 45 seconds a side, or until lightly browned. Use more oil if needed. If there is any left at the bottom of the pan when all are done, discard it. The scallops may be made up to this point and set aside.

To cook, place the veal in the pan with the rest of the ingredients. Bring to a simmer, cover the pan, and cook gently 15 minutes, turning the veal scallops twice as they cook. Serve immediately.

SERVE WITH mashed potatoes, to capture some of the sauce, or with either *Sformato* with Green Beans (page 249) or *Sformato* Bianco (page 254).

WINE SUGGESTION: a full-bodied red

Veal Scallops with Chives and Pine Nuts

1½ pounds thinly sliced veal
Flour
3 tablespoons butter
1 tablespoon olive oil
Salt and freshly ground pepper
2 tablespoons minced fresh chives
⅓ cup dry vermouth or white wine
⅓ cup pine nuts, lightly toasted

SERVES 4

I DON'T KNOW about you, but I have to go across the city to get really fine veal scallops. The rest of the markets sell thinish slices of varying size and shape, and this is the recipe to use for those.

Lightly pound veal between sheets of wax paper until ⅛ inch thick and about double the original size. Cut into pieces about the size of half a postcard. Dredge in flour.

Heat butter and oil in a large frying pan set over medium-high heat. When sputtering, slip in a layer of veal and cook until golden brown on both sides. Remove and cook the rest in the same way.

Return the veal to the pan and toss with salt and pepper to taste and chives. Add the vermouth or wine and let it cook up around the meat. Lower heat and let the liquid make a sauce. Cover the pan and cook 5 more minutes, turning twice to coat the veal.

Uncover when done, toss in nuts, stir well, and let them heat through. Serve hot.

THIS COULD be served over rice or with mashed potatoes or perhaps Green Beans Parmesan (page 169).

WINE SUGGESTION: a medium-bodied red

Veal Scallops with Fontina and Sage

4 large veal scallops
Juice of ½ lemon
Salt and freshly ground pepper
Flour
Freshly made bread crumbs for dredging (see page 325)
1 egg
2 tablespoons butter
2 tablespoons vegetable oil
Fontina cheese
2 tablespoons chopped fresh sage

SERVES 4

THIS IS one of my favorite ways to serve veal to company, and I'm very partial to fontina. It should be creamy and with a haunting, nutty flavor, so taste it—some of the Danish fontina is rather rubbery, it seems.

Place veal scallops between wax paper and pound gently until they are thin and twice their original size. Sprinkle both sides with lemon juice and let them sit about 30 minutes.

Sprinkle lightly with salt and pepper, then turn them in a plate of flour until lightly coated. Place the bread crumbs on a plate. In a bowl, beat the egg with a tablespoon of water. Dip each scallop in the egg mixture, then coat with bread crumbs. As you bread each one, lay it out on a sheet of wax paper. Refrigerate the scallops about 30 minutes to set the coating.

Heat butter and oil in a large frying pan and in batches sauté the scallops 2 to 3 minutes a side, or until lightly gold. Lay out in a baking pan as they cook. Top each with thinly sliced cheese (or if it's easier, grated cheese). Sprinkle with sage. Fresh is best here, but you can use dried, crumbled sage—not powdered—if that's all you have.

The scallops can sit, if you like, at this point. To continue, place under a preheated broiler and cook until the cheese almost starts to bubble. Serve immediately.

SERVE WITH Mushrooms Stuffed with Pine Nuts (page 196) and/or Green Beans with Shallots and Balsamic Vinegar (page 170).

WINE SUGGESTION: a medium-bodied red

Broiled Lamb Chops

8 lamb chops, about 1½ inches thick
¼ cup olive oil
1 clove garlic, peeled and thinly sliced
1 branch rosemary (or 1 teaspoon dried)
Salt and freshly ground pepper

SERVES 4

THIS IS the simplest way to prepare lamb chops at home in little time. Beef takes well to sauces, and pork and chicken and even fish are adaptable to presentation, but lamb (anyway both chops and leg) should be innocent of almost anything but plain fire and forthright seasoning.

Marinate chops in oil, garlic, and rosemary for an hour or more. Preheat broiler for 10 to 15 minutes at least, so the chops begin to sear immediately. Broil 5 to 8 minutes a side on a rack set about 2 inches from the flame. I find a total of about 15 minutes ideal for a crusty outside and pink interior, but you may like them rarer or (God forbid) well done. They can also be grilled outside in this manner.

Remove with tongs to warm plates and salt and pepper lightly. Serve at once.

THESE ARE largish chops, but even so they really need a substantial side dish—any of the gratins will work well, especially Eggplant Gratin (page 241) or Gratin of Garbanzos, Tomatoes, and Turmeric Custard (page 247).

WINE SUGGESTION: a full-bodied red

Lamb Chops Abruzzo

12 loin lamb chops, about 1
  inch thick
Salt and freshly ground pepper
¼ cup olive oil
2 sprigs fresh rosemary
1 clove garlic, lightly flattened
  and peeled
¼ cup dry white wine
Juice of ½ lemon

SERVES 4

*MOST ANY recipe will tell you to broil or grill lamb chops for
maximum succulence, but this recipe shows how easy and
delectable it is to panfry them.*

Trim chops of excess fat and sprinkle with salt and pepper. Heat oil in a large frying pan set over medium-high
heat. As it heats, add rosemary and garlic. When the
garlic turns gold, lift it out.

Place chops in the hot pan and sauté until browned on
each side, in batches if necessary. Pour in the wine
(watch, it will sputter) and continue to cook, turning
twice, until all the wine has evaporated. By then the
chops should be done, but still pink inside and ready to
serve.

Remove to warm plates and sprinkle with lemon juice.

FOR THE best of all worlds, pair these with Pumpkin
Gnocchi with Sage Butter (page 205).

WINE SUGGESTION: a full-bodied red

Lamb Chops with Red Pepper Butter

1 large, sweet red pepper, roasted (see page 331)
6 tablespoons butter
Salt
¼ teaspoon lemon juice
12 loin lamb chops, about 1 inch thick
1 clove garlic, slightly flattened and peeled
Olive oil

SERVES 4

RED PEPPERS *are milder and sweeter than green but still have as distinctive a taste. I know several dishes rescued by both green and red—though usually from behind the scene, as it were. Recently cooks have brought them forward, and this is one case I think they make a brave partner to a simply cooked lamb chop.*

Clean roasted peppers. Cut into strips, then into small dice.

Slice butter into a food processor and add about a quarter of the pepper. Process to a fairly fine puree. Add salt to taste, lemon juice, and the rest of the pepper and process until just well mixed. Scrape into a bowl and press with your hands. There will be liquid to pour off, but you don't have to be fanatic about it. Cover with plastic wrap and refrigerate.

You can cook the chops by grilling, broiling, or pan-frying. To grill or broil, rub with garlic, then brush with oil and cook about 3 minutes a side. To fry, heat the garlic in about ¼ inch olive oil and remove when golden. Fry the chops 3 minutes a side in batches.

Place chops on warmed plates and divide the pepper butter over them. The butter will have melted by the time you get to the table, and there will be a delectable mound of red pepper on top.

SERVE WITH Potatoes Maxime (page 224), Gratin Dauphinois (page 239), or superbly with Gratin of Fennel (page 246). If you wish a green vegetable, try Green Beans with Shallots and Balsamic Vinegar (page 170) or Broccoli with Buttered Crumbs (page 176).

WINE SUGGESTION: a full-bodied red

Lamb Chops with Green Peppercorns

12 loin lamb chops, about 1
    inch thick
Salt and freshly ground pep-
    per
½ cup dry vermouth or white
    wine
2 tablespoons green pepper-
    corns
2 tablespoons white wine vin-
    egar
4 tablespoons butter
Vegetable oil

SERVES 4

THIS IS ABOUT as far as I will go in the way of saucing an already admirable chop, but if you like green peppercorns, it is very good indeed.

Trim chops of excess fat, if necessary, and sprinkle lightly with salt and pepper. Put vermouth or wine, peppercorns, and vinegar in a small saucepan and cook over medium-low heat until reduced to about 2 tablespoons. Cook slowly to allow the peppercorn essence to really flavor the sauce. This may be made well ahead and set aside.

You can cook the chops by grilling, broiling, or pan-frying. To grill or broil, brush liberally with oil first. To fry, pour a film of oil in a frying pan set over high heat. Whatever the method, cook the chops about 3 minutes a side. They should be well seared on the outside and still pink on the inside—though not bloody.

While the chops are cooking, remove the peppercorns and juices from the saucepan and reserve. Add the butter and cook over medium-high heat until the butter foams up and starts to brown. Immediately return the peppercorns to the pan. Pour the sizzling sauce over the chops and serve immediately.

SERVE WITH Red Pepper Gratin (page 242), Potatoes Sablees (page 226), or Broccoli Puree with Gruyère and Madeira (page 180).

WINE SUGGESTION: a full-bodied red

Sauced and Succulent Pork and Ham

JAMES BEARD STATED it flatly: "Pork happens to be my favorite meat." I cannot be so bald about that, but I do treasure recipes where to contradict would be folly. Pork used to be considered by food pundits at most a family experience, too humble for guests. At the same time restaurants left it off the menu as not a lure for patrons, and also as taking too long to cook.

I somehow believe all these opinions and positions, at the same time claiming banners for those recipes that don't take up hours of attention. Indeed, a host of rather elegant ways have been invented, and put by, to serve up the humble pork chop, and they should be ours to use and share.

On the other hand, ham is an applauded company affair—great on the face of it—but how does the lone cook or couple use up the rest of that display for future meals? Granted, you can serve it, of fond memory, scalloped with creamy potatoes a time or two, and grind up some ham salad, with a lot of mayonnaise, a dab of mustard, and plenty of chopped pickle, but it can then become a burden and a bore. My solution is to knife prime pieces off to freeze, for tossing with some miraculous sauce down the road, like those mentioned here—ham then becomes a joy to have extra on hand.

Roast Pork Arista

4 cloves garlic
1 teaspoon salt
1 teaspoon freshly ground
  pepper
1 teaspoon fennel seeds
2 tablespoons olive oil
1½ to 2 pound pork tenderloin

SERVES 4

THIS IS NOT the only reason to keep fennel seeds on hand, but it is among the best. It absolutely perfumes the kitchen as it cooks, so that guests sit up and take notice before they even get to table. If you can't get tenderloins, the same process can be used for a 2½-pound boneless pork loin, which needs to roast an hour and a half, and will feed six.

The way they go about this in Tuscany is to grind the garlic with salt, pepper, and fennel seeds with a mortar and pestle, adding in the olive oil last. You can speed this up by running salt, pepper, and fennel seeds in a food processor fitted with the steel blade until the fennel breaks up, then dropping the garlic cloves in one by one while the machine is running. Finally, add olive oil through the tube while running. Push down and process as finely as possible, then scrape it out and continue with a mortar and pestle. This is probably no great shakes, but the essence starts to get to you as you smell the perfumes released with a little mix and grind, and you soon have a fragrant paste you'd spoon on practically anything.

Since pork tenderloins taper off at one end, they are usually packaged in twos end to end, making a tube about 2½ inches in diameter. Keep them that way, wipe dry, tie with string, and rub the fennel paste all over them. Wrap in foil or plastic wrap and let marinate several hours—or overnight in the refrigerator.

To cook, preheat the oven to 375 degrees. Unwrap the pork. If you have refrigerated it, let come to room temperature. Place in an oiled roasting pan and bake 30 minutes, or until the internal temperature is 165 degrees. Remove from the oven and cut off string. Let sit 5 to 10 minutes, then slice into ½-inch-medallions. Fan out on warm plates and serve at once.

SERVE WITH any of the *sformati*, Sweet Potato and Turnip Gratin (page 245), Pumpkin Gnocchi with Sage Butter (page 205), and/or Green Beans Parmesan (page 169).

WINE SUGGESTION: a medium-bodied red

Pork Cutlets Milanaise

4 boneless pork chops, about
   ¾ inch thick
1 egg, lightly beaten
1 cup freshly made bread
   crumbs (see page 325)
½ cup freshly grated Parmesan cheese
3 tablespoons olive oil
¼ cup dry white wine
Salt and freshly ground pepper
Lemon wedges

SERVES 4

SERVED BONE IN, with the chop pounded out around—where would one come upon such a cut unless Milan itself? While I agree in principle to the bone and would myself try the pounding, and even though I know a friendly butcher, I usually request boneless chops. You still have a classic dish, fit to serve any happy guests. Optional are a strew of chopped, seeded olives, green or black, or roasted and diced red pepper tossed in during the last ten minutes of cooking.

Trim the chops of most of their fat. Place between sheets of wax paper or plastic wrap and beat gently with a rolling pin or mallet until twice their width or more. Dip each cutlet in egg, then into bread crumbs mixed with cheese to coat. These may be prepared ahead and left in the refrigerator to set the coating.

To cook, heat oil in a large frying pan set over medium-high heat. Fry cutlets in batches, careful not to crowd the pan, just until each side is golden brown. Lift out onto a plate when they are done and pour out oil. Add wine to the pan and let it come to a boil. Return the cutlets to the pan and toss gently with salt and pepper to taste (not too much salt because of the cheese).

Cover the pan, turn down heat to low, and cook 20 minutes, turning now and again. Serve hot, with lemon wedges.

SERVE WITH mashed potatoes, and perhaps Green Beans with Shallots and Balsamic Vinegar (page 170), Italian Broccoli (page 178), or Broccoli with Ripe Olive Sauce (page 179).

WINE SUGGESTION: a medium-bodied red

Pork Fillets with Prunes

24 large prunes
Dry white wine (or Madeira)
4 boneless pork chops, well
  trimmed (about 1 pound)
Salt and freshly ground pepper
Flour
4 tablespoons butter
1 tablespoon red currant jelly
⅓ cup heavy cream

SERVES 4

FROM TOURS, originally using local prunes and Vouvray, this is finely translated with both California prunes and a white Pinot. It is one of my favorite dishes for company, particularly during autumn and winter months.

Place prunes in a bowl with wine to cover and leave to marinate 6 hours or, better, overnight.

Lightly sprinkle the pork with salt and pepper, then dust with flour. Add butter to a large frying pan and sauté chops until golden on both sides over medium heat. Lower heat, cover the pan, and cook until tender—this will depend on their thickness—not more than 20 minutes for about ½ inch. As they cook, put the prunes and wine in a saucepan and simmer about 30 minutes.

Place pork on warm plates, scoop out the prunes to lay beside them, and add the prune liquid to the frying pan. Reduce a little over high heat, then stir in the jelly. Stir in cream and reduce to a slightly thickened consistency. Add more salt and pepper to taste. Pour sauce over the meat and serve immediately.

THIS SHOULD always be served with Potato-Gruyère Cakes (page 236).

WINE SUGGESTION: a full-bodied white

Pork Loin with Mustard Sauce

4 boneless pork chops, cut ½ inch thick
Salt and freshly ground pepper
2 tablespoons vegetable oil
2 tablespoons butter
2 tablespoons grainy mustard
3 tablespoons dry white wine
½ cup heavy cream

SERVES 4

SIMPLE *but delicious.*

Trim chops, if necessary, but don't remove all the fat. Pat dry with paper towels and sprinkle with salt and pepper. Heat oil in a frying pan set over medium-high heat and sauté chops 4 to 5 minutes a side, or until golden brown and cooked through. Remove and keep warm.

Pour out the oil and put butter in. Add mustard and wine and stir a couple of minutes, then stir in cream and cook until slightly thickened. Put chops on warm plates and glaze with the sauce. Serve immediately.

THESE ARE lovely with Danish Red Cabbage (page 183) and new potatoes tossed in butter and minced parsley.

WINE SUGGESTION: a medium-bodied red or full-bodied white

Pork Medallions with Mushrooms and Marsala

1½ pounds pork tenderloin
Salt and freshly ground pep-
    per
Flour
¼ cup vegetable oil
4 tablespoons butter
2 minced shallots or green
    onions
½ pound mushrooms, sliced
    (regular or shiitake)
⅔ cup dry Marsala
⅓ cup chicken stock

SERVES 4

A VERY tantalizing dish, especially if you go all the way and get shiitake mushrooms for it.

Slice the tenderloin into ½-inch slices, then place between sheets of wax paper and flatten with a rolling pin to ¼ inch thick. Salt and pepper them lightly and dust with flour. Heat oil in a frying pan set over medium-high heat and in batches sauté the medallions about 3 minutes a side, or until golden. Remove from the pan and keep warm in a low oven.

Pour off fat and add 2 tablespoons butter to the pan. When it sizzles, add shallots and stir a minute, then add mushrooms and stir another minute or so. Add Marsala and stock and cook over high heat until reduced by about half. Taste for salt and pepper. Remove from the heat, cut remaining butter into pieces, and swirl into the sauce.

Divide the pork among 4 warm plates and pour the mushroom sauce over.

SERVE WITH *Sformato* with Green Beans (page 249), *Sformato* Bianco (page 254), or Eggplant Gratin (page 241).

WINE SUGGESTION: a medium- or full-bodied red

Pork Tenderloin with Capers and Cream

1½ pounds pork tenderloin
Salt and freshly ground pepper
2 tablespoons butter
2 shallots, minced
½ cup chicken stock
½ cup heavy cream
2 tablespoons capers

SERVES 4

NOT ALL MARKETS put out the tenderloin for sale, but they will have boneless pork chops which come to the same thing. If they are less than ¾ inch thick, though, you will want to cook them less.

Cut tenderloin into ¾-inch slices and pat dry with paper towels. Season with salt and pepper. Put butter in a large frying pan set over medium heat and sauté about 6 minutes a side. Remove from the pan and add shallots. Sauté a couple of minutes, then add stock and cream. Turn up heat and cook until the sauce reduces slightly, stirring to scrape up the meat bits. Before removing from heat, add capers and then the pork. Cook just to reheat. Serve hot.

SERVE WITH Carrots with Marsala (page 185)—the contrast between the sweetness of the carrots and the sour capers is perfect.

WINE SUGGESTION: a full-bodied white or good brut champagne

Pork Chops Nontronnaise

4 meaty loin pork chops,
    about ½ inch thick
Salt and freshly ground pep-
    per
4 tablespoons butter
1 cup freshly made bread
    crumbs (see page 325)
1 clove garlic, minced
¼ cup cornichons, chopped
½ cup dry white wine or
    chicken stock
2 tablespoons lemon juice
Minced parsley

SERVES 4

THIS IS ONE of those fine recipes for which one goes on reading Marcel Boulestin. Though he was a restaurateur and thinks in those terms by preference, it is a boon for home cooks.

Trim chops of excess fat and pat dry with paper towels. Sprinkle with salt and pepper. Heat butter in a frying pan large enough to hold all the chops and sauté over medium heat until golden on both sides.

Remove chops with a slotted spatula. Pour off all but 3 tablespoons of fat. Add bread crumbs and sauté until golden. Mix them with garlic and cornichons and spread on top of the chops. Return chops to pan. Pour wine or stock around them and sprinkle with lemon juice.

Cover the pan, lower heat, and cook another 20 minutes, or until the chops are quite tender. Serve sprinkled with parsley.

LOVELY WITH Celery Root Puree (page 190), Potatoes Maxime (page 224), or perhaps Leek and Zucchini Gratin (page 244).

WINE SUGGESTION: a medium-bodied red or full-bodied white

Pork Chops with Oranges

4 loin pork chops, cut 1 inch
  thick
2 oranges
1 clove garlic, slightly flattened and peeled
1 sprig rosemary (or ¼ teaspoon dried)
Freshly ground pepper
Dry Marsala
3 tablespoons olive oil
Salt

SERVES 4

YOU HAVE TO experiment with this chop to see how you like it. I prefer mine quite well done, but you may not. The basic thing is never to let the marinade boil quite away, at most to a glaze. Pork chops need a little moisture to stay juicy, not a lake. Also, the Marsala should not be more pronounced than the taste of orange.

Trim chops of excess fat and place in a bowl. Squeeze the juice of 1 orange over them, add ½ teaspoon grated orange rind, garlic, rosemary, a good grind of pepper, and 2 tablespoons Marsala. Let marinate several hours.

To cook, remove chops from the marinade and pat dry. Heat oil in a frying pan set over medium-high heat. Add chops and cook about 5 minutes a side, or until golden. Salt them as they cook. Add the marinade, lower heat, cover, and cook about 30 minutes, or until tender. After 15 minutes, check to make sure the marinade has not cooked away and turn the chops.

Slice the other orange, peel and all, and cut the slices in half. Fan these out on dinner plates and place a chop beside them. Add ¼ cup Marsala to the pan, turn up heat, and stir until you have a rich sauce. Strain over the chops and serve.

SERVE WITH Celery Root Puree (page 190) or *Sformato* with Green Beans (page 249).

WINE SUGGESTION: a medium-bodied red

Pork Chops Stuffed with Chèvre

4 loin pork chops, cut 1 inch
   thick
1 clove garlic
½ teaspoon dried thyme
¼ teaspoon dried rosemary
3 ounces chèvre cheese
1 cup dry white wine
¼ cup olive oil
1 cup freshly made bread
   crumbs (see page 325)
2 tablespoons butter
Salt

SERVES 4

THESE NEED ONLY a toss of chiffonade of sun-dried toma-
toes to make a trendy dish of the late eighties, but they should
remain a home specialty longer. If you can't get chèvre, try feta
cheese.

Slice the chops with a small, sharp knife held parallel to
the surface, so that a pocket is formed through the flesh
clear to the bone. Mince garlic and herbs together and
mix with the cheese. Divide the mixture into fourths and
poke into the chop pockets, smoothing the chops so
there are no bulges. Secure the openings with toothpicks, lay in a shallow dish, pour wine and oil over, and
marinate in the refrigerator for several hours. Turn the
chops now and again as they marinate.

To cook, preheat oven to 350 degrees. Take a frying
pan large enough to hold all the chops, put in the bread
crumbs, and shake them over medium heat until they
are evenly and lightly browned. Remove to a plate and
wipe the crumbs from the pan. Drain the chops (reserving the marinade for later) and turn them in the crumbs
off the fire.

Melt butter in the pan and sauté the chops over medium heat until they are crisp and golden on each side.
Add about ¼ cup of the marinade, then cover the pan
and bake about an hour—or until quite tender.

To serve, remove the toothpicks and pour any pan
juices over the chops.

SERVE WITH Rice with Pine Nuts (page 207) and/or Green
Beans with Tomatoes (page 172), or perhaps Sweet Potatoes with Lime and Sherry (page 213).

WINE SUGGESTION: a medium-bodied red

Pork Chops with Paprika and Sage Cream

4 meaty pork chops, 1 inch
  thick
Paprika (preferably sweet
  Hungarian)
Salt
Cayenne pepper
2 tablespoons butter
1 tablespoon vegetable oil
2 minced shallots or green
  onions
2 teaspoons minced fresh sage
  (or ¾ teaspoon crumbled
  dried)
½ cup dry white wine
¾ cup heavy cream

SERVES 4

FOR YEARS everyone cooked pork chops for half an hour at least, but there is new thought about this, such as in this recipe, which really only requires them to be cooked through. They are still succulent, and here sauced and spiced to perfection.

Trim chops of excess fat, if necessary, and pat dry with paper towels. Sprinkle both sides with paprika, salt, and cayenne to taste. This can be done ahead, if you like, and left to sit at room temperature.

Put a tablespoon of butter and oil in a large frying pan set over medium heat. Add chops and brown well, 3 to 4 minutes a side. Reduce heat and cook another 3 minutes a side. Remove and keep warm.

Pour fat from the pan and add remaining butter. Add shallots or onions and sauté over medium-low heat a minute or more, then add sage and stir. Add wine and boil over high heat until reduced by half, then add cream and cook over medium heat until slightly thickened. Season to taste with salt. Return chops to the pan and cook until just warmed through.

SERVE WITH noodles tossed with butter and poppyseeds, Rice and Rye Pilaf (page 209), or *Sformato* with Corn and Red Peppers (page 252).

WINE SUGGESTION: a medium-bodied red or full-bodied white

Pork Chops Charcutière

4 meaty loin pork chops,
    about 1 inch thick
Salt and freshly ground pep-
    per
2 large onions, chopped
1 tablespoon flour
1½ cups light beef stock
2 tablespoons tomato paste
1 teaspoon Dijon-style mus-
    tard
3 tablespoons minced corni-
    chons (or capers)
2 tablespoons minced parsley

SERVES 4

A CLASSIC French way with chops, and one that makes an extraordinarily fine sauce.

Trim chops of excess fat and place the trimmings in a frying pan. Melt down the fat over medium-high heat until you have 2 tablespoons, then scoop out the trimmings. Pat chops dry with paper towels, salt and pepper to taste, and sauté until browned on both sides. Put onions around them, stir a bit, cover the pan, and cook over low heat 30 minutes, or until the chops are tender and the onions cooked down. Remove chops and keep warm.

Stir in flour, turn up heat, and cook a few minutes. Then add stock and stir until you have a slightly thickened sauce. Add tomato paste, mustard, and a few good grinds of pepper. Let cook 5 minutes, then add cornichons and parsley. Pour over the chops and serve.

I ALWAYS want these with just mashed potatoes, to share some of the sauce.

WINE SUGGESTION: a full-bodied red

Ham with Madeira Sauce

2 large ham steaks (or 4 serving slices baked ham)
4 tablespoons butter
2 minced shallots or green onions
¼ cup dry Madeira
2 teaspoons tomato paste
1 teaspoon Dijon-style mustard

SERVES 4

MADEIRA COMPLEMENTS *ham superbly, but make sure you get dry Madeira, as one of the most available brands simply labels its product Madeira, and it is awful for most cooking purposes.*

Cut away any excess fat from ham. Heat 3 tablespoons of butter in a large frying pan set over medium heat and sauté the shallots until soft. Add ham in batches and sauté until it takes on a little color—careful not to burn the butter. When all are done, return to the pan, sprinkle with half the Madeira, cover, and cook over low heat 6 minutes or so. This can be done ahead and reheated if necessary.

To serve, place ham on warm plates. Add the rest of the Madeira and turn heat up high. Stir in tomato paste and mustard and whisk well. When the sauce has thickened very slightly, whisk in the remaining butter and pour over the ham. Serve at once.

THE PERFECT dish to accompany is French Creamed Spinach (page 212).

WINE SUGGESTION: a good brut champagne

Ham with Port and Mushroom Sauce

2 tablespoons butter
1 minced shallot or green onion
½ cup finely chopped mushrooms
½ cup dry white wine
¼ cup tawny port
1 tablespoon brandy
1 teaspoon tomato paste
1 cup heavy cream
Freshly ground pepper
4 serving slices baked ham

SERVES 4

DON'T THINK you need salt in this delicious sauce, for the ham will add enough later on.

Melt butter in a frying pan set over medium heat. When it foams up, stir in the shallot and cook a minute. Add mushrooms and cook another minute, then add wine and cook until it reduces by half. Stir in 3 tablespoons of port and brandy and cook a couple of minutes, then stir in tomato paste and cream. Simmer until slightly thickened—about 5 minutes. Finally add pepper to taste and ham. Cover and cook over low heat until the ham is just heated through. Uncover and stir in the last of the port. Serve hot.

A PERFECT accompaniment would be Spinach "en Branche" (page 211).

WINE SUGGESTION: a medium-bodied red

Ham Slices with Leeks

2 large ham steaks (or 4 serv-
    ing slices baked ham)
Dijon-style mustard
4 medium-size leeks
Milk or light cream

SERVES 4

MOST OF THE main dishes in this book were chosen because they take little time, and though this takes up to a couple of hours in the oven it is easy to assemble and fine to forget about while it's cooking. And it's too good to leave out!

Preheat oven to 300 degrees. Trim ham of excess fat and cut the steaks in half. Spread lightly with mustard and arrange in a baking dish large enough to hold them in one layer—with room to spare.

Trim leeks of roots and green tops. Slice them into ½-inch discs and place in a bowl of water. Swish them around to make sure any dirt is released, then place in a sieve and run water over them. Strew leeks around the ham and pour enough milk or light cream over the dish so the ham is just barely covered.

Bake, uncovered, for 1½ to 2 hours, or until all the liquid is absorbed and the ham is lightly browned. Serve the slices on warm plates, with the leeks at the side.

SERVE WITH Mushrooms Bordelaise (page 195) or any of the broccoli dishes.

WINE SUGGESTION: a full-bodied white

Ham Slices with Currant and Mustard Glaze

⅓ cup red currant jelly
3 tablespoons grainy mustard
2 large ham steaks (or 4 serv-
    ing slices baked ham)
2 tablespoons butter

SERVES 4

DELICIOUS—and what could be simpler?

Melt jelly in a small saucepan set over medium-low heat. When syrupy, remove from the fire and stir in mustard. Let sit until it cools to room temperature and has thickened up a bit.

Sauté ham in butter until the slices take on a little color. Place on a baking sheet, coat with the glaze, and broil until they begin to bubble. Serve at once.

IDEALLY THIS should be served with French Creamed Spinach (page 212), but you could also try Gratin Dauphinois (page 239) or Sweet Potato and Turnip Gratin (page 245).

WINE SUGGESTION: a fruity white

Nivernaise Ham

4 serving slices baked ham
3 tablespoons rendered ham
   fat, butter, or olive oil
1 cup chopped onion
2 tablespoons flour
1 cup beef stock
2 tablespoons tomato paste
½ cup dry white wine
1 tablespoon fresh tarragon
   (or 1 teaspoon dried)
½ cup white wine vinegar
6 peppercorns
4 juniper berries, slightly
   crushed
¼ cup heavy cream
Salt and freshly ground pepper
Minced parsley

SERVES 4

THIS IS an old French recipe, and I think one of the very best ham dishes in the world. If you don't have juniper berries on the shelf, now is the time to seek them out—you won't be sorry.

Trim ham slices of extra fat and reserve. Heat the rendered fat, butter, or oil in a large frying pan set over medium-high heat and sauté the ham until lightly browned on both sides. Remove from the pan and place on a plate.

Put ham trimmings in the pan and stir, then add onion and cook several minutes. Stir in flour and cook 2 to 3 minutes. Add stock and stir until thickened and smooth, then stir in tomato paste, wine, and tarragon. Cover, lower heat, and simmer 15 to 20 minutes. If it gets too thick, add a little more wine or water.

As this cooks, put vinegar, peppercorns, and juniper berries in a small saucepan and simmer until the liquid is reduced to a tablespoon. Add to the sauce, then stir in the cream and let cook until the flavors marry. These steps can all be done ahead.

To serve, strain the sauce and return to the frying pan. Add the ham and cook until just heated through. Taste for salt and pepper and stir in parsley. Serve at once.

I'VE NEVER got beyond serving this with anything other than mashed potatoes to share some of the wonderful sauce.

WINE SUGGESTION: a medium-bodied red

Solognote Sauce
for Ham

½ cup minced shallots
1 teaspoon minced fresh tarragon (or ½ teaspoon dried)
2 tablespoons butter
2 tablespoons white wine vinegar
½ cup dry white wine
3 egg yolks
1 tablespoon water
¾ cup heavy cream

SERVES 4

THE FRENCH SERVE THIS *over sliced, poached ham, and consider it "fit for the King," served with plain spinach and wild parasol mushrooms. When you first make it you will think, Oh, certainly this needs salt—I know I did—but it really needs none, especially considering the salt in ham, and if you have brought out the flavor of the shallots with long slow cooking.*

Sauté shallots and tarragon in butter in a saucepan set over low heat until shallots are soft and translucent—don't rush this, the procedure ought to take about 15 minutes. Add vinegar and wine, raise heat to medium, and reduce liquid by about half. Strain through a sieve into the top of a double boiler, pressing the solids well with a spoon. Whisk egg yolks with water and add them to the liquid, then stir over hot (not boiling) water until slightly thickened. Don't let them scramble, but as soon as they have just changed texture pour in the cream in a thin stream, whisking as you do so. Cook about 5 minutes, stirring occasionally, but don't let the sauce come to a boil. If necessary, the sauce can be made half an hour or so ahead and reheated.

CONSIDER THE French, and serve this with Spinach "en Branche" (page 211) and a quick sauté of shiitake mushrooms.

WINE SUGGESTION: a medium-bodied red

Mostly Chicken

BOTH AVAILABLE AND VERSATILE, chicken remains one of the first choices for entertaining, for nearly everybody. The most common plaint I hear, going around the country, is for more ways to perk up that day-to-day bird, new pizzaz. And they plead for family, as well as occasions for boss or friends next door, or relatives, for whom they wish to make it new.

True, there are recipes for other than poultry here—one for exemplary turkey, and a handful of showcase game hens and quail—but on the whole they reflect my continuing quest for simply outstanding ways to serve chicken. Looking back on the array, I am reminded, too, how in debt I am to prior cooks, numberless through the ages, who have directed and refined perfections we take for granted. Like poets they are few in any generation, for the usual chef cares no more than to amuse and beguile, rather than challenge the palate.

I have fiddled and tuned the knobs here, from classic to rustic to sophisticated modern, so that my sources stretch from Jeremiah Tower, so insolent and brave, to my effacing next door neighbor to sauces perfected back in the dawn of smoke fires around the Mediterranean. I bow and cook! To them.

Roast Chicken with Red Wine Vinegar

1 chicken (about 3 pounds)
Salt and freshly ground pepper
4 tablespoons butter, at room temperature
½ cup red wine vinegar
1 tablespoon balsamic vinegar (optional)
½ cup water
3 cloves garlic, whole, unpeeled
8 peppercorns
1 sprig fresh tarragon (or 1 teaspoon dried)
1 tablespoon tomato paste
3 tablespoons minced parsley

SERVES 4

NOTHING IN THE RECIPE will suggest to you how absolutely delicious the finished dish is. In fact, I think it's my very favorite way to roast a chicken.

Preheat oven to 325 degrees. Remove giblets and globs of fat around the cavity opening, pat chicken dry with paper towels inside and out, and salt and pepper inside and out. Put half the butter inside the chicken and truss the legs. Fold the wings back behind the chicken and rub the breast and legs with remaining butter. Place in a roaster and pour vinegar and water around it, then add garlic and peppercorns. Roast 2 hours, basting every 15 to 20 minutes.

Remove the chicken from the roaster. Set roaster over a medium flame and scrape up as much of the meaty bits as possible with the pan juices. Put through a sieve into a small saucepan, taking out the cloves of garlic and squirting the flesh from them into the saucepan. Cook with tarragon and tomato paste over high heat, stirring well, until reduced by half. Taste for salt and add rather a lot more ground pepper, then stir in parsley. Carve the chicken while the sauce is reducing and pour the finished sauce over the portions.

SERVE WITH Potatoes Maxime (page 224), Potatoes Sablees (page 226), Potato-Gruyère Cakes (page 236), or Leek and Zucchini Gratin (page 244).

WINE SUGGESTION: a dry white or medium-bodied red

Roast Tarragon Chicken

1 chicken (about 3 pounds)
Olive oil
Salt and freshly ground pepper
3 tablespoons butter
2 tablespoons minced fresh tarragon
½ clove garlic, minced
¾ cup dry white wine
2 tablespoons brandy
½ cup heavy cream

SERVES 4

TARRAGON AND CHICKEN have a delightful affinity for each other, and while there are many (especially French) recipes for the couple, this is one of the finest. Dried tarragon could be used for the cavity, but it won't do much for the sauce later. For this dish I think fresh tarragon is exactly the touch that makes it great.

Preheat oven to 325 degrees. Remove giblets and globs of fat around the cavity opening, wipe chicken inside and out with paper towels, then rub with olive oil and salt and pepper inside and out. Combine butter with 1 tablespoon of tarragon and garlic and place inside the bird. Truss the legs, tuck wings behind, and place the chicken breast up in a roaster. Pour wine around it and bake 2 hours, basting every 15 minutes.

Warm brandy in a small pan, light it, and pour flaming over the chicken. Keep the pan rotating so the brandy burns as much as possible. Remove chicken to a warm platter, add cream to the roaster, and stir over high heat a minute. Stir in remaining tarragon and cook a few minutes more. Carve the chicken and pour some of the sauce over each portion.

SERVE WITH Mashed Potatoes (page 218), *Sformato* Bianco (page 254), or perhaps Red Pepper Gratin (page 242).

WINE SUGGESTION: a dry white

Parsley, Sage, Rosemary, and Thyme Roast Chicken

1 chicken (about 3 pounds)
Salt and freshly ground pepper
2 tablespoons parsley
2 teaspoons fresh rosemary (or
  1 teaspoon dried)
½ teaspoon fresh thyme (or ¼
  teaspoon dried)
4 fresh sage leaves (or ¼ teaspoon crumbled dried)
1 shallot
¼ cup olive oil
½ cup dry white wine

SERVES 4

FOR THIS FRAGRANT DISH you should have as many of the herbs fresh as possible, though one or two may be dried with little loss of flavor.

Remove giblets and globs of fat around the cavity open-ing, pat chicken dry with paper towels inside and out, then salt and pepper inside and out. Put herbs, shallot, and oil in a food processor and whirl until you have a creamy, herb-flecked mixture. Rub this well over the chicken inside and out. This can be done ahead and the chicken covered with foil and refrigerated.

To cook, preheat oven to 325 degrees. Place chicken in a roaster, tuck wings behind, and tie the legs together with string. Pour wine around and place in the oven. Roast 2 hours, basting every 15 minutes with the pan juices. Let sit about 15 minutes before carving. Serve with some of the pan juices drizzled over.

SERVE WITH Gratin Dauphinois (page 239) or Mashed Po-tatoes with Green Onions (page 218) and/or Broccoli with Buttered Crumbs (page 176).

WINE SUGGESTION: a dry white

Roast Dijon Chicken

1 chicken (about 3 pounds)
Salt and freshly ground pepper
Dijon-style mustard
¼ cup olive oil

SERVES 4

WAIT TILL YOU TASTE the piquant, crispy skin of this chicken—and what could be simpler?

Preheat oven to 325 degrees. Discard giblets and any globs of fat around the cavity opening, wipe the chicken dry with paper towels inside and out, and salt and pepper both inside and out. Tuck wings behind and tie the legs together. Using a small brush, coat the chicken completely with mustard, making sure to get it anywhere there is skin.

Place in a roaster and drizzle oil over. Bake 2 hours, basting every 15 minutes or so. Let rest 15 minutes before carving.

SERVE PERHAPS with Mushrooms Stuffed with Pine Nuts (page 196) and Broccoli with Buttered Crumbs (page 176).

WINE SUGGESTION: a full-bodied white

Roast Chicken with Lemon, Ginger, and Coriander

1 chicken (about 3 pounds)
Salt
1 tablespoon grated fresh ginger
1 lemon
Handful fresh coriander
3 tablespoons butter, at room temperature
2 tablespoons flour

SERVES 4

ALL THESE fine aromatics make for a delightfully flavored chicken. I like to serve it garnished with sprigs of coriander.

Remove giblets and any globs of fat around the cavity opening, pat chicken dry inside and out with paper towels, and sprinkle inside and out with salt. Rub inside with ginger. Poke the lemon all over with a fork and stuff it and the coriander inside the chicken (you don't have to worry about the coriander stems here). Tie the legs together and tuck the wings behind. Let chicken sit about an hour before cooking, refrigerated.

To cook, preheat oven to 350 degrees. Rub butter over the top of the chicken. Place in a roaster in the oven and bake 1½ hours without opening the oven. Remove and let sit 10 minutes before carving. If you like, you can remove the lemon and squeeze some of the juice over the chicken.

Skim extra fat from the roasting pan, stir in flour over medium heat, and after it has cooked 3 to 4 minutes, add enough water to make a fine gravy. Let it cook another 3 to 4 minutes, then pour through a strainer into a gravy boat.

THE PERFECT partner for this would be Rice with Pine Nuts 207).

WINE SUGGESTION: a dry white

Chicken Ste. Menehould

1 chicken (about 3 pounds)
½ cup dry white wine
1 stick plus 3 tablespoons butter
1 clove garlic, slightly flattened and peeled
1 shallot, peeled and sliced
2 whole cloves
Parsley sprig
1 bay leaf
¼ teaspoon dried thyme
½ teaspoon dried basil
Salt and freshly ground pepper
2 egg yolks, lightly beaten
Freshly made bread crumbs for dredging (see page 325)
½ cup heavy cream
2 tablespoons brandy

SERVES 4

ONE OF MY great favorites for years, and one I learned first from Elizabeth David. She pictures a whole chicken coated with crumbs, which, I found early on, all fall off at carving, no matter how great it looks on a platter. So I cut the bird up—but don't fiddle around too much with a classic such as this. (Ste. Menehould, in any recipe, means coated with crumbs, much as anything Florentine means there is spinach lurking somewhere, and Doria means cucumbers.) The chicken is moist, the crust is crisp, and the sauce is one of the best I know.

Cut chicken into 2 breast portions and 2 portions of leg and thigh. Put them in a pot with wine, stick of butter, garlic, shallot, cloves, herbs, and salt and pepper to taste. (Use the rest of the carcass and giblets for stock.) Bring to a boil, turn heat down, cover the pot, and simmer for about 30 minutes, basting every 10 minutes. Test breast pieces for doneness—the juices should run clear, not rosy, when poked with a knife. The breast pieces will be done about 5 minutes before the thigh and leg pieces. When done, remove the chicken to a plate. If necessary, these can be cooked ahead, tented with foil, and left to sit at room temperature.

A few minutes before serving, preheat the broiler. Melt remaining butter in a saucepan, then brush the chicken with egg yolks, roll in bread crumbs, and drizzle with melted butter. Boil the cooking juices down a little, strain them, and return them to the pan. Add cream and stir over high heat until slightly thickened, then stir in brandy. Broil the chicken pieces until golden, place on warm plates, and pour the sauce over them.

SERVE THIS simply with Mashed Potatoes (page 218), with a sprinkle of the succulent crumbs and sauce over.

WINE SUGGESTION: a full-bodied white

Chicken Sauté with Fines Herbes

1 chicken, cut up (or 4 half-
  breasts or leg and thigh
  portions)
Flour
4 tablespoons butter
Salt and freshly ground pepper
2 tablespoons fines herbes
  (*parsley, chives, tarragon,
  and chervil minced
  together—forget the chervil
  if you don't have fresh*)
½ cup dry white wine
½ cup crème fraîche (*see page
  327*) or sour cream
1 tablespoon minced chives

SERVES 4

ONE OF THOSE *dishes that really prove that simplest is often best. It is for those who keep a few pots of fresh herbs on the back step or windowsill, though you can get by with dried tarragon in a pinch.*

I prefer to use either white or dark pieces for this, as the breast meat takes less time to cook, but if you use both, simply take the breasts out about 5 minutes before the dark pieces are done.

Wipe the chicken with paper towels and dredge with flour. Place butter in a frying pan set over medium-high heat. Add the chicken and sauté the pieces until lightly golden on both sides—salting and peppering as you turn them.

Turn skin side up and scatter herbs over. Add half the wine around the edges and let it bubble up. Then turn heat down, cover the pan, and cook until just tender—25 to 30 minutes. To test them, poke with a small, sharp knife and see if the juices run clear rather than pink. I think the current passion for underdone chicken is detestable. . . .

Remove the chicken to a platter and keep warm. Add the rest of the wine, turn heat up, and cook, stirring, for a few minutes until the juices are reduced a little. Add cream and chives and stir into the sauce. Pour over the chicken and serve immediately.

SERVE WITH Potatoes Maxime (page 224) or Gratin Dauphinois (page 239).

WINE SUGGESTION: a dry or fruity white

Chicken Sautéed with Artichokes

1 chicken, cut up (or 4 half-
    breasts or leg and thigh
    portions)
Salt and freshly ground pep-
    per
4 tablespoons butter
1 clove garlic, slightly flat-
    tened and peeled
½ cup dry white wine
1 9-ounce package frozen arti-
    choke hearts
⅔ cup heavy cream
3 egg yolks
1 teaspoon lemon juice

SERVES 4

AN ELEGANT DISH, even if you do use frozen artichoke hearts to speed up the process—of course, if you have the time to cook four artichokes and slice up their hearts, it's even better.

Pat chicken dry with paper towels and sprinkle with salt and pepper. Put butter in a large frying pan set over medium-high heat. Sauté chicken until golden on both sides, lowering heat if butter darkens. Add garlic and then wine, cover, and let simmer 25 minutes for breasts and 15 minutes longer for the dark meat.

Drop artichokes into boiling water and blanch for 1 or 2 minutes. Drain and add to the chicken during the last 5 minutes of cooking.

Remove chicken and artichokes to warm plates and discard the garlic. Boil down the liquid in the pan until almost syrupy. Beat cream with egg yolks and add to the pan. Stir over low heat until this thickens slightly, but do not let it come to a boil, for the egg will curdle. Add lemon juice to taste, check for salt, and pour over the chicken. Serve at once.

SERVE WITH Potatoes Sablees (page 226) or *Sformato* Bianco (page 254).

WINE SUGGESTION: a full-bodied white or good brut champagne

Chicken Normande

1 chicken, cut up (or 4 half-breasts or leg and thigh portions)
Salt and freshly ground pepper
4 tablespoons butter
4 apples, peeled, cored, and sliced
½ cup Calvados (or applejack)
3 tablespoons minced parsley

SERVES 4

MOST NORMANDY CHICKEN recipes use a lot of native cream as well for this delicious dish. This is not only less caloric, but the real appleness shines through better.

Preheat oven to 375 degrees. Pat chicken dry with paper towels and sprinkle with salt and pepper. Put butter in a large frying pan set over medium-high heat. Sauté chicken 5 or 6 minutes a side, or until lightly browned. The butter shouldn't burn. Place chicken and butter in a baking dish and add apples and Calvados. Light the Calvados, being careful, as it will flame up brightly. Tip the pan this way and that so the flames are fed.

Cover the pan and bake 25 minutes for the breasts and 5 minutes longer for the dark meat. Place on warm plates and sprinkle with parsley.

SERVE WITH Mashed Potatoes with Green Onions (page 218) and/or Broccoli with Bacon Maxime (page 177).

WINE SUGGESTION: a fruity white, Normandy cider, or a pilsner beer

Tuscan Chicken with Lemon and Fennel

4 chicken leg and thigh portions
2 tablespoons olive oil
Salt and freshly ground pepper
2 tablespoons lemon juice
4 strips lemon peel
2 bay leaves
1 clove garlic, slightly flattened and peeled
½ teaspoon fennel seeds
¼ cup brandy (optional)

SERVES 4

SOME FOLKS, I know, don't care for the anise flavor of fennel, but I am very fond of it if it's not overdone. Here, I believe it's just right.

Pat chicken dry with paper towels. Put oil in a large frying pan set over medium-high heat. Sauté chicken until lightly browned on both sides, sprinkling with salt and pepper as you go. Add all the other ingredients, turn heat down, cover the pan, and cook 30 minutes. Turn chicken once during cooking.

To serve, discard lemon peel, bay leaves, and garlic. If you like, pour warmed brandy over, light with a match, and move the chicken around until the flames die down. Serve hot.

SERVE WITH *Sformato* with Green Beans (page 249) or perhaps Eggplant Gratin (page 241).

WINE SUGGESTION: a dry white

Chicken with Olives and Pine Nuts

4 chicken leg and thigh portions
Salt and freshly ground pepper
2 tablespoons butter
2 tablespoons olive oil
1 medium-size onion, coarsely chopped
½ teaspoon dried crumbled sage (not powdered)
1½ teaspoons minced fresh rosemary (or ½ teaspoon dried)
2 bay leaves, finely crumbled
1 cup dry white wine
1½ cups chicken stock
16 pitted green olives, sliced
½ cup lightly toasted pine nuts

SERVES 4

THIS IS ONE of those welcome Italian dishes that remind there is more to Italy than tomatoes, garlic, and basil.

Pat chicken dry with paper towels and sprinkle with salt and pepper. Melt butter and oil in a large frying pan set over medium-high heat. Brown the chicken about 5 minutes a side. Remove the chicken to a plate and add onion to the pan. Stir over medium heat several minutes, adding the herbs as you do so. When onion softens, add wine, turn up heat, and cook until the wine has almost evaporated. Stir in stock and cook until it is reduced by half.

Return the chicken to the pan, cover, lower heat, and cook 20 minutes, or until chicken is moist and tender and there is no red at the bone. Stir in olives and cook another 10 minutes, tasting the sauce for seasoning, then stir in pine nuts and let heat through. Serve hot.

SERVE WITH Polenta (page 203) or *Sformato* Bianco (page 254).

WINE SUGGESTION: a dry white

Chicken with Dried Mushrooms

1 ounce dried porcini mushrooms
4 chicken leg and thigh portions
2 tablespoons vegetable oil
2 tablespoons butter
Salt and freshly ground pepper
1 medium-size onion, chopped
½ cup dry white wine
2 tablespoons tomato paste

SERVES 4

I AM LUCKY to have a friend who brings great bags of the best-quality dried porcini back from Italy once a year, and she kindly shares some with me. They are easily found nowadays in superior markets, and though expensive they are well worth it. Look for ones that are light brown and in large pieces, for the darker small chips may be less expensive but don't have as much flavor.

Put mushrooms in a small bowl and add hot tap water to cover. Let soak about half an hour, then filter the water they have soaked in through a paper towel placed in a sieve and reserve. Wash mushrooms thoroughly to remove any grit, then chop coarsely.

Pat chicken dry with paper towels. Heat oil and butter in a large frying pan set over medium-high heat. When the butter foams up, add chicken and sauté until golden on both sides, salting and peppering as you go. Remove to a platter and add onion to the pan. Cook over medium-low heat until a light gold, then return chicken to the pan. Stir in mushrooms and their soaking liquid, then add wine stirred with tomato paste.

Cover the pan and simmer over low heat 30 minutes, or until the chicken is well done. Serve on warm plates with the sauce poured over.

SERVE WITH wedges of Polenta (page 203).

WINE SUGGESTION: a full-bodied white or medium-bodied red

Chicken Piquant

4 chicken leg and thigh portions
Flour
¼ cup olive oil
1 medium-size onion, chopped
½ cup dry white wine
1 tablespoon tomato paste
Salt and freshly ground pepper
½ cup white wine vinegar
1 teaspoon anchovy paste or
minced anchovy
3 gherkin pickles
1 tablespoon capers
1 small clove garlic
2 tablespoons parsley

SERVES 4

ONE WOULD THINK *all these flavors would elbow each
other in a disharmonious rout, but instead they meld together
beautifully.*

Pat chicken dry with paper towels and shake in flour.
Heat oil in a large frying pan set over medium-high heat
and sauté chicken several minutes a side—just to sear.
Remove from the pan and add the onion. Cook several
minutes, then return chicken to the pan. Add wine
stirred with tomato paste, then season to taste with salt
and pepper. Cook, covered, over low heat about 30
minutes—or until quite tender.

Meanwhile, simmer vinegar in a small saucepan until
reduced by half. Mince together anchovy, pickles, capers, garlic, and parsley and add to the vinegar. Stir
well. Add this to the chicken during its final 10 minutes
of cooking. Serve hot.

WITH ALL this piquancy you need something bland like
Polenta (page 203) or even plain Mashed Potatoes (page
218).

WINE SUGGESTION: a dry white

Chicken Breasts with Basil-Tomato Cream

2 chicken breasts, halved, boned, and skinned
4 tablespoons butter
1 shallot, minced
½ cup garden or canned chopped tomatoes
½ cup dry white wine
½ cup heavy cream
Salt and freshly ground pepper
¼ cup fresh basil, cut into strips
Whole fresh basil for garnish

SERVES 4

THERE'S NO ACCOUNTING for the lively flavor of this very simple dish. Part of it is the fresh basil, of course, but even without garden tomatoes it sparkles.

Pat chicken breasts dry with paper towels. Place between wax paper and pound lightly with a rolling pin so they spread out a bit—they should not be thinner than ¼ inch. Keep in wax paper and refrigerate.

To make the sauce, melt 2 tablespoons of butter in a saucepan set over medium-high heat. Add shallot and stir a minute, then add tomatoes and cook another minute. Add wine, turn up heat, and let reduce by half. Add cream and simmer over low heat until thick enough to coat a spoon. Add salt and pepper to taste. Stir in ¼ cup basil, remove from heat, cover, and let sit until needed. This sauce can be made hours ahead, and it will only gather flavor. It might be necessary, however, to thin it with a little more cream at serving time.

To serve, gently reheat sauce. Melt remaining butter in a large frying pan set over medium-high heat. When it stops sizzling, add the breasts and cook 2 to 3 minutes a side, sprinkling with salt and pepper as they cook. They should be springy to the touch and no longer pink inside. Place on warm plates, ladle sauce over, and decorate with several large basil leaves.

SERVE WITH Rice with Pine Nuts (page 207).

WINE SUGGESTION: a dry or full-bodied white

Chicken Breasts with Mustard and Mushrooms

2 chicken breasts, halved
Flour
4 tablespoons butter
2 tablespoons vegetable oil
Dijon-style mustard
1 medium-size onion, finely
    chopped
½ cup finely chopped mush-
    rooms
2 tablespoons minced parsley
Salt and freshly ground pep-
    per
1 cup heavy cream
Lemon juice

SERVES 4

ONE OF MY FAVORITE company dishes over the years, with just the right balance of flavors—simple to prepare yet complex enough for any gourmet to admire.

Preheat oven to 350 degrees. Pat chicken dry with paper towels and dust lightly with flour. Heat butter and oil in a frying pan set over medium-high heat and sauté the chicken until browned on both sides. Remove from the pan to a baking dish and spread the tops with mustard.

Add onion to the pan and cook a few minutes to soften, then stir in mushrooms for another minute. Add parsley and salt and pepper to taste (not too much pepper because of the mustard), then add the cream. Let it bubble up, then pour over the chicken. If necessary, the dish can be prepared up to this point and kept covered.

To continue, bake 30 minutes, or until the chicken is quite tender. Taste the sauce for salt and add a few drops of lemon juice to perk it up. Serve hot.

SERVE WITH plain rice, to share the sauce, and Green Beans with Sesame and Pimiento (page 173) for color.

WINE SUGGESTION: a full-bodied white

Chicken Breasts with Sherry Vinegar

2 chicken breasts, halved, boned, and skinned
Salt and freshly ground pepper
4 tablespoons butter
2 shallots, minced
3 tablespoons sherry vinegar
¼ cup heavy cream, or crème fraîche (see page 327)

SERVES 4

I REMEMBER MY FIRST imported sherry vinegar about fifteen years ago, found only at a wine importer as a very, very special item—though an inexpensive one. Nowadays it is found nearly everywhere. You might also use other specialty vinegars in this fine and easy recipe.

Pat chicken dry with paper towels. Locate the white tendon on the undersides of the breasts, and with the aid of a small, sharp knife pull it out. Sprinkle lightly with salt and pepper. Add butter to a frying pan set over medium-high heat. When it melts, add the breasts and turn to coat them thoroughly. Cook about 4 minutes a side. They will be ready when the flesh is opaque and a little springy when you press with a finger. Remove to a plate.

Add shallots to the pan and toss a minute or so, then add vinegar and cook another minute. Stir in cream and let thicken slightly. Add chicken, turning in the sauce, and let heat through. Serve at once.

SERVE WITH Green Beans with Walnuts and Walnut Oil (page 174) or Broccoli with Ripe Olive Sauce (page 179).

WINE SUGGESTION: a dry white or medium-bodied red

Chicken Breasts with Madeira and Pecans

2 chicken breasts, halved,
  boned, and skinned
1 cup dry Madeira
Flour
Salt and freshly ground pepper
1 egg
1 tablespoon water
⅔ cup pecans, finely ground
3 tablespoons butter

SERVES 4

THIS IS A TRICK taught me by a Southern cook who uses the finest fresh pecans and Sercial Madeira. It makes a ravishing dish.

Pat chicken breasts dry with paper towels. Place chicken breasts between wax paper and pound lightly just to relax them a bit—don't pound out thinly. Place in a nonreactive bowl with Madeira and marinate an hour or more in the refrigerator. Remove from marinade and reserve the liquid. Roll chicken in flour seasoned with salt and pepper, dip in egg beaten with water, and then roll in pecans. Press the nuts well into the breasts, then refrigerate, covered with plastic wrap, an hour or more to set the coating.

To cook, melt half the butter over medium-high heat in a frying pan large enough to hold all the breasts in a single layer. Sauté about 3 minutes a side, or until golden and springy to the touch. Don't overcook. Remove to plates and keep warm. Add marinade to the pan, raise heat high, and cook until the wine thickens slightly. Remove from the heat and stir in remaining butter, whisking to make a smooth sauce. Pour over the chicken and serve.

SERVE WITH Broccoli Puree with Gruyère and Madeira (page 180) or Asparagus with Walnut or Hazelnut Oil (page 168).

WINE SUGGESTION: a dry or fruity white

Chicken Breasts with Capers

2 chicken breasts, halved,
　　boned, and skinned
Salt
Juice of ½ lemon
Freshly made bread crumbs
　　for dredging (see page 325)
4 tablespoons butter
½ cup dry white wine
½ cup heavy cream
1 tablespoon capers
1 teaspoon caper juice

SERVES 4

AN EXCELLENT all-purpose company dish. Sometimes I like to add also a tablespoon of green peppercorns—they look just like capers but of course with a difference in taste and texture.

Pat chicken breasts dry with paper towels. Place between wax paper and pound slightly with a rolling pin—they need only be flattened slightly. Sprinkle with salt and lemon juice. Roll in bread crumbs, cover with plastic wrap, and refrigerate for 30 minutes or more to set the coating.

Heat butter in a frying pan set over medium heat. When it starts to sizzle, add the breasts and cook about 4 minutes a side. Remove to a plate. Add wine and cook down over high heat until syrupy, then add cream and cook down until it makes a light sauce. Add capers, caper juice, and salt to taste. Return chicken breasts to the pan and let warm through over low heat. Serve immediately.

SERVE WITH Mushrooms Stuffed with Pine Nuts (page 196) or Red Pepper Gratin (page 242).

WINE SUGGESTION: a full-bodied white

Chicken Torcello

2 chicken breasts, halved,
   boned, and skinned
Salt and freshly ground pepper
2 tablespoons vegetable oil
2 tablespoons butter
1 clove garlic, minced
½ pound mushrooms, sliced
1 large shallot, minced
½ cup dry white wine
¾ cup heavy cream
½ cup sun-dried tomatoes,
   cut into slivers

SERVES 4

THIS WAS DISCOVERED several years ago in a departed friend's recipe file left to me in honor of all our years' talk about food and cooks and restaurant fare. I must say it was one of the best legacies for which I could have asked.

Pat chicken breasts dry with paper towels. Place between wax paper or plastic wrap and flatten to about a ¼-inch thickness with a mallet or rolling pin. Cut each breast in half and sprinkle with salt and pepper.

Heat oil and butter in a large frying pan set over medium-high heat. Fry the breasts in batches about a minute a side, then remove to a plate.

Add garlic and mushrooms to the pan and stir for 4 to 5 minutes, then lift out with a slotted spoon to the chicken plate. Add shallot to the pan and cook a minute. Add wine, turn up heat, and reduce it by half. Add cream and stir until it thickens slightly—3 to 4 minutes.

Stir in the tomatoes, add the mushrooms and chicken pieces, and turn to mix thoroughly. Let warm through over low heat another 3 to 4 minutes.

SERVE WITH Rice Pilaf (page 208) or Zucchini-Stuffed Baked Potatoes (page 232).

WINE SUGGESTION: a dry white

Chicken Breasts Stuffed with Brie

2 chicken breasts, halved,
    boned, and skinned
2 tablespoons butter, at room
    temperature
Salt and freshly ground pep-
    per
4 ounces Brie cheese, white
    crusts removed (about ½
    cup)
Flour
1 egg, lightly beaten
Freshly made bread crumbs
    for dredging (see page 325)
2 tablespoons melted butter

SERVES 4

DON'T LIMIT THESE to visiting royalty, though they would do very well for such an occasion. They are ineffable. You might substitute Camembert here, or even creamed cheese mixed with a scrap of garlic and minced herbs, but Brie is best.

Pat chicken breasts dry with paper towels. Place between wax paper or plastic wrap and pound lightly with a rolling pin or mallet until about ⅛ inch thick. Spread the undersides with butter. Sprinkle lightly with salt and rather well with pepper, then divide Brie among them and spread to within half an inch from the edges. Roll them up from the short end, tucking in the ends as well as possible.

Lay out a plate with flour, a bowl with egg, a plate with bread crumbs, and a baking dish large enough to hold the breasts in one layer. Dip the rolls in flour, then into egg, then roll in bread crumbs and place in the baking dish. These can sit for an hour or more, covered with plastic wrap and refrigerated, until ready to cook.

To continue, preheat oven to 350 degrees. Drizzle with the melted butter, salt lightly, and bake 20 minutes.

SERVE WITH Gratin of Potatoes and Shiitake Mushrooms (page 240) or Green Beans with Shallots and Balsamic Vinegar (page 170).

WINE SUGGESTION: a full-bodied white

Italian Turkey Scallops

4 ¼-inch-thick slices turkey
    breast (about 1 pound)
Salt and freshly ground pep-
    per
Flour
3 tablespoons olive oil
1 clove garlic, slightly flat-
    tened and peeled
1 small branch rosemary (or
    ½ teaspoon dried)
1 lemon
¾ cup dry Marsala
1 cup coarsely grated fontina
    cheese
¼ cup grated Parmesan or
    Romano cheese (or a combi-
    nation)
2 tablespoons butter

SERVES 4

I'VE FRANKLY GOTTEN bored with turkey, and except for this exciting dish, where turkey is just an excuse for all the gilding, I never serve it to guests. It may seem a little fussy, all that layering, but it is really quite simple when you get down to it, and your guests will heap compliments on the cook.

Pat turkey slices dry with paper towels. Place between sheets of wax paper and flatten with a rolling pin to about ⅛ inch thick. Don't worry if these fall apart a bit, it won't matter later. Sprinkle lightly with salt and pepper and dust with flour, shaking off any excess. Heat oil with garlic and rosemary in a large frying pan set over medium heat. When the garlic turns golden (don't brown it), remove along with the rosemary. Turn heat up to medium-high and sauté the turkey (if necessary in batches) only a minute or so a side. They don't have to brown, only take on a little color and "seize up." As they cook, remove to a baking pan large enough to hold them all in a single layer.

Slice lemon as thinly as possible and cut out the peel with a small pointed knife. Cut each slice into quarters and divide among the turkey. Add Marsala to the pan and cook down over high heat, stirring until almost syrupy. While this is reducing, sprinkle the breasts first with fontina, then with Parmesan. Pour the Marsala sauce over. This can be done ahead, cooled to room temperature, covered with plastic wrap, and refrigerated.

To continue, heat oven to 375 degrees. Dot breasts with butter and bake 5 to 7 minutes, or until golden and bubbly. Serve at once.

I LIKE to serve this with angel hair pasta, simply buttered, salted, and peppered, with a toss of Parmesan.

WINE SUGGESTION: a full-bodied white or medium-bodied red

Rock Cornish Game Hens with Cream Cheese and Grapes

2 Rock Cornish game hens
Salt and freshly ground pepper
Butter
6 ounces cream cheese
½ cup heavy cream
½ pound seedless green grapes

SERVES 2 TO 4

USUALLY A CORNISH HEN is thought to serve only one, but if you choose largish birds, and with all this cream cheese and cream, I find half a satisfying portion—it's up to you, the world is filled with people with larger appetites than mine.

Preheat oven to 350 degrees. Remove and discard giblets. Wash hens and pat dry with paper towels. Sprinkle well with salt and pepper inside and out, then rub with softened butter. Divide cheese and stuff the hens with it. Place in a buttered roasting pan breast down.

Bake 15 minutes, then place breast up and bake another 30 to 45 minutes, basting with cream now and again. Wash grapes and stem them, then slice in half. Add them during the last 10 minutes of cooking.

To serve, halve the hens, cutting first around the backbone (discarding it), then down through the breastbone, and spoon the pan juices and grapes around them.

SERVE WITH Rice Pilaf (page 208) or Wild Rice, Barley, and Mushrooms (page 210).

WINE SUGGESTION: a fruity white

Rock Cornish Game Hens with Sage and Fontina

2 Rock Cornish game hens
1 tablespoon dried crumbled
　　sage (not powdered)
1 clove garlic, minced
2 tablespoons lemon juice
Olive oil
Fontina cheese
Salt and freshly ground pep-
　　per

SERVES 2 TO 4

I USED TO find game hens rather blah, until my friend Dorothy Neal served me up some superb ones, and finally convinced me for good.

Preheat oven to 375 degrees. Remove and discard giblets. Wash the hens and pat dry with paper towels. Combine sage, garlic, lemon juice and 2 tablespoons olive oil. Slip fingers under the breast skin and loosen it all over. Spread the sage mixture over the breast meat. Thinly slice cheese and insert slices under the skin so the entire pocket is covered. Sprinkle the hens inside and out with salt and pepper and rub olive oil all over. Tuck the wings behind, and if you wish, tie the legs together. This can be all done well ahead and refrigerated.

Roast about 50 minutes, or until crisply golden. Remove from the oven and halve by cutting on either side of the backbone (discarding it), then down through the breast bone. Serve while hot.

SERVE WITH Broccoli with Buttered Crumbs (page 176) or Green Beans with Sesame and Pimiento (page 173) and/ or Rice and Rye Pilaf (page 209).

WINE SUGGESTION: a dry white

Glazed Quail with Sherry Vinegar

8 quail
Salt and freshly ground pepper
2 tablespoons butter
1 tablespoon vegetable oil
3 tablespoons sherry vinegar
Pinch of sugar

SERVES 4

MANY SUPERMARKETS these days carry pen-raised quail, and they make a delicious nibble picked up with the fingers. There's really no other way—the reason restaurants always go for boned quail.

Preheat oven to 400 degrees. Starting at the top of the backbone, cut each quail in half from inside. Then turn and cut through the breast from the inside as well. Pat dry with paper towels and salt and pepper lightly. Heat butter and oil in a large frying pan. Sear the quail in batches, (if necessary) until golden brown. Add vinegar and sugar and toss to coat. This can be done ahead and refrigerated.

To continue, place quail in a baking dish and bake about 10 minutes, or until heated through. Serve at once.

SINCE YOU have to pick these up with your fingers, I serve them with Classic French Fries (page 219) and make it all finger food. However, they would be excellent with Wild Rice, Barley and Mushrooms (page 210).

WINE SUGGESTION: a dry white or medium-bodied red

Braised Quail with Shiitake Mushrooms

8 quail
Salt and freshly ground pepper
Flour
4 tablespoons butter
1 cup chicken stock
Pinch of dried thyme
1 bay leaf
4 ounces shiitake mushrooms
¼ cup dry Madeira
4 slices bread, brushed with butter, pan-fried, and crisped in a warm oven

SERVES 4

THIS IS ONE of the best quick game dishes I know, and I serve it often now that quail are available at the corner market, along with fine mushrooms. If the mushrooms are expensive, remember the quail are relatively cheap, so it makes a very reasonable dish rather than the extravagance it appears.

Split quail in half. The best way to do this is to insert a boning knife through them and cut down through the backbone from the inside. Then turn and cut through the breast from the inside as well. It takes only a second. Pat them dry with paper towels. Sprinkle with salt and pepper and shake in a bag of flour.

Heat butter in a large frying pan set over medium-high heat. Sauté quail in batches 3 to 4 minutes a side, until they are golden. As they cook lift out to a stovetop casserole.

Add stock to the frying pan and let bubble up, scraping the bits from the bottom. Pour over quail, add thyme and bay leaf, and let come to a boil over medium heat, stirring so juices thicken. Clean mushrooms well and remove and discard stems, then cut tops into ¼-inch slices. Add to the casserole along with Madeira, stir, and taste for salt and pepper. This can be done ahead and reheated.

To serve, warm through, then arrange 4 quail halves side by side on each plate. Place the crisped bread beside them and top with mushroom slices, then pour the sauce over both. Serve hot.

THIS PLATE doesn't need much but a tuft of greenery, but it is excellent with Dandelion Greens Provençale (page 192).

WINE SUGGESTION: a dry white or medium-bodied red

CONSIDERABLE
SIDE DISHES

Lively Vegetables

VEGETABLES, AS SOMETHING TO BE AD-mired on their own, not just as a stodgy side to a plate or heaped in a stew, are almost an invention of the present century. Now we love them for their own taste and texture, and as it were—independence. We like them still as partners, but like Tracy and Hepburn, a jostling free-for-all, forkful by forkful. My theory is they should be just a bit unexpected, as to choice of sauce, herb, spice, or combination thereof.

I remember my mother remarking about a family, poor due to the Depression, where the wife happened to mention she failed to understand why her family wouldn't eat turnips, especially as they used to like them so much. Upon enquiry, it turned out she had served a meal of only buttered turnips, and it was unimaginable to her that it was just too much of a good thing. I think some of this kind of thing is behind children or even grown-ups who say they don't like vegetables of one kind or another. They have come to believe carrots only come sweetly glazed, green beans only almondine, cauliflower only cheese sauced, and their tastebuds simply rebel.

Here are some of the ways to make the unsuspecting carrot or stalwart green bean and its cousins sit up and take notice. My only theory has been to complement the taste of the pure vegetable itself, for there is no need to whelm with too much sauce or fussy preparation. I believe, in fact, one of the signs of a fine restaurant, or home cook, is how much love and respect has gone into the side dishes.

Asparagus with Walnut or Hazelnut Oil

1½ pounds asparagus
¼ cup walnut or hazelnut oil
Salt and freshly ground pepper
1 lemon, cut into wedges

SERVES 4

THE NEWLY AVAILABLE nut oils shine on cooked asparagus as well as salad. The hot vegetable brings out their delicate nutty taste to perfection. I don't think they even need lemon this way, but your guests might, and a couple of wedges bring a bright note to the plate.

Wash asparagus and snap off the lower stalk (or if you like them neater, cut off all the same length). Some books advise tying these in bundles, to stand stalk down in a tall pan so only the tops steam, but that is really unnecessary. Simply drop in a large frying pan filled with a couple of inches of boiling, salted water. Time will depend on the thickness of the stalks—barely 5 minutes for medium. Test for tenderness with the tip of a small knife and drain immediately.

Toss while hot with oil and salt and pepper to taste. Serve with lemon wedges at the side.

Green Beans Parmesan

1 pound green beans
4 tablespoons butter
Salt
¼ cup freshly grated Parmesan cheese

SERVES 4

WHEN YOU WISH to serve a green vegetable, this is both one of the simplest and most versatile. It can accompany anything not already slathered with cheese, and the Parmesan here only gives a lift, not a push, to the beans. If your beans are not top-notch, you might add a squeeze of lemon to perk them up, or a few scrapes of nutmeg.

Trim the beans and drop into a large pot of boiling, salted water—a large pot helps them cook more evenly and ensures a bright color. Let cook just until they are done, but still with a little "bite" to them. Drain and run cold water over to stop the cooking. Melt butter, place beans in a bowl, and toss with butter and salt to taste. Divide beans into 4 bundles and place on a baking dish. Sprinkle with cheese. This may be made ahead, covered, and kept at room temperature. Don't refrigerate, for it changes the taste of the beans.

To serve, place in a heated oven (this can be at almost any medium to hot temperature if you are cooking other dishes—though the cheese shouldn't brown). Bake until beans are heated through and the cheese melts. Serve at once.

Green Beans with Shallots and Balsamic Vinegar

1 pound green beans
4 tablespoons butter
1 large shallot, minced
1 tablespoon plus 1 teaspoon
  balsamic vinegar
Freshly ground pepper

SERVES 4

A LOT OF TO-DO has been raised recently about the uses of balsamic vinegar, so potent it can overpower a tender salad, but sometimes perfect in cooking to give a complex resonance we cannot quite put a finger on. This is one such, though you could use aged sherry vinegar with equal aplomb.

Top and tail beans and leave them whole unless they are very large. In that case, cut them diagonally into 1-inch pieces. Drop into a large pot of boiling, salted water and cook just until they lose their raw taste—4 to 5 minutes. Immediately drain and run cold water over to stop the cooking. These can be done well ahead and kept at room temperature.

To serve, put 1 tablespoon of butter in a frying pan set over medium heat. Sauté shallot for a couple of minutes, then toss beans into the mixture. As you cook them, put the remaining butter and vinegar in a small saucepan. Heat over medium heat, stirring until the butter browns—2 to 3 minutes. Immediately stir into the beans, sprinkle with pepper, and serve.

Green Beans with Mustard and Crumbs

1 pound green beans
2 teaspoons Dijon-style mustard
2 tablespoons butter
1 cup freshly made bread crumbs (see page 325)
¼ teaspoon dried summer savory
Salt and freshly ground pepper

SERVES 4

CRUSTY, AND—YES—SAVORY (summer savory being one of the best herbs with green beans), these make a superb last-minute addition to almost any plate.

Top and tail beans and cut diagonally into 1-inch lengths. Drop into a large pot of boiling, salted water and boil for 4 to 5 minutes, or until just done. Immediately drain and run cold water over to stop the cooking. These can be done ahead, covered and kept at room temperature.

To continue, stir mustard into the beans. Heat butter in a frying pan set over medium-high heat. When it sizzles, add bread crumbs and toss until they start to take color. Add savory and salt and pepper to taste and cook until golden. Add beans and toss until they are warmed through. (Or place beans in a shallow buttered, baking dish and top with the crumbs, then heat in a moderate oven.) Serve immediately.

Green Beans with Tomatoes

1 pound green beans
¼ cup olive oil
¼ cup minced green onion
1 clove garlic, minced
1 cup canned tomatoes,
   drained and coarsely
   chopped
¼ cup juice from the tomatoes
Salt and freshly ground pepper
¼ cup chopped fresh basil

SERVES 4

ALL OVER THE MEDITERRANEAN young beans are cooked with garden fresh tomatoes—sometimes, unfortunately, they are swimming in oil and the beans are almost brown with the acid from the tomatoes. However, done properly, this is a very lively dish. If you have garden tomatoes you're ahead already, but canned Italian plum tomatoes work fine, and you can even use dried basil if you add it to the tomatoes as they cook. A particular bonus is that the beans are just as good at room temperature, so they can be prepared ahead.

Trim beans and leave whole if small—larger beans should be cut diagonally into 1-inch pieces. Heat oil in a small frying pan set over medium heat and sauté onion and garlic until limp. Add tomatoes with juices and cook 5 to 6 minutes. Add beans, sprinkle with salt and pepper to taste, turn heat low, cover the pan, and cook until beans are just tender. Uncover the pan now and again, turn the beans, and test for doneness. At the very end stir in basil. Serve hot or at room temperature.

Green Beans with Sesame and Pimiento

1 pound green beans
2 tablespoons sesame seeds,
   lightly toasted
2 tablespoons olive oil
1 tablespoon lemon juice
2 ounces chopped canned pimientos
Salt and freshly ground pepper

SERVES 4

IMAGINE A LITTLE more oil and lemon, and this would be a salad—as is, it makes a perfect vegetable dish to prepare in advance with no hassle.

Top and tail the beans and drop into a large pot of boiling, salted water. Depending on their size, cook only 3 to 4 minutes, or just until they lose their raw flavor. Immediately drain and run cold water over to stop the cooking. Drain well in a colander.

Place beans in a bowl and toss with sesame seeds, oil, lemon juice, pimientos, and salt and pepper to taste. The dish can be made 1 or 2 hours in advance, covered, and kept at room temperature—it should not be refrigerated.

Green Beans with Walnuts and Walnut Oil

1 pound green beans
2 tablespoons walnut oil
½ cup coarsely chopped wal-
    nuts
Salt
Several drops lemon juice

SERVES 4

ONE ENCOUNTERS *green beans and almonds so often that this makes an exciting change. They could also be prepared with hazelnuts and hazelnut oil.*

Trim beans and cut diagonally into 1-inch pieces. Drop into boiling, salted water and cook 4 to 5 minutes—or until tender but still with a bit of crispness. Immediately drain and run cold water over to stop further cooking. These can be done ahead and kept at room temperature.

To continue, heat oil in a frying pan set over medium-low heat. Add nuts and stir-fry 2 to 3 minutes. Turn up heat and add beans and stir-fry another 2 to 3 minutes. Sprinkle with salt to taste and a little lemon juice, just enough to perk up the beans—they should not be lemony. Serve hot.

Baked Beets with Tarragon Butter

8 medium-size beets
3 tablespoons butter
1 tablespoon minced fresh tarragon
Salt

SERVES 4

THIS IS ONE of those vegetable dishes so delicious it's almost best served as an individual course with good crusty French bread. Beets, in France, are often sold baked like this, but even there they are somehow tastier done at home. Baking intensifies and clarifies their flavor in a way boiling can never attain. Try this recipe as a tonic side dish for a lamb or pork chop.

Preheat oven to 375 degrees. Trim off beet tops, leaving about half an inch attached. Don't bother with the root end. Place on a sheet of foil, fold it up around beets, and center in a baking dish. Make a few slits in the top of the foil so the beets don't just steam. Bake an hour or more, depending on their size. Test by simply running a small, sharp knife through the foil into the center of a beet.

When tender, remove from the oven, unwrap, and let cool to room temperature. Top and tail the beets and peel them. At this point they can be used in any recipe, but they will be better just enough to make a difference!

When cool, slice the beets. Melt butter in a saucepan set over medium heat. When it sputters, stir in tarragon. Add beets and toss until coated and warmed through, adding a sprinkle of salt on the turn.

Broccoli with Buttered Crumbs

I've often thought it would be interesting (and instructive) to have a cookbook where all the fine food writers gave up for a moment their measuring cups and spoons and simply explained the dishes they cook by instinct, without any hard rules. Mashed potatoes would be one of mine, certainly, and also this secret for making the very best buttered crumbs. To begin, trim a head of broccoli into 1-inch florets and steam them in a collapsible steamer that fits into a large saucepan. Then lift them out and sprinkle while hot with a few squeezes of lemon, a grind of pepper, and a pinch of salt. For ease, I position them for steaming long before dinner, and if my timing is off a little it really won't matter: They can be hot or tepid, so long as they are emerald green and still a little crisp. The important thing is the crumbs.

Actually, the crumbs themselves *are* the recipe. These are what I call "fresh bread crumbs" in a recipe—they should not be store-bought sawdust. I always keep a sliced loaf of homestyle bread in the freezer, and it only takes a few minutes to thaw and trim slices, then whirl in a food processor for light, fluffy, delectable crumbs. You need about one slice per serving. (When a recipe calls for dry, fine bread crumbs, you must crisp them in a slow oven and whirl again—but not for buttered crumbs.)

For each slice, heat a small nut of butter in a frying pan, dump in the crumbs, and quickly stir them to distribute the butter evenly. Toss over medium-high heat until they are crisp, golden, and separate. If they tend to clump together there's too much butter, and another strewing of crumbs is called for. Salt them a little, toss, and let sit. If your instinct is to snack them all before dinner, they will be perfect for your vegetable. To serve, place broccoli (or green beans, cauliflower, asparagus, or even an omelet) on a warm plate, then warm up crumbs and sprinkle them over. Serve with a lemon wedge, and sit back with pride.

Broccoli with Bacon Maxime

1 pound broccoli
3 slices bacon, cut into small
  strips
2 to 3 tablespoons butter
Salt and freshly ground pepper
Freshly grated nutmeg

SERVES 4

FROM THE FABLED Maxime's in Paris. I have adapted this only a smidgen, as they tend to cook the vegetable limp where we would want it still a little toothsome. Don't overdo the nutmeg—this is the time to keep in mind Maxime's original idea that a dish should be seasoned only as much as to give a little mystery to the tastebuds.

Cut the florets from the broccoli, separating any extra-large ones so they will cook evenly. (The stems may be saved, to peel and blanch for salad another day.) Either steam the florets or poach them in water until just tender. They are done when a small, sharp knife easily pierces them. Immediately drain in a colander and run cold water over to stop the cooking. These may be prepared ahead, covered, and kept at room temperature.

Place bacon in a small pan of boiling water and let simmer 6 to 8 minutes, then drain and reserve. This process approximates French bacon, which is not smoked.

To continue, place bacon and butter in a frying pan and cook over medium heat until the bacon starts to crisp. (The butter should not burn, nor should the bacon be cooked to dry-crisp.) Add the broccoli and toss to coat, sprinkling with salt and pepper to taste. Add only a suggestion of nutmeg, for it should not overwhelm.

Cook 3 to 4 minutes, or until the broccoli is warmed quite through. Divide among 4 plates and serve hot.

Italian Broccoli

¼ cup olive oil
½ teaspoon dried red chile
   flakes
1 teaspoon anchovy paste or
   mashed fillets
1 clove garlic, slightly flattened and peeled
1 pound broccoli
Salt and freshly ground pepper
Juice of ½ lemon

SERVES 4

NOT ONLY DOES THIS have a very lively flavor, with the taste of anchovy extremely subtle, it also makes a fine summer dish, easy to serve since it doesn't have to be cooked at the last minute.

Place oil, pepper flakes, anchovy, and garlic in a small saucepan. Heat over low heat until the garlic turns golden. Let sit until it cools to room temperature.

Cut florets from the broccoli, separating any extra-large ones so they will cook evenly. Peel the stems with a swivel vegetable peeler and cut them into matchstick lengths. Either steam the broccoli or cook in boiling, salted water until just tender—don't overcook. They should have a little bite to them. Drain immediately and run cold water over to stop the cooking. Place in a bowl and pour oil mixture through a sieve over them. Toss with salt and pepper to taste and lemon juice. Serve hot or at room temperature.

Broccoli with Ripe Olive Sauce

½ cup olive oil
2 cloves garlic, slightly flattened and peeled
½ cup minced ripe olives
1 to 2 teaspoon lemon juice
Salt and freshly ground pepper
1 bunch broccoli

SERVES 4

ONE OF THE TIMES *the mild American ripe olives are actually preferable to the more gutsy Italian or Greek ones—but it is best to use a very fruity virgin oil if possible. This is a delicious dish to set before any company.*

Heat oil in a small saucepan set over medium-low heat. Add garlic and cook, stirring now and again, until cloves turn a light gold—don't brown them. Remove the garlic and add olives, lemon juice to taste, and rather a lot of salt and pepper. Let cook 1 or 2 minutes, then turn off heat and let sit.

Trim broccoli, cut off large stems, and divide into equal-size florets. Just before serving, either steam the broccoli or drop into boiling, salted water. Turn on flame under the olive sauce. When just tender, drain the broccoli and place on plates, then pour sizzling hot olive sauce over.

Broccoli Puree with Gruyère and Madeira

1 bunch broccoli (1½ pounds)
4 tablespoons butter
1 minced shallot or green onion
3 tablespoons dry Madeira
⅓ cup grated Gruyère cheese
Salt and freshly ground pepper
Several drops of lemon juice (optional)

SERVES 4

WHEN RESTAURANTS STARTED serving trios of purees on every plate a few years ago, the critics started yelling "Baby Food!" No one in his right mind would call this baby food.

Cut broccoli florets down to the main stem. Peel stems with a small, sharp knife or vegetable peeler and slice into 1-inch pieces. Drop these into a pot of boiling, salted water and cook about 8 minutes. Add tops and cook another 8 minutes, or until they both test soft. Drain and empty into a food processor.

Heat butter in a medium saucepan set over medium-low heat until it sputters a little, then stir in shallot or onion. Cook slowly, stirring now and again, until limp. Add to the food processor along with Madeira and cheese and whirl until pureed. Taste for salt and pepper, scrape back into the saucepan, and cover.

To serve, heat gently. When warm, taste again for seasoning—a few drops of lemon juice, perhaps?

Brussels Sprouts with Grapes and White Wine

1½ pounds Brussels sprouts
1½ cups chicken stock
1 cup seedless green grapes
2 tablespoons butter
⅓ cup dry white wine
Dash of Tabasco sauce or
    white pepper

SERVES 4

AN UNLIKELY COMBINATION from the old Waldorf-Astoria, which apparently served Brussels sprouts in as many ways as potatoes. Elegant looking, with its two kinds of green ovals, it serves splendidly aside roast game or pork.

Trim sprouts and remove any loose leaves. Cut an X in the root end with a small knife (this is to let them cook quicker). Bring the stock to a boil in a large saucepan and add the sprouts. Cover and cook over low heat 10 minutes, or until almost tender. Stir in grapes, butter, wine, and Tabasco. Cook another 5 minutes. Lift out the sprouts and grapes with a slotted spoon and put in a bowl. Raise heat and reduce the cooking liquid to the consistency of a light sauce.

To serve, return sprouts and grapes to the pan and let just heat through. Serve hot.

Brussels Sprouts in Parmesan Cream

1 pound Brussels sprouts
3 tablespoons butter
Salt and freshly ground pepper
Freshly grated nutmeg
½ cup crème fraîche (see page 327) or heavy cream
3 tablespoons grated Parmesan cheese

SERVES 4

ESPECIALLY IF YOU USE crème frîche, this makes the most of what can be a rather indelicate vegetable. If you use ordinary cream, it's perhaps best to scoop out the sprouts with a slotted spoon and then boil the liquid down a little before pouring over the vegetable. Sprouts are served a good deal with holiday meals and with roast game, and they make a fine pair with Carrots with Cognac (page 184).

Trim sprouts and remove any loose leaves. Cut an X in the root end with a small knife (this is to let them cook quicker). Drop into a pot of boiling salted water and cook over medium heat about 10 minutes. The time will depend on the size of the sprouts—they should be just tender if a small knife is inserted at the base.

Drain, return to the pot, and add butter, salt and pepper to taste, and a whisper of nutmeg. Stir over medium heat until coated, then add cream and cheese. Let heat through, then place in a hot dish and serve.

Danish Red Cabbage

1 pound red cabbage
¼ cup red wine
¼ cup red currant jelly
2 tablespoons red wine vinegar
3 tablespoons butter (or goose
  fat)
Salt

SERVES 4

THE USUAL RECIPE for red cabbage calls for it to be cooked with apple, red wine, and in the grandest version—chestnuts. That can be superb, but I think the Dane's method has a purer, sharper flavor, and even more intense color. It is excellent with pork, duck, or goose. Buttered and parslied potatoes make a fine contrast on the plate, too.

Strip cabbage of any tired leaves, core it, and cut into chunks. Whirl in a food processor in batches until finely minced. Place in a saucepan with the rest of the ingredients (salt to taste), cover the pan, and simmer over very low heat 2 hours or more. Stir now and again. Serve hot.

Carrots with Cognac

8 medium-size carrots
½ teaspoon sugar
2 tablespoons butter
2 tablespoons cognac
1 tablespoon minced parsley
Salt

SERVES 4

GENERALLY IN A RECIPE I just specify brandy, but this is the name of the recipe given me, relinquishing with one taste its secret of a good slosh of the very, very best. Any honest homegrown brandy will get you by here, though, and it's certainly the easiest carrot recipe you could hope for.

Preheat oven to 350 degrees. Scrape carrots and trim them into strips about 3 inches long and ¼ inch thick. For older carrots you might have to cut out the woody core.

Lay a sheet of foil in a baking pan and place the carrots in the center. Sprinkle with the rest of the ingredients (salt to taste) and make a tight package of the foil. Bake an hour, or until the carrots are tender. Serve hot.

Carrots with Marsala

1 pound carrots
4 tablespoons butter
¼ cup dry Marsala
1 teaspoon sugar
Salt

SERVES 4

THIS MAKES AN almost unidentifiable flavor to glazed carrots, perfect with many a meat. It is also a fine way to treat the new baby carrots we find in the market these days, though these should be left whole.

Scrape carrots, cutting off tops and tips. Slice diagonally into 1-inch pieces. Drop into a pot of boiling, salted water just until tender—5 to 6 minutes—then drain. These can be done ahead.

To serve, melt butter in a small frying pan set over medium heat. When it sizzles, stir in carrots and cook a minute or so, then add Marsala, sugar, and salt to taste. Cook another 5 minutes or so, turning carrots now and again. The sauce should reduce slightly and glaze the carrots. Serve hot.

Flemish Carrots

1 pound carrots
1 hard-boiled egg yolk
3½ tablespoons melted butter
Salt and freshly ground pepper
¼ teaspoon white wine vinegar
2 tablespoons minced parsley

SERVES 4

THIS SIMPLE, easy sauce is also fine with asparagus, broc-coli, green beans, or perhaps even beets. If you make it ahead it will solidify as the butter cools, but this won't matter to the final dish. It can certainly dignify a simple chop any day at my house.

Scrape carrots and cut into strips about 3 inches long and ¼ inch wide, discarding any woody cores. Drop into boiling, salted water until just tender—8 to 10 minutes. Drain.

While the carrots cook, mash the egg yolk in a small bowl and whisk in butter by the tablespoon. This will quickly make a sauce like mayonnaise. Add salt and pepper to taste and then whisk in vinegar. Toss with warm carrots and parsley and serve immediately.

Cauliflower with Cheese and Browned Butter

1 medium-size head cauli-
flower
Salt and freshly ground pepper
6 tablespoons butter
½ cup freshly grated Parmesan or Romano cheese

SERVES 4

NEAR THE TOP of most anyone's list of comfort dishes is cauliflower with a flowing, creamy cheese sauce. This is almost equally seductive while being simpler to turn out.

Cut off the outer leaves, then core the cauliflower, leaving the head intact. You can boil this in a large pot with about an inch of salted water, but the best way is to steam it, covered, on a rack over water. Steaming takes 10 to 12 minutes, depending on size, and boiling will take 1 or 2 minutes longer. Cook just until a sharp knife can penetrate the stems. Sprinkle with salt and pepper to taste—to my mind cauliflower needs a good bit of salt, particularly among the inner branches. Keep warm.

Melt butter in a small saucepan set over medium heat, shaking the pan now and again until the foam dies down and the butter is a light nut brown—don't let it burn. Sprinkle cheese over the cauliflower, then pour the sizzling butter over the top. This can be served immediately, or if you must, let it sit at room temperature and reheat in a moderate oven.

Minted
Cauliflower

½ cup white wine vinegar
¼ cup finely chopped fresh
    mint
2 tablespoons sugar
1 medium-size head cauli-
    flower
Salt

SERVES 4

BOULESTIN IS QUITE PRECISE in his recipe: "Having boiled the cauliflower and drained it well, put it in the serving dish and pour over all a good quantity of mint sauce." Of course, you must know how to prepare English Mint Sauce (as for lamb—not our terrible mint jelly). The florets are, indeed, one of the finest accompaniments to lamb chops, or for a leg of lamb you might serve a whole head of cauliflower, which having absorbed the sauce can be garnished with mint sprigs and then presented at the table to cut like a pie. It is something to remember for those who want maximum flavor with a minimum of fat.

Heat vinegar in a small saucepan and stir in mint and sugar off the flame. Let this sit at least half an hour to gather flavor.

To cook, core the cauliflower and separate the branches into equal 1-inch florets. Drop into boiling, lightly salted water and cook until just tender—5 to 6 minutes. Test with a knife and drain thoroughly. These can be made ahead, if you like, and steamed a little to reheat before tossing with the mint sauce. Serve hot or at room temperature (but toss with sauce while hot).

Celery with Mustard Butter

4 cups celery, sliced diago-
    nally into 1-inch pieces
2 tablespoons butter
2 teaspoon Dijon-style mus-
    tard
Salt and freshly ground pep-
    per
Freshly grated nutmeg

SERVES 4

CELERY HAS A DELICATE yet pervasive flavor that makes it a natural, along with carrots, for making stocks. Served on its own it needs little but this kind of kick to make it a fine partner for chops or steaks.

Drop celery into boiling, salted water and cook 8 to 10 minutes, or until done but still a little crispy. Drain it well. This step can be done well ahead.

To continue, melt butter over medium heat and stir in mustard. Add celery and toss over medium-high heat with salt, pepper and nutmeg to taste. Serve hot.

Celery Root Puree

2 pounds celery root
2 medium-size potatoes
Salt and freshly ground pep-
    per
3 tablespoons butter
¼ cup milk or cream
2 tablespoons minced parsley

SERVES 4

THIS SHOULD BE in any fine cook's file, and yet you see celery root (knob celery, celeriac) on the market shelf with no one buying. Take courage and start yourself with this, which can be served anywhere you'd ordinarily go for mashed pota- toes. Try it first perhaps with your next roast turkey, for holidays, and watch them ask for more.

Peel celery root well and cut into 1-inch pieces. Do the same for the potatoes. Boil them separately in lightly salted water until tender. When a fork pierces them eas- ily, drain well, return to their pans, lay a double sheet of paper towel over, cover the pan, and let steam 5 min- utes.

Put them together through a food mill or a ricer—this will remove any little fibers celery root sometimes has. Place warm in a food processor and whirl with salt and pepper, butter, and milk. The mixture should be very light and fluffy. Whirl in the parsley. The puree can be made ahead to this point.

To serve, warm in the top of a double boiler.

Cucumbers with Mushrooms

3 medium-size cucumbers
1 cup sliced mushrooms
2 tablespoons butter
Salt and freshly ground pepper
2 tablespoons minced chives, parsley, or tarragon

SERVES 4

A FINE, delicious dish with simple fish or chicken. It comes together in just a couple of minutes, only showing the mushrooms to the fire before they leak juices. You might also like a few drops of lemon at the very final toss.

Peel cucumbers and slice in half lengthwise. Scoop out the seeds with a small spoon and cut into ¼-inch slices. Drop them into a pot of boiling, salted water for 3 minutes, then drain and run cold water over to stop the cooking. This can be prepared ahead.

Wipe mushrooms and cut off the stems, then cut into ¼-inch slices. This can be prepared ahead.

Melt butter in a frying pan, add the cucumbers, and toss just until heated through. Add mushrooms, cook another minute, and sprinkle with salt and pepper to taste and the chives. Serve while hot.

Dandelion Greens Provençale

½ cup freshly made bread
   crumbs (see page 325)
1 clove garlic, peeled
1 shallot, peeled
2 tablespoons parsley
Salt
2 tablespoons olive oil
2 good bunches dandelions

SERVES 4

THIS CAN BE DONE with most any green—mustard, kale, or collards—so long as they are cooked just tender, although they won't make pretty nests like the dandelion greens. Another way is to use either curly endive or escarole, for which you should separate the leaves and cook just a minute.

Place crumbs in a food processor. Drop in garlic, then shallot, then parsley through the tube as you pulse. Add salt to taste, then the oil.

Remove stems from dandelions (so you have mostly leaf) and wash them well. Bring about an inch of water to a boil in a large frying pan, sprinkle in some salt, add the dandelions all facing the same way, cover the pan, and cook about 10 minutes over medium-low heat. Test for doneness. Drain and let cool to room temperature.

Divide the leaves into 4 portions. With your hands, curl them into 4 nests. Place on a baking dish greased with a little olive oil. Divide the bread crumb mixture among them, crowning each nest with a smooth pile. These can be made well ahead.

To cook, preheat oven to 350 degrees. Bake the dandelion about 25 minutes, or until light gold on top. Serve them either hot or at room temperature.

Braised Fennel

2 bulbs fennel (about a pound each)
3 tablespoons butter
½ cup chicken stock
Salt and freshly ground pepper
Freshly grated Parmesan cheese

SERVES 4

I WAS READING a similar recipe recently which used about six cloves of garlic. As much as we all love garlic, surely this is a case of overkill to the delicate anise flavor of fennel. Serve with pork, lamb, or grilled chicken.

Preheat oven to 350 degrees. Trim stems and feathery tops from fennel bulbs (it's nice to save the feathers to garnish the finished dish). Slice bulbs in half lengthwise, then slice these halves into 4 sections

Use some butter to grease a baking dish large enough to hold the fennel in a single layer. Place the fennel in cut sides down, pour stock over and sprinkle with a little salt and pepper. Strew generously with cheese. Dot with remaining butter.

Bake uncovered for 40 to 45 minutes, or until the fennel is tender. Serve hot or warm.

Leeks with Puffed Noodles

2 large leeks
Vegetable oil
Chinese rice stick noodles
Salt

SERVES 4

LIVING IN SAN FRANCISCO with its extensive Oriental community, I eat out more than cook at home this cuisine that holds surprises all along the way. I learned how to cook these noodles for a Chinese chicken salad, and then came up with this East-West dish, which is so simple and impressive, if I had a restaurant again I would turn this into a signature dish. Try it first on your family, so you get the hang of it—it's really more complicated to explain than to cook. It's a particularly fine partner with steaks, sauced or not.

Cut the stem ends off leeks and then the green tops. Slice in half vertically, then into thin vertical strands. Place in a bowl of water. This step can be done ahead.

To cook, heat oil in a deep-fat fryer, or at least an inch deep in a heavy, medium-size frying pan. Drain leeks and pat dry. The oil should be 350 to 375 degrees. Drop in the leeks and fry for several minutes, or until lightly crisped and starting to turn gold. Remove with the fryer basket or a slotted spoon to paper towels.

Break up the strands of noodles into about 3-inch pieces and fry a handful at a time—don't try too many at once, for they won't puff evenly. At the proper temperature rice noodles explode at once into a mass of white fluff. It's hard to estimate how much you will need until they cook up, but this will be approximately 2 cups expanded noodles per serving. As they cook, lift them out and place with leeks on paper towels. Salt both lightly and toss. Serve hot.

Mushrooms Bordelaise

1 pound fresh mushrooms
2 tablespoons vegetable oil
4 tablespoons butter
3 minced shallots or green
   onions
¼ cup freshly made bread
   crumbs (see page 325)
Salt and freshly ground pepper
¼ cup mixed fines herbes or
   parsley

SERVES 4

IF YOU HAVE ALL THE INGREDIENTS handy, this is a dish that goes like the wind, or at least during the last turn of a broiled chop. The French use these to border many a fancy platter, as well as a simple method to show off different varieties of wild mushrooms—try it with shiitakes or chanterelles. As a plus they have fewer calories than french fries!

Buy mushrooms, if possible, all of a size. Brush off any dirt and trim the stems just where they are darkened— they don't have to be trimmed to the cap. Button mushrooms can be left whole and large ones quartered.

Heat oil and butter in a large frying pan. When it sputters, toss in the mushrooms and cook over high heat for 3 minutes or so, until lightly browned. Stir in shallots and bread crumbs and toss a couple of minutes more. Season to taste at the last minute with salt, pepper, and herbs. Toss and serve immediately.

Mushrooms Stuffed with Pine Nuts

Large mushrooms
Lemon juice
Olive oil
Freshly grated Parmesan cheese
Lightly toasted pine nuts

SERVES 4

THESE ARE ABOUT THE MOST SIMPLE yet proud garnish for a main dish I know. They can pair with almost any meat, fish, or fowl not already replete with mushrooms. Best of all, they can be prepared in the time it takes you to dish up the meat.

Choose 4 mushrooms per guest if about a good inch, or 3 for inch-and-a-half's. Snap out their stems to save for another use. Rub the caps with lemon juice, then turn in olive oil. Set in a gratin dish. These can sit a while.

To cook, preheat oven to 400 degrees. Sprinkle a little cheese in each cap, top lightly with a filling of nuts, then make a little snowcap of cheese. Drizzle a little olive oil over, then bake 10 minutes, or until lightly browned. Serve hot or warm.

Shiitake Mushrooms with Pâté de Foie Gras

4 shiitake mushrooms (*about 2½ inches in diameter*)
1 tablespoon butter
Salt
1 tablespoon cognac
2 ounces pâté de foie gras

SERVES 2 TO 4

THIS IS CALLED OVERKILL, but why not if your pocket can afford the ingredients? However, don't economize with canned pâté made with inferior ingredients, just go to your nearest gourmet shop and get a slice of the real McCoy. It makes a perfect accompaniment for a simple steak or slice of rare prime rib.

Remove stems from mushrooms. Heat butter in a frying pan just large enough to hold them all in a single layer. Sauté over medium heat about 2 minutes a side, or just until they start to become tender. Don't overcook. Salt lightly as they cook and add the cognac. Ignite with a match and shake the pan until the flame dies down. Place them in a baking dish and spread a thin layer of pâté in each cap, then pour over the pan juices. These can be made ahead and kept at room temperature.

To continue, place in a moderate oven and just heat through. Serve hot.

Sweet-Sour Red Onions

4 large red onions
Red wine vinegar
Butter
Sugar
Salt
2 tablespoons red currant jelly

SERVES 4

NO RECIPE CAN DESCRIBE how enticing these smell, look, and taste. You'll have to try them yourself.

Preheat oven to 350 degrees. Choose flattish onions so they sit well. Peel and trim carefully, trying not to strip too much flesh away or too much off the root ends. Drop into a pot of boiling, salted water. Simmer 10 minutes, then remove with a slotted spoon and let cool until you can handle them. Slice in half parallel to the root end. Place each half in a square of foil and bring the foil up around the sides. Top each with about a teaspoon of vinegar and butter, then a pinch of sugar and a sprinkle of salt. Close them tightly. Bake 35 to 40 minutes, or until a small knife enters them easily.

Melt jelly in a small saucepan set over low heat, then brush the tops of the onion halves with it. These can be made well ahead, covered, and kept at room temperature.

To continue, preheat oven to anywhere from 325 to 375 degrees. Place onions in a small baking dish, pour the juices from the foil around them, and bake, uncovered, until heated through and slightly glazed on top. Serve hot or at room temperature.

Orzo with Green Onions and Parsley

1 cup orzo
1 clove garlic, slightly flattened and peeled
1½ tablespoons olive oil
¼ cup minced green onions,
  with part of tops
1 tablespoon minced parsley
  or fresh coriander

SERVES 4

ORZO IS A RICE-SHAPED PASTA that makes a pleasant change of pace when you are contemplating a starch. While usually cooked in chicken stock, like a rice pilaf, and then tossed with butter and Parmesan, you'll find this recipe is lighter and has an almost Oriental touch. It could be served with almost any main dish, but it is particularly fine with delicate fish.

Drop orzo into 2 cups of boiling, salted water. Add garlic, return to a boil, cover, and simmer 10 minutes, or until the pasta is tender. Drain any excess liquid and remove the garlic. Toss with oil, onions, and parsley or coriander. Serve immediately

Of Garden Peas

Peas ephemeral, peas delectable! Like picked corn, they quickly lose sweet and savor off the vine. Those gardenless, harvesting only market crop, are up for inevitable disappointment at the table, especially if they themselves have ever picked a dinner's worth. With the exception of the British, whose peas resemble cotton marbles, European markets offer a fine seasonal city crop from the local countryside—why can't we?

At other times the French content themselves with canned petits pois—another vegetable entirely. So is the frozen pea with us, excellent of its kind, but no substitute for the absolutely real, picked that day by the gallon, in the glare of the sun, with only a small emerald bowl to show. But obtainable year round are snow peas, which you must admit very good indeed. Increasingly, also, a "sugar snap pea" may be had, which would seem to breed the best of the two, with edible peas inside an edible shell.

Snow peas, I think, should be done as simply as possible, just like the real thing. They need to have their tops pinched off and the small thread attached down the flat side pulled out. If shriveled, pinch off the curl at the bottom tip as well. This is easiest done by hand. To serve, drop into boiling, salted water (or steam them) not much more than a minute. With a squeeze of lemon, a dash of salt and pepper, and a melting knob of butter tossed in, they make an ideal quick way to balance with some crispy greenery on a plate of meat and potatoes.

Peas Braised with Cucumbers

1 cucumber
2 tablespoons butter
Salt and freshly ground pepper
1 teaspoon minced chives or parsley
Pinch of sugar
¼ cup chicken stock
1 10-oz package frozen tiny peas

SERVES 4

WHEN ALL ONE CAN GET is frozen peas, this comes to the rescue at a trot, if not a grand gallop. It's a recipe I found during research for my American Table, *and I use it constantly.*

Peel cucumber and cut it lengthwise into quarters. Scoop out the seeds and cut into ¼-inch dice. Place in a saucepan with butter, cover, and cook over medium heat 4 to 5 minutes. Add salt and pepper to taste, chives, and sugar. Add stock, bring to a boil, and then add peas. When they again come to a boil, cook covered another 2 minutes. Serve hot.

Snow Peas with Tree Oyster Mushrooms

¾ pound snow peas
2 tablespoons butter
1 minced shallot or green onion
½ pound tree oyster mush-
   rooms, cut into strips
Salt and freshly ground pepper

SERVES 4

THESE MUSHROOMS ARE very delicate and are perfect with snow peas, whereas the more meaty shiitake mushroom would overwhelm the peas. Sugar snap peas may also be used.

Pinch tops off peas and pull out the tiny thread attached down the flat side of the pea. If shriveled, pinch the curl at the bottom as well. Drop into a pan of boiling, salted water, cook 2 minutes, and then drain.

Melt butter in a frying pan set over medium-high heat. When it sputters, stir in shallot and cook for a minute, then stir in mushrooms with salt and pepper to taste. Cook a minute or so, then stir in peas and cook another minute. Serve hot.

Polenta

¾ cup coarse-milled polenta
4 cups water
Salt
3 to 4 tablespoons freshly
  grated Parmesan or Ro-
  mano cheese

SERVES 4

THE COMMON METHOD of pouring polenta into boiling water can be tricky (and makes for lumps), so I prefer this. Also, I have discovered recently that if you cook it in the top of a double boiler, it practically eliminates stirring, though it will take about 15 minutes longer.

Combine polenta and water in a large saucepan, turn on the heat, and bring to a boil, stirring now and again. As it begins to thicken, stir steadily so that no lumps are formed. Turn heat low until the polenta makes just a gentle *plop plop* as it cooks. Stir every 5 minutes or so. If the polenta seems too thick and begins to stick to the sides of the pan, add a little more hot water. Cook 30 to 45 minutes, depending on the mill of the meal used. Polenta is done when it's a thick and creamy mass with individual particles still with a little bite to them. About 5 minutes before the end, add salt to taste and the cheese.

In Italy, the polenta is poured out on a slab, usually marble, and cooled slightly, then cut with a thread into wedges. This is not necessary—I pour into 2 lightly wetted pie pans and cut with a knife.

Polenta Cups
with Gorgonzola
and Pine Nuts,
or Chèvre and
Sun-Dried
Tomatoes

*1 recipe polenta, using 1 cup
    meal and 5 cups water (see
    page 203)*
*4 ounces Gorgonzola cheese or
    chèvre*
*4 tablespoons butter, at room
    temperature*
*3 tablespoons pine nuts or
    slivered sun-dried tomatoes*
*Freshly grated Parmesan or
    Romano cheese*

SERVES 4

EITHER OF THESE is a kind of tour de force *presentation we expect more from restaurants than home cooks, but they are really quite simple to assemble and cook.*

Pour prepared polenta into a wetted 8-x-8-inch square baking dish. Refrigerate until cold—at least an hour. Cut into 3-inch rounds with a large biscuit cutter or drinking glass and scoop out the centers with a small spoon, being careful to leave at least ½-inch sides and bottom. For variation 1, cream Gorgonzola and butter and fill the cups, then sprinkle with nuts and grated cheese. For variation 2, cream chèvre and butter, then work in sun-dried tomatoes. Fill the cups and sprinkle with grated cheese. These can be made well ahead, covered and kept at room temperature.

To continue, preheat oven to 400 degrees. Bake 10 minutes, or until heated all the way through and beginning to brown. Serve hot or warm.

Pumpkin Gnocchi with Sage Butter

1 pound canned pumpkin
2 eggs
¾ cup flour
½ teaspoon baking powder
Salt
Freshly ground nutmeg
½ clove garlic, minced (optional)
4 to 6 tablespoons butter
½ teaspoon crumbled dried sage leaves (not powdered sage)
Freshly grated Parmesan cheese

SERVES 4 TO 6

A COUPLE OF YEARS AGO restaurants all over started turning these out, but they are just as easily prepared at home. And do use a can of pumpkin rather than the remains of the Halloween one (not bred for taste, and quite watery). I like these especially with Lamb Chops Abruzzo (page 118) or Roast Pork Arista (page 122).

Mix pumpkin with eggs, flour, baking powder, salt to taste, and a good sprinkle of nutmeg. If you add garlic it should not be obtrusive. Let sit at least an hour, covered with plastic wrap.

To cook, bring a pot of salted water just to a simmer. Place large spoonfuls of the mixture on a floured board and lightly roll them into a cylinder about the width of a thumb. Cut into 1½-inch lengths and drop into the water. The water should never come to a boil. When the gnocchi are done, they will rise to the surface. Remove them with a slotted spoon to a plate.

Melt butter with sage. When it starts to bubble, remove from the fire. Spread some of it in individual ramekins or a shallow baking dish large enough to hold the gnocchi in a single layer. Lay them in and drizzle the rest of the butter mixture over. Sprinkle well with cheese. These may be made ahead to this point, covered, and kept at room temperature.

To continue, preheat broiler and place gnocchi under just until they start to bubble and take on color. Serve immediately.

Red Radishes with Raspberry Vinegar

2 bunches radishes
1 tablespoon butter
1 tablespoon vegetable oil
1 tablespoon raspberry vinegar
Salt and freshly ground pepper

SERVES 4

PERHAPS MORE A GARNISH than a real side vegetable, these have a sprightly flavor and add color to a plate if snuggled in between the usual green vegetable and the meat.

Choose bunches with radishes all more or less the same size, if possible. Trim and wash them and cut into quarter wedges.

Heat butter and oil in a frying pan set over medium heat. Add radishes and toss to coat well. After a few minutes sprinkle the vinegar over and then salt and pepper to taste. Cook 10 to 12 minutes, tossing now and again. When done, they should be a beautiful red, and still a little crisp when you bite in. Serve hot.

Perfect Rice

There are as many basic recipes for rice as there are pots and peoples. The Chinese want it slightly sticky so as to stick to chopsticks, the Italians breed a special pearly grain to make risottos with a creamy outside, but at the center of each grain a toothsome kernel. Recipes in the United States hold a dry and separate quality the ideal. I have only one word to add about all this: Basmati. You can buy it these days in specialty stores, or in health food outlets where it's cheaper than Uncle Ben's, and its nutty fragrance and taste make you dissatisfied with any other.

The simplest recipe will suffice. Measure twice the boiling, salted water to rice: say, ½ cup rice to 1 cup of water. Cover, turn heat low, and just simmer 20 minutes. You can't beat that. If your timing is off it can sit a while, too. Stir in some butter, or even olive oil scented with a clove of garlic previously simmered and discarded. Serve—that's just about it.

VARIATION 1

Shake a fistful of pine nuts in sizzling butter until they turn pale gold. Stir into the rice before serving.

VARIATION 2

Lightly toast some sesame seeds in a dry frying pan set over low heat. Stir them into the rice when you add the butter.

Rice Pilaf

3 tablespoons butter
¼ cup finely chopped onion or
  2 shallots, minced
¾ cup long-grain or Basmati
  rice
1½ cups chicken stock
Salt and freshly ground pepper

SERVES 4

RISOTTO IS the talk of the town these days, but let us re-member it takes half an hour of last-minute fussing to get it on the table, and it really is a course on its own, like pasta. A pilaf, on the other hand, you can almost forget as you assemble dinner, and it is definitely a side dish to complement the meat. I recently served it to a poet and his French wife with some-thing like a game hen, and instead of asking for the recipe for the interesting first course or smashing dessert, she asked po-litely for the rice recipe. I told her it's just like her mother made it, but with Basmati rice.

Melt butter in a saucepan set over medium-low heat and add onion or shallots. Stir until soft, then add rice and stir until the grains are coated with butter and starting to turn opaque—do not brown the rice. Add stock, turn up heat, bring to a boil, and taste for seasoning. If the stock is seasoned well you won't need much salt. Cover, turn heat low, and simmer 20 minutes. If necessary, this can sit a while and be reheated gently. Fluff with a fork before serving.

Rice and Rye Pilaf

½ cup rye "berries"
Salt
2 tablespoons butter
2 green minced onions, with
    part of tops
½ cup long-grain rice
1 cup chicken stock

SERVES 4

RYE BERRIES ARE the kernels of the grain, to be found in health food stores—and probably in Dean and Deluca in New York City. Not only is it nutritionally admirable, it is plain delicious combined with rice.

Put rye kernels in a small saucepan with ¾ cup water and a pinch of salt. Bring to a boil, lower heat to a bare simmer, cover the pan, and cook 45 to 50 minutes. The water should be absorbed when they test done—a little chewy-tender. This can be done ahead.

To continue, heat butter in a medium-size saucepan, stir in onion until softened, and then stir in rice until it turns slightly opaque—a matter of 3 to 4 minutes. Add rye and chicken stock, then add salt to taste. Bring to a boil, lower heat, cover, and steam 20 minutes. Stir before serving. If necessary, it can sit and be gently reheated to serve.

Wild Rice, Barley, and Mushrooms

¼ cup wild rice
Salt
2 tablespoons butter
1 minced shallot or green on-
    ion
1½ cups chicken stock
½ cup pearl barley
1 cup mushrooms, sliced
Freshly ground pepper

SERVES 4

I DON'T KNOW ABOUT YOU, but I find wild rice a rather overpraised delicacy, though I admire its texture. Here it is combined with another texture in the barley, and with mushrooms for further flavor. It is a dish to serve with lamb, game hens, pork chops, or even turkey.

Wash rice thoroughly and place in a saucepan with 1 cup water and a dash of salt. Bring to a boil, turn heat low, cover the pan, and simmer 45 to 50 minutes. Melt 1 tablespoon of butter in another saucepan set over medium-low heat. Stir in the shallot and cook several minutes. Add stock and barley, turn heat low, cover the pan, and cook 25 to 30 minutes. The liquid in the rice should have been completely absorbed, but if not, drain it and stir the rice into the barley. This can be done well ahead.

Toward serving time, put remaining butter in a small frying pan set over medium-high heat. Add mushrooms, toss to coat with butter, and cook several minutes, or just until they start to exude juice. While they cook, sprinkle with a little salt and pepper. Stir these into the rice-barley mixture and reheat gently.

Spinach "en Branche"

The simplest way to treat yourself to fresh spinach is this method, and one of the best. I first had it in one of London's best grills (nothing fancy, just choice meats, crisp fries, good beer), and paid more attention to the spinach than the chop. For years I tried to produce a similar mound at home, by just wilting it with the water on its leaves. No, the secret seems to be in drying it as you would lettuce for a salad. Paper towels, a spin dryer if you have one. . . . To cook them is a process so easy as not to be a recipe at all.

Take a large bouquet of fresh spinach, pinch the leaves off, maybe even leaving an inch of tender stem. Drop them into a bowl and fill it to the brim with cold water. Swish the leaves around and let sit a few minutes to let dirt and sand settle. Carefully lift out into a colander, with your hands or a slotted spoon, leaving sediment behind. To be safe, repeat the process. Dry as above.

Only a few minutes before table, heat a large frying pan with enough olive oil, butter, or bacon fat to generously film the bottom—start only with a tablespoon or so. After a few minutes over medium-high heat it should just start to sputter. Throw the spinach in and toss quickly, just until the mass seems about to sink—a matter of seconds. Quickly remove from heat, toss again with salt, pepper, and maybe a blessing of nutmeg. A sprinkle of lemon is the final touch, but these should be in wedges at the side for guests to sprinkle at will.

French Creamed Spinach

2 pounds fresh spinach
4 tablespoons butter
2 teaspoon flour
Salt and freshly ground pep-
    per
Freshly grated nutmeg
1 cup heavy cream
1 tablespoon dry Madeira

SERVES 4

ONE OF THE WORLD'S *great classic glories, and though cleaning spinach takes a little time, it's worth it just for that tiny edge of flavor over frozen spinach. No other recipe I've seen has the final touch of Madeira, which lifts it even a tad higher.*

Stem the spinach and wash according to the preceding recipe. Bring water to a boil in a large saucepan and drop spinach in. Cook 3 to 4 minutes, then remove with a slotted spoon to a colander (this assures any dirt or sand left will settle to the bottom of the pan). Immediately run cold water over, then squeeze water out with your hands. Mince it finely.

Melt 3 tablespoons of butter in a saucepan set over medium heat and stir in spinach. Cook several minutes, stirring, until it begins to stick to the bottom of the pan. Stir in flour and cook another couple of minutes. Season with salt and pepper to taste and a suggestion of nutmeg. Add cream and stir until the spinach is smooth and bubbling. Stir in Madeira and cook another minute, tasting for seasoning. This can be prepared ahead, kept covered for an hour or so, and reheated gently until bubbling, adding more cream (or milk) if necessary.

To continue, stir in remaining butter. Serve immediately.

Sweet Potatoes with Lime and Sherry

2 pounds sweet potatoes
3 tablespoons butter
Salt and freshly ground pepper
2 tablespoons lime juice
2 tablespoons dry sherry
Sour cream

SERVES 4

THE OTHER DAY I was in the market listening to a considerable rumpus being made by an elderly lady at the vegetable counter. She was making sure, by asking everyone around, that she did not get yams, but sweet potatoes. This continued all the way to the checkout counter, where she reiterated to one and all how she disliked the sweetness of yams. It was only as I was scooping up my change that I heard The Recipe. It was worth all the fuss.

Peel potatoes and cut into ¼-inch slices. Drop into a pan of boiling, salted water and cook until soft—about 8 minutes. Drain well, place a sheet of paper towel over the pan, cover with the lid, and let steam several minutes.

Put potatoes through a ricer and mash in butter, then add salt and pepper to taste, lime juice, and sherry. This can be done ahead and reheated in the top of a double boiler. To serve, heat well and place a dollop of sour cream on each portion.

Tomatoes Provençale

2 large garden tomatoes (at
    least 3 inches wide)
Salt and freshly ground pep-
    per
½ cup freshly made bread
    crumbs (see page 325)
1 clove garlic
1 shallot or green onion
2 tablespoons parsley
1 tablespoon fresh basil (or 1
    teaspoon dried)
⅛ teaspoon dried thyme
¼ cup olive oil

SERVES 2 TO 4

WHEN TOMATOES ARE IN SEASON, I serve these often with many a different main course, but all that wonderful stuffing does little toward making the mealy, watery supermarket tomato palatable. It is a classic dish, and deservedly so.

Cut tomatoes in half horizontally and gently squeeze out seeds and juice. Salt and pepper lightly. Put bread crumbs, garlic, shallot, parsley, basil, and thyme in a food processor and process until everything is finely minced. Add about half the oil and salt to taste and spin a little. Divide the bread crumb mixture among the tomatoes, stuffing down into the holes and smoothing over the tops. Use a little of the oil to grease a baking dish large enough to hold all 4 halves. Drizzle the rest of the oil over the tops. These can be made well ahead and kept covered with plastic wrap at room temperature.

To continue, preheat the oven to 400 degrees and bake 10 to 15 minutes. The tomatoes should not be cooked so much that they start to lose their shape. Serve hot or warm.

Baked Yams with Black Walnuts

The dark-skinned sweet potatoes that are called Jewel yams can be baked like any ordinary potato, at medium to high heat, just until soft. Unlike baked potatoes, though, they can sit ages and then be reheated, split, and buttered. After years of not understanding why perfectly sensible folk eat sweet potatoes with lots of brown sugar—or topped with even sweeter marshmallows (or pineapple!)—over the holidays, I have invited and even invented a few new ways for this delightful tuber. White potatoes, or what is called the Irish potato, are more versatile and have spread the globe. The New World also gave us the sweet potato, but it has pretty much stayed home.

Of all my quest and culinary effort, I really am content with just a baked yam with its perfectly smooth, sweet flesh hardly even in need of butter. But for special company I like to surprise by sizzling the butter with some chopped black walnuts. With their strong fragrance, mated with the silky textured yam, you have a truly New World experience. They also take almost inhuman patience to crack, and so are usually only found in the Midwest where they are treated like truffles.

I grew up with a dozen across the street, to be used as cowboy projectiles along with staining your face to play Indian. But also to gather in, wait until shriveled black, then to shuck and dry and at last on winter nights, to crack, pick out, and wait for cake or pie or these delightful yams.

A Little Potato Anthology

FORKING UP ALMOST any memorable potato dish, I think, Yes, I'm, after all, that Stodge we hear of, the meat-and-potato guy. I've even contemplated scribbling the Compleat Potato Book, and my files hold dozens of suggestions. I stand by what I wrote in *The American Table:* "The potato is a magical vegetable, quick to take on new character with every marginal change in shape or twist in cooking."

As an avid collector, I find even most of the favorite, trusted cookbook authors are likely to skimp over the six or seven standards, as if that were all. Of the crop, I've tested some very unlikely recipes in my time. But with simplicity and ease as our goal here, I've narrowed my gamut to the range of the amateur cook. No tricky Pommes Soufflés, or little marbles scooped out with a melon baller. (One of my favorite recipes, even *I* have never cooked, is one for the deep-fried remains of that holey potato all the marbles were cut from, saved, and served, for family only, at the queen of England's table.)

Still, there are crowning glories. Perfect as the standards can be, beyond the mashed potato made in heaven and the celestial french fry, there are shapes and crusts and textures any cook might summon without much ado from this plainest of vegetables. My only theory is that whatever hocus-pocus you pull on it, a cooked potato ought to taste like potato.

NOTE: See also Gratin Dauphinois (page 239) and Gratin of Potatoes and Shiitake Mushrooms (page 240).

Perfect Mashed Potatoes

I use two instruments not ordinarily associated with mashed potatoes: a ricer and a double boiler. The ricer gives a lighter texture than mashing, and it assures you will never be accused of having lumps. You'll see how the double boiler comes in handy all along the way.

Take a good-size potato (baking potatoes are fine, but the ordinary bag potato is usually what I use) per serving and cook in the bottom of the boiler in salted water until a fork or sharp knife can pierce easily to the center. Drain the pot, cover with 2 layers of paper towels, cover with the lid, and let sit several minutes to dry out. This is essential for perfection. Then peel potatoes and put through a ricer set over the top part of the boiler. Add about a tablespoon of butter for each potato.

Heat about ½ cup of milk per potato (it's difficult to say exactly because potatoes differ so in size, but it's better to heat too much than too little) in the bottom of the boiler. When it starts to form tiny bubbles around the edge, stir it bit by bit into the potatoes until they are very creamy—just a little more liquid than you might expect, but not soupy. Add salt and pepper to taste. Put some water in the bottom of the boiler (there's no need to wash the milk residue out), set the potatoes on top, cover with the lid, and keep over barely simmering water for 15 to 20 minutes. They can sit longer, even up to an hour, but they will puff up a little and some of the creaminess will be lost.

Serve with a pat of butter to melt on top of each mound. These are my secrets for success.

Variation 1

Rather than discarding them, take peels, stack them, and cut into fine strips. Toss with just enough melted butter to coat. Bake at 425 degrees for 15 minutes, or until crisp as chips. Serve warm over mashed potatoes.

Variation 2

Mince a good-size green onion for every potato you cook and add to the cold milk as it heats up. After you rice the potatoes, mash the potatoes with the onion-milk mixture and butter. This is perhaps the very best potato dish of all.

Classic French Fries

Take a medium-size baking potato per person and cut in ¼-inch strips. Peel or not as you wish, but if you like skins on you should scrub well before. Put in a good bowl of cold water to wash off surface starch and hold until you need them.

Drain potatoes and pat dry with paper towels. Heat vegetable oil to 325 degrees. For 2 potatoes I just put a couple inches of oil in a cast-iron frying pan, but for more I suggest a deep-fat fryer with a basket and instructions. At temperature, throw them all in bubbling fat to cover and cook until flabby and ivory colored—about 5 to 6 minutes. Scoop out with a slotted spoon (or the basket) and drain on paper. I just use yesterday's newspaper, but you could be more fastidious with paper towels. These can be held about 30 minutes.

To serve, heat oil to 375 degrees (notice the higher temperature). Drop fries back in and cook until crisp and golden, about another 8 to 10 minutes at even temperature. Drain again on paper, sprinkling with salt while hot.

This is the way most restaurants turn out fries, if they know what they're about, and it also saves the harried host at home, for they only need be turned out at the last moment while you slice the meat.

Baltimore Fries

1½ pounds red potatoes,
   about 2 inches round
Vegetable oil
Salt

SERVES 4

I DISCOVERED these when I was doing research for The American Table, *and I use them constantly with any dish you would ordinarily expect french fries. They are crisp, delicious, and different—one of the true classics.*

Scrub the potatoes and cut into quarters. Drop into boiling, salted water and simmer over medium-low heat 15 minutes, or until almost done but not really soft. Drain and dry on paper towels. These can be made ahead and kept, covered loosely, at room temperature.

To serve, heat at least an inch and a half of oil in a frying pan (or use a deep-fat fryer). When it starts to shimmer—but not smoke—add a potato quarter to test. In 5 minutes it should be golden brown all over. If so, cook the rest, and drain on paper towels, immediately salting. Serve hot.

Potato-Shell Fries

4 medium-size Idaho baking
    potatoes
Vegetable oil
Salt
Freshly grated Parmesan
    cheese
Sour cream
Chives

SERVES 4

THIS IS A RECENT DISCOVERY. I was testing a recipe for something like this, but baked then broiled with a coating of grated Cheddar. They weren't as crisp as I would have liked them, and the Cheddar made a kind of glue. So I tried this and came out with an instant favorite.

These can be baked at any medium or hot temperature, if you are cooking another dish. Scrub the potatoes well with a stiff brush. Poke with a jab of a small knife and lay on the oven rack to cook. Test now and again. They will be done when they yield between the fingers. Take them out and let cool enough to handle. Cut in half lengthwise and scoop out flesh from the middle leaving only about a ⅓-inch shell. If your spoon slips, pat some flesh down around the shells. These can be reserved and tented with plastic wrap until cooking time.

To fry, heat enough oil to come up over the shells to about 350 degrees. It is important to have the oil really hot. Fry the shells about 5 minutes, or until crisp and golden brown. Lift out to drain on paper and immediately sprinkle with salt and a shower of cheese. Serve hot, with a dollop of sour cream in the boat. A few snipped chives won't hurt either.

Fried Potatoes with Shallot-Parsley Butter

2 large baking potatoes
Vegetable oil
1 tablespoon melted butter
1 shallot, minced
1 tablespoon minced parsley
Salt and freshly ground pep-
    per

SERVES 4

A SPECIALTY OF the San Ysidro Ranch in Montecito, California, and very good, too, with practically any simple meat.

Wash potatoes and cut in half lengthwise, then cut into thin slices crosswise. Peel them if you wish, but I like them with the skin on. In a deep-fat fryer, heat oil to about 375 degrees. Fry in batches, if necessary, until gold and crisp and drain on paper towels. While hot, sprinkle with butter, shallot, parsley, and salt and pepper to taste.

Potatoes Sautéed in Goose Fat

8 2½-inch-round new potatoes
   (preferably White Rose)
Goose fat
Salt and freshly ground pepper

SERVES 4

THE ORDINARY SAUTÉED POTATO *is done in clarified butter, but goose fat—if you have it—lifts it into another realm. I generally cook a goose for holidays, and it renders enough fat to keep me in business for the rest of the year (the fat refrigerated and tightly sealed). It's also possible to use goose fat rather than meat drippings when you cook ordinary roast potatoes. They are particularly fine with chicken.*

Peel potatoes and cut into smooth ovals—you don't have to be a fanatic about this, but they will cook more evenly if approximately all the same size and cut smoothly. Do not wash the potatoes, simply wipe and wrap in a towel.

Heat up about one-sixteenth inch of fat in a frying pan large enough to hold all the potatoes in a single layer. When fat is hot, add potatoes and let cook over medium-high heat 1 or 2 minutes, then turn them over. After another 1 or 2 minutes, shake the pan to flip the potatoes and continue to cook for 4 to 5 minutes, or until seared all over a pale gold. Sprinkle with salt and pepper, cover the pan, lower heat, and cook 15 to 20 minutes. Shake the pan every now and again to prevent sticking and ensure even color. They are done when a small knife pierces them easily. Serve hot.

Potatoes Maxime

4 medium-size potatoes
½ cup melted butter
Salt and freshly ground pepper

SERVES 4

AT MAXIME'S IN PARIS these are prepared with more than twice this amount of butter, but if the potatoes are tossed so they are completely coated they cook the same without swimming in a lake. They are a kind of free-form Potatoes Anna (where the scallops are elaborately arranged in concentric circles), baked in lovely copper oval pans and turned out onto an oval platter exactly the right size. Home cooks will want to simply cut them up into serving portions in the kitchen and place them beside the meat—they are so crisp and delicious your guests won't miss the visuals.

Preheat oven to 425 degrees. Peel potatoes and wash and dry them. Very thinly slice into a bowl, then pour butter over and toss well with a sprinkling of salt and pepper. Spread in a shallow baking dish large enough to hold the potatoes in a layer of no more than half an inch. Bake 40 minutes, or until crisp and golden.

Potatoes Roasted with Whole Shallots

4 medium-size potatoes
12 shallots, peeled
¼ cup olive oil or butter, or half of each
Salt and freshly ground pepper
2 bay leaves, broken in half

SERVES 4

THESE ARE QUITE A LIFT *from the ordinary roast potato, and are just as easy to prepare. I cook them at 325 degrees since that is the temperature I use to roast chicken, and I most often use them as a side dish there. But they could roast at 350 degrees just as well.*

Preheat oven to 325 degrees. Peel potatoes and cut into quarters. Drop into a pot of boiling, salted water and cook 5 minutes, then drain and pat dry with paper towels. Place with all the other ingredients in a baking dish large enough to hold them all in a single layer. Toss to coat well. Bake 40 to 50 minutes, turning the potatoes 3 times, so they crisp on all sides. Discard the bay leaves if you wish. Serve hot.

Potatoes Sablees

8 red potatoes, about 2 inches
  in diameter
2 tablespoons butter
¼ cup freshly made bread
  crumbs (see page 325)
Salt

SERVES 4

LIKE THE BEST POTATO RECIPES, this seems very simple and has to be tasted to be believed. It reaches a kind of apex in dining if you can find very tiny new potatoes that can be cooked whole as the French do.

Plunk potatoes into a pot of boiling, salted water and cook 12 to 15 minutes, or until a knife pierces them easily. Drain and cut in half—leaving the skins on or not, as you choose. Melt butter in a frying pan large enough to hold them in a single layer. When it sputters, add the potatoes cut side down. Cook over medium-high heat several minutes to develop a little crust, then add bread crumbs and a sprinkle of salt and toss another few minutes, until the crumbs make a crispy, golden brown crust.

Savory Potatoes Roasted in Foil

8 red potatoes, about 2 inches
  in diameter
1 clove garlic, minced
1 shallot, minced
Salt and freshly ground pepper
2 tablespoons olive oil
2 tablespoons butter
1 branch fresh rosemary,
 . thyme, basil, tarragon, or
  bay leaf

SERVES 4

WAIT UNTIL YOU SMELL THESE as you slit the foil! They are superb with practically any dish, and a whiz to turn out.

Preheat oven to 350 degrees. Tear off a large sheet of foil and lay it in a shallow baking pan. Wash potatoes and cut them, unpeeled, into quarters. Place them on the foil with all the rest of the ingredients and toss lightly to coat. Seal up the packet, folding well to seal perfectly. Bake an hour, remove from the foil, discard rosemary, and serve immediately.

Potatoes in Red Pepper Butter

2 medium-size red peppers
4 tablespoons butter
Salt
8 red potatoes, about 2 inches
   in diameter

SERVES 4

A DELIGHTFUL AND DIFFERENT potato which can accompany many a meat or fish dish.

Cut peppers in half and lay cut side down on a sheet of foil. Broil until the skin chars black, then place in a paper bag to steam for 10 minutes. Scrape off the char, cut out seeds, and place in a food processor with butter. Whirl until pureed and add salt to taste. This can be made hours ahead.

To serve, drop potatoes into a pan of boiling, salted water and cook until a small, sharp knife penetrates easily. Drain, return to the pan, cover with a paper towel, cover with the lid, and let dry out several minutes. Peel them and cut into quarters. Toss in the pan with the red pepper butter and serve at once.

Cumin or Caraway Seed Potatoes

8 red potatoes, about 2 inches
    in diameter
Cumin or caraway seeds
Salt
½ cup melted butter

SERVES 4

THESE ARE BURSTING WITH FLAVOR (*if you admire cumin or caraway—if not, try a sprinkling of sweet Hungarian paprika instead*) *and are particularly fine with pork dishes. Don't, however, serve them to guests you suspect might have dentures.*

Preheat oven to 350 degrees. Wash potatoes and cut, unpeeled, in half. Place seeds on a small plate and dip the cut side of the potatoes so there is a light scattering on the flesh, then sprinkle with salt. Lay cut side down in a baking pan brushed with some of the butter. Drizzle the rest of the butter over and sprinkle with more salt. If necessary, this can be done an hour or so ahead.

Bake for about 30 minutes, basting once with the pan butter. When done, they should be soft inside with a golden crust of skin.

Polish Dill Potatoes

8 red potatoes, about 2 inches
    in diameter
4 tablespoons butter, at room
    temperature
Salt
½ cup buttermilk, at room
    temperature
1 tablespoon minced fresh dill
    (or 1 teaspoon dried)

SERVES 4

THESE ARE PARTICULARLY DELIGHTFUL *with fish dishes. Try them even if you think you don't like buttermilk, and I think you'll be very pleased.*

Scrub potatoes, cut into quarters, and drop into a pot of boiling, salted water. Simmer about 15 minutes, or until tender. Drain, return to the pot, place a paper towel over, then cover with a lid. Let sit several minutes to dry.

Add butter and stir potatoes to coat, salting lightly. Stir in buttermilk and dill. Serve at once.

New Potatoes with Mustard Cream

2 pounds tiny new potatoes
   (or 2-inch red potatoes)
4 tablespoons butter
1 tablespoon Dijon-style mustard
3 tablespoons heavy cream
2 tablespoons minced parsley
Salt and freshly ground pepper

SERVES 4

TRY THESE SOMETIME beside a grilled steak with Mushrooms Bordelaise (page 195), and you will have something to really crow about.

Drop potatoes into boiling, salted water and cook until tender. Drain them and let cool—the small potatoes can be left whole, but larger ones should be quartered. Heat butter in a large frying pan set over medium heat. When it sizzles, add potatoes and turn to coat them well. Cook about 5 minutes, turning until lightly browned. Add mustard mixed with cream and turn up heat. Toss to coat, adding parsley and salt and pepper to taste. Serve hot.

Zucchini-Stuffed Baked Potatoes

2 large baking potatoes
2 tablespoons butter
2 medium-size zucchini,
  coarsely grated
Salt and freshly ground pepper
Freshly grated Parmesan or
  Romano cheese

SERVES 4

NOT ONLY DO THESE look and taste wonderful, they are much less caloric than the usual baked potato with butter, sour cream, and chives. Also, they finely combine a starch and vegetable in one easy package.

Scrub and bake the potatoes—this can be done at any medium to hot temperature, if you are cooking other items. When soft, remove from the oven, slice lengthwise, and scoop out the flesh into a bowl. Reserve the potato shells. Either mash the potatoes or put through a ricer.

Melt butter in a small pan. When it sputters, toss the zucchini into it, stirring over medium heat 3 to 4 minutes. Add salt and pepper to taste. Fold lightly into the potatoes, then spoon back into the shells. Sprinkle with cheese. These can be held, covered, for an hour or more before baking.

To continue, preheat oven to 425 degrees and bake potatoes 8 to 10 minutes, or until heated through and the tops are lightly browned.

Bookbinder Potatoes

4 medium-size baking potatoes
12 tablespoons butter, melted
¾ cup freshly grated Parmesan cheese

SERVES 4

THESE TAKE A LITTLE TIME and a lot of butter, but they are better than any baked potato you've ever eaten. I promise.

Preheat oven to 350 degrees. Peel potatoes, wash, and cut into ⅛-inch slices not quite through the potato. Press together and snuggle in a baking dish so they fit closely together. Fill the pan with enough water to come halfway up the potatoes, then pour butter over and sprinkle with cheese.

Bake 1½ hours, basting every 15 minutes. It is important to keep the potatoes moist. When done, they should be soft and golden. Serve hot.

Baked Potatoes with Shaved Hazelnuts

2 large baking potatoes
¼ cup hazelnuts
¼ cup butter
Salt and freshly ground pepper

SERVES 4

YEARS AGO I heeded the advice of a French cook that a baked potato was even better served amandine. I found this sound advice, for you could serve only half a potato with relatively little fat and maximum flavor. Once I had a packet of shaved almonds which proved delicately better, and once there were only hazelnuts at hand which seemed best of all.

Bake potatoes at any medium to high temperature. They are done when you can pinch a crackling crust through to a soft interior. Don't fret about timing—I suppose it's possible to overcook a baked potato, but I've never heard of it.

While the potatoes cook, shave the nuts into slices with a swivel vegetable peeler, being careful of your fingers. (If this sounds like too much work, go ahead and chop them.) Heat butter in a small saucepan and add nuts at the first sizzle. Lower heat and stir until the butter and nuts go from straw colored to light hazel. Remove from the heat immediately. Cut each potato in half lengthwise, then run a sharp knife through the flesh and pinch them out so they fluff up a little. Sprinkle with salt and pepper, and pour hot hazelnut butter over them and serve.

My Mother's Creamed Parmesan Potatoes

3 medium-size baking potatoes
3 tablespoons butter
Salt and freshly ground pepper
½ cup freshly grated Parmesan or Romano cheese
2 tablespoons minced parsley
½ cup heavy cream

SERVES 4

THIS DEAR RECIPE somehow got left out of my American Table, and I'd like to remedy that. They have a kind of ivory appearance, and maximum flavor, making them a dish you can serve to any company, grand or not. Try baking them in individual packets, to warm up on the grill when you cook outside.

Preheat oven to 450 degrees. Peel potatoes and cut into equal ¼-inch lengths, as you do french fries. Pull about 2 feet of foil over a baking sheet and pile the potatoes on it. Dot with butter, season with salt and pepper, then sprinkle with cheese and parsley and toss. Fold up sides of the foil and pour cream in, then fold foil carefully around the potato pile to make a fairly compact, airtight package.

Bake an hour. Remove from the oven, slit an X in the foil package, and remove the potatoes to plates or a serving dish.

Potato-Gruyère Cakes

2 large baking potatoes (about
   1¼ pounds total)
1 tablespoon butter
1 medium-size onion, finely
   chopped
2 eggs
⅓ cup flour
½ cup grated Gruyère cheese
½ cup milk
Salt and freshly ground pepper
Freshly ground nutmeg
1 teaspoon vegetable oil

SERVES 4

I SERVE THESE as the perfect foil for Pork Fillets with Prunes (page 124), but they are so good you may want to try them alongside a steak.

Peel potatoes and wipe with a paper towel—don't wash them. Finely grate or slice the potatoes and grate in a food processor. Melt butter in a frying pan set over medium heat. Add onion and cook until limp and starting to turn color. Add these to the potatoes and lightly wipe out the pan with a paper towel.

Add eggs, flour, cheese, milk, salt and pepper to taste, and a very little nutmeg to the potatoes and combine with a few on/off pulses of the food processor. If the mixture sits a while it will turn gray, but that won't make much difference to the final product.

Heat oil in the frying pan set over medium heat and heap in large spoonfuls—about 2 inches in diameter—of the mixture. Cook about 5 minutes a side, or until they are golden brown. They may be kept in a warm oven for 15 minutes or so before serving.

Gratins and *Sformati*

SOME OF THE MOST memorable vegetable dishes of all are gratins, their tops golden and glistening, turned out in a lovely oval dish, often melting with Gruyère or rich cream absorbed into the whole goodness. Best of all for the harried cook, they take little effort other than assembly, and can sit a good while both before and after cooking. Most, in fact, are often ideal at room temperature.

An array of gratins opens before you in any good cookbook, but you have to dig hard to find *sformati*. Recently a friend flew to Chicago, where his Italian family firmly believes he starves, and arrived back with a hunk of the finest aged Parmesan and a bag of dried porcini mushrooms to share. Best of all, he brought a description of a green bean side dish served at room temperature—light, delicate, but with much character. Skeptically thumbing cookbooks, I realized that it must be there in Ada Boni's "String Bean Pudding," and even in Elizabeth David—neither making any great claim for it.

The most common indeed was for green beans, but variations using other vegetables occurred when you knew what to look for. Then, asking around Italian cooks and rolling up my sleeves to experiment, with promise of so much variation and ease of preparation, I came to believe *sformati* are quite simply an overlooked classic.

In Italy, I find, they are almost always tipped out bottom up on a serving dish to bring to table. This can be very tricky, so I just cut into wedges and slide onto dinner plates in the kitchen. Sometimes a sauce is poured over as well, but except for the *Sformato* Bianco (page 254) I think this distracts from their purity of flavor.

The Bianco is a separate case. Here, the béchamel is a little thicker, egg whites are whipped, and it turns out more like a soufflé. It can be served any place you might expect a simple pasta, perhaps with a fresh tomato sauce or pesto. In Parma it is either served with a meat sauce or with a vegetable such as asparagus, parboiled, cooked in a little butter, and then strewn with Parmesan. Try it just as is first for your family, and see what you think. I like it plain and simple, like mashed potatoes.

Don't worry about making too much of either a gratin or *sformato*, for either is a treat warmed up for lunch the next day.

Gratin Dauphinois

1 to 2 cloves garlic
1 tablespoon butter
1½ pounds new potatoes
Salt and freshly ground pepper
1½ cups milk
⅔ cup heavy cream
½ teaspoon flour

SERVES 4

GRATIN DAUPHINOIS is really old-fashioned scalloped potatoes with a hint of garlic, but properly prepared with thinly sliced waxy potatoes (not baking potatoes)—oh the difference! There is much controversy in France even about whether or not this dish should include cheese or even eggs. Eggs they can certainly do without and though the most common version served in this country uses Gruyère, with fine potatoes and cream even that is unnecessary—particularly when served as a side dish to meats. Try it this way and I almost guarantee you will think the cheese superfluous.

Preheat oven to 375 degrees. Peel garlic and either very finely mince or put through a garlic press. The amount will depend on how garlicky you like your potatoes. Use some of it to rub the bottom and sides of a gratin dish large enough to hold about a 1-inch layer of potatoes. When it has dried a bit, use butter to grease the dish.

Peel and very thinly slice potatoes. The French use a *mandoline* here, but if you don't own the gadget try using the side slot on your grater. These can make the slices a little sloppy, so cut the last potato carefully with a swivel vegetable peeler to make perfect slices for the top of the gratin. Layer the potatoes, sprinkling with a little salt and pepper as you go. Use more garlic here, if you like. Add the final layer of attractively overlapped slices, then heat milk to bubbling and pour over. You should have enough to come almost to the top of the potatoes, but they should not be covered. Mix cream with flour and pour over.

Bake 45 to 50 minutes, or until all the liquid is absorbed and the top is golden brown. If it starts to brown too quickly, cover loosely with foil. If the dish must wait, remove from the oven before all liquid is absorbed and then return to a hot oven for 10 minutes to finish cooking.

Gratin of Potatoes and Shiitake Mushrooms

½ pound fresh shiitake mushrooms
6 tablespoons butter
Salt and freshly ground pepper
4 medium-size potatoes
1 clove garlic, slightly flattened and peeled
1 cup heavy cream
½ cup milk
1 teaspoon flour

SERVES 4

I THINK MUSHROOMS added to potatoes is a much more delightful combination than a lot of cheese. Oyster or other fresh mushrooms might be used too—or even in combination—but they should not overpower the taste of the potatoes.

Preheat oven to 350 degrees. Cut stems of mushrooms and discard. Cut caps into ¼-inch slices. Melt 2 table-spoons of butter in a frying pan set over medium-high heat. Add the mushrooms and toss 3 to 4 minutes with salt and pepper to taste. Remove from the heat.

Peel potatoes and cut into ¼-inch slices. Rinse and pat dry with paper towels. Rub the garlic over insides of a good-size gratin dish. When dry, use a little of the butter to grease it. Add potatoes and mushrooms, tossing with a little additional salt. Pour cream over and then the milk mixed with flour. Dot with remaining butter.

Bake 40 to 45 minutes, or until the liquid is absorbed and the top of the gratin is starting to brown. Serve hot or warm.

Eggplant Gratin

1 medium-size eggplant
   (about 1½ pounds)
4 tablespoons butter
2 tablespoons flour
1 cup milk, heated
Salt and freshly ground pepper
Freshly grated nutmeg
1 clove garlic, slightly flattened and peeled
½ cup freshly made bread crumbs (see page 325)
½ cup grated Gruyère cheese

SERVES 6

I KNOW THERE ARE some folks who say they don't like eggplant, but I think if they allowed themselves just one taste of this dish they would be changed forever.

Preheat oven to 375 degrees. Top and peel the eggplant and cut into 1-inch chunks. Drop into a large pot of boiling, salted water and cook 5 minutes, or until soft. Drain in a colander and press lightly to extract water.

Melt 2 tablespoons of butter in a small saucepan, then stir in flour over medium heat. Stir several minutes, then pour in milk all at once. Stir until the sauce is smooth and bubbly. Lower heat and cook 4 to 5 minutes more, adding salt, pepper, and nutmeg to taste. Either mash the eggplant or whirl until smooth in a food processor. Stir eggplant into the sauce.

Place garlic in a small frying pan with remaining butter and cook over low heat until the garlic turns golden, then discard garlic. Use some of this to grease a gratin dish or pie pan. Add bread crumbs to the garlic butter and stir until golden. If the crumbs are not lightly separated, or if there seems too much butter, add a few more bread crumbs—this all depends on the consistency of the bread crumbs you use.

Sprinkle cheese over, then sprinkle with bread crumbs. This can be made ahead and cooked later.

To cook, bake 30 minutes or until bubbly. Serve hot or warm.

Red Pepper Gratin

4 large red peppers, roasted
  (see page 331)
1 cup freshly made bread
  crumbs (see page 325)
2 cloves garlic
2 tablespoons parsley
Olive oil
Salt and freshly ground pepper
1 teaspoon wine vinegar

SERVES 4

ONE OF THE BEST WAYS *to use red peppers, this makes a vibrant dish to serve with almost any main dish. It also could be a first course, if you like.*

Peel them of charred skin, and seed roasted peppers and cut into quarters. Preheat oven to 350 degrees. Put bread crumbs, garlic, and parsley in a food processor and process until well minced, then add enough olive oil just to moisten the mixture and salt and pepper to taste. Oil a gratin dish large enough to hold the peppers in a single, crowded layer and place the peppers on it skin side down. Drizzle with a little vinegar, then top evenly with bread crumb mixture. Bake 30 minutes, or until the crumbs are lightly golden. Remove from oven and let cool to room temperature before serving.

Cauliflower and Arugula Gratin

1 medium-size head cauliflower

4 tablespoons butter

4 tablespoons flour

2 cups milk

Salt and freshly ground pepper

2 cups arugula leaves, washed, stemmed, and coarsely chopped

½ cup coarsely grated Gruyère cheese

SERVES 4

EVER SINCE arugula became widely available for salads, I've thought it might make a wonderful addition to some cooked dishes, with its meaty, nutty taste. Here it certainly does. If you can't get arugula or grow it (also called rocket or roquette), you might use watercress leaves.

Cut off outer leaves and core cauliflower. Separate the florets into approximately the same size and drop into a large pan of boiling, salted water. Cook only about 5 minutes, or until a knife pierces them easily. Immediately drain in a colander. If you've let florets cook a little too much, run cold water over them to make sure the cooking stops. Butter a gratin dish large enough to hold them all in a single layer and arrange the cauliflower round tops up.

Melt butter in a saucepan set over medium heat. Stir in flour and cook 2 to 3 minutes, then add milk all at once, stirring until smooth and thick. Lower heat and cook about 5 minutes. Season to taste with salt and pepper. Stir in arugula and half the cheese and cook only 30 seconds or so. Pour evenly over the cauliflower and sprinkle with the rest of the cheese. This can be made ahead, covered with plastic wrap, and kept at room temperature.

To continue, preheat oven to 375 degrees. Bake 20 minutes, or until bubbling and lightly gold on top. Serve hot or warm.

Leek and Zucchini Gratin

4 medium-size zucchini
Salt
4 medium-size leeks
4 tablespoons butter
⅔ cup heavy cream
1 egg
¼ cup finely grated Gruyère
cheese

SERVES 4

THE ZUCCHINI GIVES *a little color to the leeks, and the leeks give flavor to the zucchini, and the cheese melds it all together for a very fine gratin. It is particularly welcome with roast chicken.*

Wash and tip the zucchini and grate coarsely into a bowl. Salt liberally, toss, and place in a colander set over the bowl. This should sit 10 minutes or more to extract the juices. Meanwhile, cut the green tops and root ends off leeks and slice into 1-inch pieces. Wash them well to remove any grit, drain, and pat dry with paper towels. Place in a large frying pan with 2 tablespoons of butter and sauté over medium-low flame for about 5 minutes. They should only just soften a bit. Add water to cover, turn heat up high, and cook, partially covered (with the lid left just a little off to the side), until the water evaporates and the leeks begin to sizzle in the butter. Uncover, toss, and let cook a few more minutes over low heat to let the leeks take a little color. Let sit until cooled a little.

Scrape leeks into a food processor (do not clean the frying pan) and process until pureed. Add cream, egg, and 2 tablespoons of cheese, then process until creamy and smooth. Squeeze zucchini with your hands to extract any liquid, taste for salt, and if too salty, run water over and squeeze again. Place in the frying pan that held the leeks, turn heat to medium-high, and toss for 1 or 2 minutes. Combine with the leek mixture and taste for seasoning.

Melt remaining butter and use some to grease a gratin dish large enough so the mixture is about 2 inches deep. Scoop in the mixture, sprinkle with the rest of the cheese, and drizzle the rest of the melted butter over. This may be made well ahead and covered.

To cook, preheat oven to 375 degrees. Bake 40 minutes, or until the top is bubbling and golden. Serve hot or warm.

Sweet Potato and Turnip Gratin

1 pound sweet potatoes
1 pound turnips
Salt
4 tablespoons butter
2 tablespoons flour
1 cup milk, heated
Freshly ground pepper
Freshly grated nutmeg

SERVES 4 TO 6

THE COMBINATION OF these two distinct flavors is intriguing, and it makes a particularly fine holiday dish to serve with turkey. It also complements roast pork very well.

Choose potatoes and turnips about the same size around. Peel both and cut in ¼-inch slices, then cut the slices in half. The best way is to steam them, but if you don't have a steamer drop into boiling water—first the potatoes, then the turnips. Steaming takes less time, but in either case, cook the slices only until just done—remember they will keep on cooking a little. Salt the slices lightly.

Butter a gratin dish large enough to hold them all in overlapping layers, then place the slices in, alternating potatoes and turnips decoratively. Melt 2 tablespoons butter in a small saucepan set over medium heat. When it sizzles, add flour and stir several minutes. Add milk all at once and stir until the sauce is thick and smooth. Turn heat low and cook several minutes, seasoning to taste with salt, pepper, and a suggestion of nutmeg. Pour over the vegetables so they are coated evenly. Melt remaining butter and drizzle over the top. This can be made ahead and covered with plastic wrap. If you refrigerate it, bring to room temperature before cooking.

To cook, preheat oven to 375 degrees. Bake 40 to 45 minutes, or until bubbly and golden. Serve hot or warm.

Gratin of Fennel

2 large fennel bulbs (about 2
   pounds total)
3 tablespoons melted butter
Salt and freshly ground pepper
1 cup heavy cream
¼ cup grated Parmesan or
   Romano cheese

SERVES 4

THE DELICATE LICORICE FLAVOR of fennel can be easily overpowered in those recipes that call for stock and garlic and whatnot. Just mellowed with cream, as in this recipe, though, I think the vegetable shows to its best. Serve it with roast chicken or pork or lamb.

Preheat oven to 375 degrees. Trim bulbs, slice vertically into ¼-inch slices, and drop into a pot of boiling, salted water. Turn heat down and simmer 5 minutes, then drain in a colander. Use a tablespoon of butter to grease the bottom and sides of a gratin dish large enough to hold slices in 2 to 3 layers. Put slices in evenly, salting and peppering lightly as you go. Pour cream over, drizzle remaining butter over, and then sprinkle with cheese. This can be made ahead and covered, if you must.

Bake 40 to 50 minutes, or until the cream is mostly absorbed and the top is golden. Serve hot or warm.

Gratin of Garbanzos, Tomatoes, and Turmeric Custard

Olive oil
1 cup canned tomatoes, drained and coarsely chopped
1 clove garlic, minced
Salt and freshly ground pepper
1 16-ounce can garbanzos (chick-peas), drained
½ cup feta cheese, crumbled (optional)
1 cup milk
2 eggs
½ teaspoon turmeric
3 tablespoons minced parsley

SERVES 4

THIS CAN BE put together in no time with a couple of cans, and the result is a sumptuous blend of colors and textures. I like it particularly with lamb.

Preheat oven to 350 degrees. Place 2 tablespoons oil in a medium-size frying pan set over medium heat. Add tomatoes and garlic and stir in salt and pepper to taste. Let cook 5 minutes, or until all the liquid has boiled away. Oil a gratin dish large enough to hold 1½ to 2 inches of the mixture. Pour in the garbanzos, then stir in tomatoes and cheese, if desired. Beat milk and eggs with turmeric, adding a little salt to taste. Pour over the mixture. Sprinkle with parsley and drizzle a little more oil over.

Bake 30 minutes, or until the custard is set and the top golden. Serve hot or at room temperature.

Queen Mary
Onion Flan

2 cups sliced onions
2 tablespoons butter
2 eggs, lightly beaten
½ cup heavy cream
Salt and freshly ground pepper
¼ cup freshly grated Parmesan cheese

SERVES 4

THE VESSEL ITSELF, lodged as a "convention center and tourist attraction," nightly lit at Long Beach, California, is really now just a concession stand. But in its seagoing days, the Queen Mary *turned out plain but succulent fare, as in this recipe. You can sprinkle with good paprika as the chef of the* Mary *did, or you might slip in some rosemary or a fine grating of nutmeg on a whim. It is a most useful dish.*

Toss onion slices with butter melted in a large frying pan. As soon as they sizzle, turn heat down to medium-low and toss again. Cook 15 to 20 minutes, turning them occasionally. They will release juices and then start to color lightly. When they turn almost translucent, remove from heat. Combine eggs, cream, and salt and pepper to taste. Grease a small gratin dish, a pie plate, or a quiche dish and put onions in. Pour the egg mixture over. This can sit, covered, if need be.

To cook, heat oven to 350 degrees and bake 35 to 40 minutes, or until richly gilded on top. Serve hot or at room temperature.

Sformato *with* Green Beans

1 pound green beans
6 tablespoons butter
Lemon juice
1½ tablespoons flour
1 cup milk, heated
Salt and freshly ground pepper
Freshly grated nutmeg
2 eggs
2 tablespoons freshly grated Parmesan or Romano cheese
Freshly made bread crumbs (*see page 325*)

SERVES 4

I TAKE THIS as a model for all other sformati *(except the Bianco, which has no vegetables), in that you will need 1 to 1½ cups pureed or minced cooked vegetables. With that in mind you might well wish to make up one or two of your own, but before exploring, try this one first as an ideal to shoot for.*

Preheat oven to 375 degrees. Trim beans and cut into 1-inch lengths. Drop into a pot of boiling, salted water and cook 8 to 10 minutes. They should be softer than you would ordinarily serve. Drain and finely chop them. If you use a processor, don't puree them, just mince. Put 2 tablespoons of butter in a saucepan, add the beans, and cook over low heat 3 to 4 more minutes, adding a few drops of lemon juice.

While the beans cook, put another 2 tablespoons of butter in a saucepan set over medium heat. Stir in flour and cook a few minutes, then add milk. Stir until the sauce is smooth and thickened, then lower heat and cook a few minutes more. Season to taste with salt, pepper, and nutmeg.

Lightly beat eggs in a bowl. Stir in cheese, then stir in beans, then add the white sauce. Melt remaining butter and use some to grease a baking dish. Sprinkle with bread crumbs, then scoop the mixture in. Sprinkle with more bread crumbs, drizzle the rest of the melted butter over, and bake 40 to 45 minutes—the top should be puffed and golden. Let sit at least 5 minutes before cutting into wedges. Or if you wish, serve at room temperature.

Celery Sformato

5 to 6 ribs celery
6 tablespoons butter
Salt
¼ teaspoon celery seed
Lemon juice
1½ tablespoons flour
1 cup milk, heated
Freshly ground pepper
2 eggs
2 tablespoons freshly grated
   Parmesan or Romano cheese
Freshly made bread crumbs
   (see page 325)

SERVES 4 TO 6

"AH, CARDONE!" an Italian cook exclaimed, on asking her the best of sformati. (We call these cardoons, when and if we find them in the market.) They are so rare I worked around with the ubiquitous celery, to make one she might extol as well.

Preheat oven to 375 degrees. Wash and trim celery stalks. For outer stalks, peel with a swivel vegetable peeler to remove tough strands. Cut into 1-inch pieces, place in a food processor, and whirl until finely chopped. Melt 2 tablespoons of butter in a saucepan set over medium heat. When it sizzles, add celery. Toss, turn heat low, cover, and cook about 15 minutes, adding a little salt and celery seed toward the end. Turn off heat and add a few drops lemon juice.

Melt 2 tablespoons of butter in another saucepan and cook over medium heat until sizzling, then stir in flour for another few minutes. Add milk all at once and stir until the sauce is thickened and smooth. Lower heat and cook a few more minutes, then season to taste with salt and pepper. Beat eggs lightly with cheese and stir in along with the celery.

Melt remaining butter and use some to grease bottom and sides of a soufflé dish. Sprinkle with bread crumbs, then scoop the celery mixture in. Sprinkle with more bread crumbs and drizzle the rest of the melted butter over. Bake 40 to 45 minutes, or until the top is puffed and golden. After 5 minutes, cut into wedges and serve. Or you may serve it at room temperature.

Sformato *with* Peas and Lettuce

1 10-ounce package frozen
  peas
6 tablespoons butter
1½ tablespoons flour
1 cup milk, heated
Salt and freshly ground pepper
1 minced shallot or green onion
2 cups lettuce, cut into ribbons
2 eggs
2 tablespoons grated Parmesan cheese
Freshly made bread crumbs
  (see page 325)

SERVES 4

THIS IS A VERY DELICATE sformato, *and one place frozen peas do admirably. I like to serve it especially with roast chicken.*

Preheat oven to 375 degrees. Cook peas according to package directions, then drain them and puree through a food mill.

While they cook, put 2 tablespoons of butter into a saucepan set over medium heat. Stir in flour and cook a few minutes, then add milk all at once. Stir until the sauce is thick and smooth, then lower heat and cook a few minutes more. Season to taste with salt and pepper.

Place another 2 tablespoons of butter in a saucepan and sauté shallot over low heat for several minutes. Add lettuce, stir well, and cook just until it wilts. Remove from heat and stir in the puree of peas. Season to taste with salt and pepper.

Lightly beat eggs in a bowl, stir in cheese, then the pea and lettuce mixture. Melt remaining butter and use some to grease a baking dish. Sprinkle with bread crumbs, then scoop the mixture in. Sprinkle with some more bread crumbs and drizzle the rest of the melted butter over. Bake 40 to 45 minutes, or until puffed and golden. After 5 minutes or so out of the oven, cut into wedges and serve. Or you may serve it at room temperature.

Sformato *with* Corn and Red Peppers

3 ears fresh corn
6 tablespoons butter
1 tablespoon water
Salt and freshly ground pepper
1 red pepper, cut into small pieces
1½ tablespoons flour
1 cup milk, heated
2 eggs
2 tablespoons grated Parmesan cheese
Freshly made bread crumbs (see page 325)

SERVES 4

A SFORMATO *bursting with flavor and color, and one not at all Italian, that goes beautifully with pork or lamb.*

Preheat oven to 375 degrees. Shuck corn and rub to remove the silks. Hold upright over a bowl and cut the kernels down with a sharp knife, then scrape ears with the back of the knife to remove all the juices. Place 1 tablespoon of butter in a saucepan and add corn, water, and salt and pepper to taste. Cook, uncovered, over low heat about 15 minutes, or until done to taste. Check several times as the corn cooks to make sure it has enough moisture—if not, add a bit more water.

Put another tablespoon of butter in a small frying pan and cook pepper over low heat for about 7 minutes, or until tender.

Scrape corn into a bowl, clean out the saucepan, and add another 2 tablespoons of butter. Let it come to a sizzle over medium heat, then stir in flour and cook a few minutes. Add the milk all at once and stir until you have a smooth, thick sauce. Let cook a few more minutes over low heat, then stir into the corn. Lightly beat eggs in a bowl, stir in cheese, and then stir in the corn mixture and the red pepper.

Melt remaining butter and use some to grease a baking dish. Sprinkle with crumbs and drizzle the rest of the melted butter over the top. Bake 40 to 45 minutes, or until puffed and golden. Let settle for at least 5 minutes out of the oven, then cut into wedges and serve. Or you may serve at room temperature.

Sformato *of*
Artichokes

3 medium-size artichokes

½ lemon

4 tablespoons butter

2 tablespoons flour

1 cup milk, heated

Salt and freshly ground pepper

2 eggs, separated, at room temperature

3 tablespoons grated Parmesan cheese

Freshly made bread crumbs (see page 325)

SERVES 4

PERHAPS THE MOST delicate and delicious of all. It pairs well with fish, especially salmon.

Trim the stems off the artichokes and drop them into a pot of boiling, salted water. Squeeze the lemon in and throw in the lemon rind. Cook over medium heat 25 to 30 minutes, or until a pointed knife can pierce the bottoms easily. Drain them and place upside down on a plate to cool. When they can be handled easily, pull away the leaves and discard the first couple of rows. Scrape the flesh off the rest into a bowl as you go. Scoop out the chokes and slice the hearts into the bowl.

Preheat oven to 375 degrees. Melt 2 tablespoons of butter in a saucepan set over medium heat. Stir flour in and cook a few minutes, then add milk all at once. Stir until the sauce thickens and is smooth, then lower heat and cook a few more minutes. Season to taste with salt and pepper.

Scoop the artichoke flesh into a food processor or blender, add a dollop of the white sauce, and process until you have a puree. Stir this back into the sauce and let simmer 1 or 2 minutes. Remove from the heat.

Beat egg yolks lightly with 2 tablespoons of cheese. When the sauce is no longer hot, stir the yolks in. In a clean bowl, whip egg whites just until they hold a peak and fold the sauce mixture gently into them.

Melt remaining butter and use some to grease the bottom and sides of a soufflé dish. Sprinkle with bread crumbs, then scoop the soufflé mixture in. Sprinkle with more bread crumbs and the remaining cheese, then drizzle the rest of the melted butter over.

Bake 40 to 45 minutes, or until the top is puffed up to the rim of the dish and is golden. Remove from the oven and let sit until it settles back into the dish. Cut into wedges and serve, or you may serve at room temperature.

Sformato
Bianco

4 tablespoons butter
2 tablespoons flour
1 cup milk, heated
Salt and freshly ground pepper
Freshly grated nutmeg
2 eggs, separated, at room temperature
3 tablespoons grated Parmesan cheese
Freshly made bread crumbs (see page 325)

SERVES 2 TO 4

AS I MENTIONED in the introduction, this can be served with a light fresh tomato sauce or with pesto. Or it can simply be used as you would mashed potatoes, beside some meat or fish cooked with enough sauce to pour some over the sformato.

Preheat oven to 375 degrees. Melt 2 tablespoons of butter in a saucepan set over medium heat. When it bubbles, stir in flour and cook several minutes. Add milk all at once and stir until you have a smooth, thick sauce. Season to taste with salt, pepper, and a little nutmeg. Remove from the heat.

When the sauce is cooled a bit, stir egg yolks with 2 tablespoons of the cheese and whisk them into the sauce. Melt remaining butter and use some to grease a soufflé dish, then coat with bread crumbs.

Beat egg whites in a clean bowl until they just hold a peak. Fold them lightly into the sauce and scoop the mixture into the dish. Sprinkle with a little more bread crumbs and the remaining cheese, then drizzle the rest of the melted butter over.

Bake 40 to 45 minutes, or until puffed up to the rim of the dish and golden on top. Remove from the oven and let sit until settled back into the dish. Cut into wedges and serve. Or serve at room temperature.

A FINALE OF

SWEETS

Special Fruits and Creams

NO FEAST COULD BE so called without a sweet to follow, I reckon. Night after night, they would be sheer excess, but, ah! for the special occasion— yes. As the expectation of guests, your crowning *coup* should be served up with a certain nonchalance, as if you did this all the time, nothing to it. A startling simple fruit dish might, perhaps, balance the first course, for freshness, after a complex main effort. Or a last, smooth creamy cup might fill in after a meal where you indulged no cream before.

Only great households, and restaurants, can afford a selection of excellent cheeses, to serve with that perfectly ripe garden pear plucked off the espalier that afternoon. Though to me the first apricots russet with the sun, stolen off a backyard tree, and eaten out of pocket, can't be beat. I've never had the like of those perfect apricots since my childhood, even on the shiniest table.

The very idea of a sweet is indulgence, and should produce a shudder of guilt at some lusciousness we might, or might not, choose. Treats would not be treats if we had them every day. But let us slice ripe pineapple, store pears up in red wine, peel forth peaches in plenty, stem green grapes, slice and toast up the nuts, stir custards, and melt chocolate for evermore—or at least for the next guest down the road.

Bananas Kirsch

The other night I had to snatch a sweet, as it were, out of the passing air. Without much thought, I peeled and sliced up a couple of speckled bananas at hand, tossed them with a sprinkle of sugar and a splash of kirsch, then just before serving, a little heavy cream spooned to coat. It was superb.

Next day I decided this was surely a recipe, not something come from the blue. After a few stabs at possible parents, such as Mapie or Pomianne, Elizabeth David was pulled off the shelf to find a treasure from years before, in a recipe she attributes to Edmond Richardin, under the title "Bananes Baronnet." Tables of my past swam back.

This was part of my culinary history, a recipe so simple and somehow right, it could be passed through generations without losing a whiff. Unless, in time, kirschwasser is no longer extracted from cherry pits and the last banana crop is gathered in.

Berries in Caramelized Cream

2 cups raspberries, blueberries, blackberries, or halved strawberries (or preferably a mixture)
¼ cup sugar
3 tablespoons water
1 cup heavy cream
1 teaspoon vanilla

SERVES 4

A SIMPLE, elegant way to treat fresh berries—every bit as good as it sounds.

Pick through berries, stem, if necessary, and refrigerate. Place sugar and water in a large saucepan and cook over medium-high heat, without stirring, until the syrup starts to turn amber in color, then remove from the heat. Heat cream with vanilla, add to the caramel syrup, and stir with a wooden spoon—the mixture will bubble up fiercely. Return the pan to low heat and cook until the cream reduces a bit and is thick enough to coat the back of a spoon. This tends to cook up very high along the edges of the pan (the reason for a large one), so regulate the heat carefully until it steadies. This can be made ahead and reheated until it just starts to bubble.

To continue, divide the berries among bowls and pour the warm cream over. Serve at once.

Cherries and Raspberries with Mascarpone

2 cups pitted sweet cherries
1 cup raspberries
3 tablespoons sugar
1 tablespoon kirsch
6 ounces mascarpone

SERVES 4

MASCARPONE IS ONE of the best cream cheeses in the world—so smooth and almost ivory with the richness of cream. It makes a beautiful foil for almost any fruit, but this combination is one of my favorites.

Combine cherries, raspberries, sugar, and kirsch and let sit for at least 30 minutes. To serve, divide the mascarpone among 4 dessert plates and surround with fruit.

Cherries Vienna

1 pound Bing cherries
¼ cup sugar
2 strips lemon peel
½ cup black currant jelly
¼ cup kirsch
Unsweetened whipped cream
  or vanilla ice cream

SERVES 4

THIS DISH doesn't have all the flamboyant service of Cherries Jubilee, brought flaming to the table, but it has, I think, a much better flavor. Just remember to tell your guests the cherries still have stones!

Wash and stem the cherries. It's not necessary to stone them, but do so if you like. Put sugar and lemon peel in a saucepan with enough water to cover the cherries, bring to a boil, drop in the fruit, and cook 4 to 5 minutes over medium-low heat. They should just soften but not split. Drain them and put in a bowl.

Melt jelly in a small saucepan and pour over the fruit, then add kirsch and toss well. Refrigerate an hour or more before serving with a dollop of whipped cream or over ice cream.

Fresh Figs Benedictine

16 ripe figs
½ cup heavy cream
2 tablespoons Benedictine

SERVES 4

WHEN YOU CAN get ripe white or black figs, try this recipe. There is an enzyme in the figs that causes the lovely Benedictine cream to thicken and coat the figs completely. They are like eating the clouds of Raphael.

Stem and peel figs and place in a bowl. Mix cream with liqueur and pour over the figs. Let stand an hour or more at room temperature before serving.

Fresh Figs with Raspberry Cream

1 pint raspberries
¼ cup sugar
1 cup heavy cream
12 ripe figs

SERVES 4

ONE OF THE MOST beautiful fruit presentations I know, and the taste is incomparable.

Measure out 1 cup of berries and combine with sugar in a food processor. Puree thoroughly and pass through a sieve to remove the seeds. This can be made anytime ahead.

To serve, whip cream until it makes soft billows—it doesn't need to be stiff. Add the raspberry puree and stir until it makes stripes through the cream. Divide among 4 dessert plates. Stem figs and cut each vertically into eighths. Open them up like a flower and settle them into the raspberry cream. Scatter the remaining whole berries over the top and serve.

Green Grapes with Honey and Brandy

1 pound seedless green grapes
¼ cup brandy
¼ cup honey
2 teaspoons lemon juice
1 sprig fresh rosemary
Unsweetened whipped cream

SERVES 4

I TAKE THIS from an old recipe which says at the end: "Serve in a cut crystal bowl," but even without that bowl it makes a wonderful cup—the secret being the rosemary.

Wash grapes and drain well. Cut in half and place in a bowl. Add brandy, honey, lemon juice, and rosemary and stir to coat. Refrigerate several hours, stirring now and again.

To serve, remove the rosemary, divide among 4 bowls, and top with a dollop of whipped cream.

Oranges Marinated in Pomegranate Juice

4 large navel oranges
½ teaspoon orange flower
  water
1 large pomegranate

SERVES 4

ABOUT THE TIME strawberries and raspberries become out-of-season, expensive delicacies, pomegranates come to the rescue with a dessert fit to be served in a Pasha's garden.

Peel oranges, removing as much white pitch as possible. Slice and arrange in overlapping rings on a serving platter. Sprinkle with orange flower water. Cut the pomegranate in half and squeeze over the oranges, letting some of the seeds fall out to decorate the fruit.

Cover with plastic wrap and refrigerate at least an hour before serving to gather flavor.

Peach Meringues

4 large peaches
Currant jelly
Brandy or crème de Cassis
2 egg whites
3 tablespoons sugar
¼ teaspoon almond extract

SERVES 4

FOR TOTAL EFFECT, this is about as little time you can spend in the kitchen to delight your guests. My only advice is to perhaps cut a small slice from the bottom round of the peach, so it sits still as a guest's fork attacks it. The first I served hit a necktie with a good splat.

Drop peaches into simmering water for a minute or so, then slip off their skins. Cut in half and discard the pits. Place on a pie plate and put a dollop of jelly in the center of each, then sprinkle with brandy or Cassis. These can be made to this point and then quickly cooked at the end of the main course.

To continue, preheat oven to 425 degrees. Whip egg whites until light and frothy. Continue to beat and add sugar bit by bit. Beat only until the meringue holds a glossy peak, then stir in almond extract. Top the peaches with the meringue, whirling with a fork to make swirls on top. Bake 10 minutes, or until the meringue is nicely browned. Serve on dessert plates.

Pears in Butter Sauce

4 ripe pears
Lemon juice
1 cup sugar
2 cups water
2 strips lemon peel
2 egg yolks
2 tablespoons sugar
2 tablespoons Poire William
  or kirsch
6 tablespoons unsalted butter

SERVES 4

THIS IS WORTH HAVING Poire William in the cupboard— for it is a kind of essence of the fruit as framboise is of raspberries and kirsch of cherries. It makes a heavenly combination. The sauce can be made with kirsch, however, and still be wonderful, and wonderful too over other stewed fruit (especially apricots).

Stem and peel pears, slice them in half, and scoop out the seeds with a small spoon. Drop into a bowl of water with a squeeze of lemon juice in order to keep them from browning.

Combine sugar, water, and peel in a large saucepan set over medium-high heat. When sugar dissolves, cook about 5 minutes to make a light syrup, then add pears and poach over low heat until tender. The time will depend on the kind and ripeness of the pears. The pears can be done ahead, left to steep in the syrup, and chilled.

To serve, drain pears and place on plates. Bring water under a double boiler to a boil with the top in place, then turn off heat. Whisk in yolks, sugar, and Poire William together until thickened. This takes only a minute—if it looks like the eggs are thickening too quickly, remove the top of the boiler off the heat. You really want to do this over generous warmth rather than real heat. When thick, whisk in butter tablespoon by tablespoon. Pour warm over cold pears.

Peach Melba

2 large peaches (or 4 small)
2 cups sugar
1 cup water
1 teaspoon vanilla
1 10-ounce package frozen
    raspberries in syrup,
    thawed
Vanilla ice cream

SERVES 4

THIS DISH, created for the singer Nellie Melba, seems to have gone out of fashion, though I can't imagine why, as it is simple, colorful, and makes a sensuous combination. The original sauce was heated, slightly thickened, and sweetened, with a dash of currant jelly stirred in. I throw all that to the winds and make what is these days called a "raspberry coulis"—much better, really. Also, if I had fine Georgia peaches I wouldn't even poach them.

Drop peaches into boiling water for a few seconds, then slip off their skins. Halve them and remove the pit. In a small saucepan combine sugar and water and boil 5 minutes to make a syrup. Add vanilla and then the peach halves and cook over medium-low heat about 10 minutes. Remove peaches from the syrup and chill them.

Put berries in a food processor and whirl until pureed, then run through a sieve to remove the seeds. Chill.

To serve, place a peach half in a serving bowl, top with a scoop of ice cream, then ladle the raspberry sauce over.

Pears Baked in Red Wine

4 large pears (preferably Bosc)
⅔ cup sugar
2 cups dry red wine
Crème fraîche (see page 327)

SERVES 4

THESE CLASSIC PEARS are a delight to have on hand: They can be cooked up in any amount, they don't have to be (indeed, shouldn't be) soft ripe, and they only get better as they sit in the refrigerator. In my restaurant we used to put up a large crock of them at a time, and they made an easy, elegant dessert—perfect after a rich repast. This is also one time that crème fraîche is perfect, since neither regular cream nor sour cream is the right texture or taste.

Preheat oven to 300 degrees. Peel pears, leaving the stem on. Place in a casserole of a size to hold them snugly in a single layer, pour sugar and wine over, and add enough water just to cover.

Bake about 6 hours, gently turning them over every hour or so when the liquid starts to cook down. When done, they should be soft and mahogany colored, and the liquid should be reduced by about half. Chill, then serve with some of the juice and a dollop of crème fraîche.

Poached Pears with Chestnut Cream

4 pears
Lemon juice
1¼ cups sugar
2 cups water
2 strips lemon peel
4 egg yolks
1¾ cups milk, scalded
1 tablespoon vanilla
1 14-ounce jar chestnuts in syrup

SERVES 4

CHESTNUTS IN SYRUP are to be found in specialty stores, and are worth keeping on hand for this recipe (and secret nibbles—they are superb over ice cream, for instance). I find this dessert great for holiday repasts, where the food is bounteous and rich, and you really couldn't face a mince pie.

Peel and stem pears. Cut in half, scoop out the seeds, and cut out the stem fiber and blossom end. Drop into a bowl of water with some lemon juice squeezed in. Put ¾ cup sugar in a saucepan along with water and lemon peel and bring to a boil. Add pears, bring again to a boil, lower heat, and simmer until tender. This will depend on the size and ripeness of the fruit. When a small knife enters them easily, turn off heat and let them return, uncovered, to room temperature in the syrup. Drain and refrigerate, covered with plastic wrap.

To make the sauce, beat yolks with ½ cup sugar until pale yellow. While beating, add milk bit by bit. Place in the top of a double boiler and stir over simmering water until the sauce thickens enough to coat the back of a spoon. Remove from the heat, let cool to room temperature, stir in vanilla, cover with plastic wrap, and chill.

To serve, place pear halves on serving plates and put a whole chestnut in each cavity. Chop ½ cup chestnuts and add to the sauce with ¼ cup chestnut syrup. Pour over the pears and serve.

Fresh Pineapple with Rum Sauce

1 ripe pineapple
12 tablespoons unsalted butter
3 egg yolks
4 tablespoons sugar
4 tablespoons dark rum
Salt

SERVES 6

THE ORIGINAL RECIPE FOR THIS DELIGHT, as I remember, advised fellow Parisians to marinate their pineapple in rum and stir the sauce with ground almonds—all, I believe, pure overkill. Tart, cold pineapple served with such a rich warm sauce is about all I could ask for a sweet. At most, I'd go to a small packet of those shaved almonds they sell, apparently so you can stick them onto the sides of a cake like bakeries. These I would toast until straw colored in the oven, and then I'd strew them like flower petals across the plates.

Top pineapple and slice into rounds. Cut the skin off evenly and slice into half-moons. Cover and let sit refrigerated until serving time.

Put butter in the top of a double boiler set over simmering water. After it melts, remove from the heat and whisk in yolks, then sugar, then rum and a whisper of salt. Return to the double boiler. Whisk only a few minutes, until you have a smooth and slightly thickened sauce. Overcooking will only make the sauce grainy (but still delicious). Remove from heat and reserve at room temperature until needed, then reheat the sauce gently for a minute or so before continuing.

To continue, place a row of overlapping half-moons on dessert plates, then pour warm sauce over pineapple and serve immediately.

Baked Plums (or Apricots) with Vanilla Sugar

1 pound freestone plums or
    apricots
¼ cup dry white wine
¼ cup sugar
1 1-inch piece vanilla bean

SERVES 4

FOR THIS YOU WANT *either plums or apricots that are not dead ripe, for they will be too soft. It is a perfect way to serve either, for in the market these days they tend to insipidity since they aren't picked tree ripe. Either will literally sing this way.*

Preheat oven to 350 degrees. Cut plums in half along their natural seam and pit them. (You can use any plum for this except ones you can't pit easily.) Place them cut side up in a glass or ceramic baking pan large enough to hold them in a single, tight layer—an 8-inch square pan is ideal, unless the plums are very small. Pour wine around them. Put sugar in a small bowl and split vanilla bean, scraping out the inner seeds into the sugar. With your fingers, rub the seeds well into the sugar and sprinkle over the plums.

Bake 30 to 40 minutes, depending on the size and ripeness of the plums. When done, they should be soft and the juices should make a bubbling syrup. Remove from the oven and let cool. Serve warm, at room temperature, or chilled, preferably with a dollop of crème fraîche, sour cream, or—best of all—mascarpone.

Spring Rhubarb and Strawberries

⅔ cup sugar
1 cup water
1½ pounds rhubarb
1 cup heavy cream
1 pint strawberries

SERVES 4

WHEN BOTH STRAWBERRIES AND RHUBARB come in early spring it has always been a temptation to use them both at once, though rhubarb can easily be stewed to death and strawberries don't take well to cooking of any kind. This is a delicious answer.

Put sugar and water in a saucepan. Bring to a boil and stir until sugar dissolves. Wash rhubarb and cut off any green parts, then cut into ½-inch pieces and drop into the syrup. When it comes back to a boil over medium heat, cook only 1 or 2 minutes, or until the rhubarb is slightly tender. Remember, it will continue to cook in its own heat, and if cooked too much it becomes mush. Pour in a sieve set over a bowl and let drain well. Chill the rhubarb.

Return syrup to the pan and boil over medium heat until reduced a bit—about 10 minutes. Let cool to room temperature. If you've reduced it too much and it stiffens, simply add a little more water and stir over low heat a minute or so.

A couple of hours before serving, whip the cream until it forms soft peaks, then beat in ⅓ cup rhubarb syrup until the cream is stiff. Fold the rhubarb in and refrigerate. Wash and stem berries and cut vertically into quarters. Place in a bowl and drizzle the rest of the syrup over. Toss and refrigerate.

To serve, divide the rhubarb among 4 dessert plates and then spoon strawberries over.

Rhubarb Fool

4 cups sliced rhubarb
2 tablespoons water
1 cup sugar
1 tablespoon butter
1 cup heavy cream

SERVES 4

FOOLS ARE SAID to be possible from most any fruit puree, but at finest I think they should be made from very acid fruits, just sweetened lightly. The best of these is gooseberry, but they are difficult to come by these days, so I stick with rhubarb. (Good fools also make fine ice creams.)

Put rhubarb and water in a saucepan. Bring to a boil, cover, lower heat, and cook 5 minutes, or until the rhubarb softens and is falling apart. Place a sieve over a bowl and scrape the fruit into it. Let drain, pressing gently with a spoon to release as much liquid as possible.

Place warm rhubarb, sugar, and butter in a food processor and whirl until it is a fine puree. Scrape into a bowl, cover with plastic wrap, and refrigerate at least an hour.

Whip cream stiff and fold the rhubarb into it gently. Spoon into serving bowls and again refrigerate until cold.

Strawberries Romanoff

1½ pints strawberries
3 tablespoons Grand Marnier
   or Cointreau
¼ cup sugar
1 cup heavy cream
½ teaspoon vanilla

SERVES 4

IT HAS BECOME USUAL in this country to whip cream, fold it along with some orange juice or liqueur into softened vanilla ice cream, and then fold in the strawberries. Somehow it all becomes too much cream, not enough berries—definitely de trop. The classic recipe is much simpler, and needs no amplification, for it is one of the most sumptuous ways to serve strawberries ever devised. The only thing better would perhaps be tiny wood strawberries with a spoonful of Devonshire cream served on the lawn at an English "strawberry tea," but that is another time, another country.

If necessary, wash the berries—it's always best not to if you can bring yourself to it. Cut off the crowns and leave whole unless very large, then cut in half. Place in a bowl with the liqueur and 2 tablespoons of the sugar. Toss well, cover with plastic wrap, and refrigerate for an hour or more.

To serve, whip cream until it holds soft peaks. Whip in the rest of the sugar and vanilla. Divide berries among bowls, spoon whipped cream over, and serve.

Cream Tangerines

4 large tangerines or tangelos
1 pint good vanilla ice cream,
   slightly softened
2 tablespoons kirsch

SERVES 4

WHEN I SERVED THESE ONCE, a guest remarked, "Oh, just like the Bohemian Club." He tasted, then added, "But why can't the Bohemian Club make them this good?" Probably the most prestigious rich man's powerbroker club in the world today—they no longer admit any real bohemians—surely could, and should, turn this out at top form, but they probably scrimp on the kirsch.

Use tangerines as large as oranges here and slice off the tops and reserve. With a grapefruit knife, then cut gently all around the flesh, leaving the shells intact, then cut a crisscross through the flesh. With a spoon (or easiest, I think, with your fingers) scoop the flesh out leaving the shells as clean as possible. Do this over a bowl to catch the juices. Also clean out the tops. Place the shells upside down on paper towels.

Scoop ice cream into a bowl and add ¼ cup tangerine juice (saving the rest to drink), then stir in kirsch. Beat quickly together (the best instrument for this is the good old potato masher). Spoon mixture into the tangerine shells, replace the lids, place on a pie plate, and freeze.

Before serving, allow to stand at room temperature for 5 minutes or so. They look nice with a small green leaf sticking out from under each lid.

Summer Macédoine of Fruits

1 ripe pineapple
3 tablespoons sugar
¼ cup framboise or kirsch
1 cup raspberries
¼ cup pistachio nuts, minced

SERVES 6

IN ONE OF HIS COOKBOOKS, the late James Beard presented a kind of "Carmen Miranda" dessert, consisting of a whole pineapple elaborately knifed out and then restuffed with pineapple flesh and raspberries, a sniff of aromatic brandy, and a scoop of sugar. This miracle, he adds, should be stood on a serving platter surrounded with raspberries dusted with confectioners' sugar and a few finely chopped pistachios. I've never aspired to all that, but even my abbreviated version rates as a fruit cup to make most others seem pale.

Top and peel the pineapple, cutting out any brown tucks. Slice it and cut into spoon-size bits, cutting out the tough core. Place in a bowl and toss with sugar and the framboise or kirsch. Cover and chill for a couple of hours, tossing when you think about it.

Thirty minutes before serving, toss with the raspberries. To serve, toss again well and spoon into dessert cups. Sprinkle with nuts just before table.

Late-Season Macédoine of Fruits

1 10-ounce frozen package
  raspberries in syrup,
  thawed
2 tablespoons orange juice
1 tablespoon lemon juice
¼ teaspoon grated orange
  rind
1 pint strawberries
1 tablespoon Grand Marnier
  or Cointreau
1 tablespoon sugar
1 cup sliced, seedless green
  grapes

SERVES 4

SPOONING THIS UP you forget these must be late-season strawberries and raspberries long gone. You forget the whipped cream . . . you remember the grapes.

Whirl raspberries in a food processor, then put through a sieve to remove the seeds. Add orange juice and lemon juice to the puree, then add the orange rind. Stir well, cover, and refrigerate.

Stem the strawberries, and unless they *must* be washed, simply cut in half into a bowl. Toss with Grand Marnier and sugar and let sit, covered, in the refrigerator. Toss whenever you open the refrigerator door.

To serve, mix the strawberries with grapes and place in serving bowls. Pour raspberry syrup over them and serve.

Frozen Honey Mousse with Kiwi

6 egg yolks
⅓ cup dark honey (buckwheat or other)
1 cup heavy cream
2 kiwi fruits, peeled and sliced

SERVES 6

THIS RESULTS IN A SMOOTH, rich-tasting cream with a flavor so subtle as to be almost indefinable. Look for honeys with a strong burst of flavor for best results. And though I tasted it first with a crown of raspberries, I want to put it forth as the absolute best way to present the new bounty of kiwi, so often used only for its light jade color. Here, I think, it becomes a flavor at last.

Put yolks and honey in an electric mixer and beat 6 to 8 minutes, or until the mixture is the texture of meringue. Whip cream in another bowl until it holds soft peaks, then fold it into the yolk-honey mixture.

Spoon into 1-cup bowls, cover with plastic wrap, and freeze about 3 hours before serving. These will last several days in the freezer, if necessary.

To serve, uncover and top with kiwi fruit.

Chocolate Pots de Crème

1 cup light cream
½ pound sweet chocolate
3 egg yolks

SERVES 4

USE IMPORTED CHOCOLATE for this—Lindt or Tobler, say—and it is one of the best simple chocolate desserts ever invented. The French usually serve it just as is, but you could pass a pitcher of more cream to pour on top, or surround it with a few bright strawberries.

In a saucepan or double boiler, scald the cream. Break up chocolate in pieces and add it, stirring until melted completely. Beat egg yolks until thick and pale, then pour the chocolate mixture in slowly, stirring until blended. Pour through a fine sieve into 4 *pots de crème* containers or into ¼-cup ramekins. Chill, covered, in the refrigerator.

Improved Mont Blanc

1 ounce unsweetened or semi-
    sweet chocolate
1 8¾-ounce can chestnut
    spread
1 tablespoon brandy
2 egg whites
Whipped cream

SERVES 4

YOUNG, AND MY FIRST TIME IN FRANCE, I doted on this sweet served everywhere just as it came from the can, topped with plain whipped cream. It is shipped all over the world in tins, a paste by-product of the little pieces left from whole Marrons Glacés, *absolutely delicious, I thought then. Nowadays I still keep it on the shelf as one of the easiest desserts you can turn out on quick notice. With a little chocolate to cut the sweetness, and whipped egg whites to lighten it, this can almost be pulled out of your secret gourmet hat as if to say, "Oh, we always eat like this."*

Melt chocolate in a double boiler set over simmering water—this can be done in its paper wrapping. Scrape the chestnut spread into a bowl and stir in brandy and chocolate. Beat egg whites until stiff but not dry and fold into the mixture. Divide into 4 ½-cup ramekins or dessert cups, cover with plastic wrap, and chill 30 minutes or more.

Serve topped with a dollop of unsweetened whipped cream.

Custards Orangerie

1 orange
1 cup heavy cream
1 cup milk
1 cup sugar
2 tablespoons water
3 eggs
2 egg yolks
2 tablespoons Grand Marnier

SERVES 6

THIS LOVELY SWEET makes one orange do the work of hundreds.

Preheat oven to 325 degrees. Peel about 6 long strips from the orange with a swivel vegetable peeler. Heat them with cream and milk in a saucepan set over low heat. When bubbles appear around the edges, turn off heat and let stand.

Put ½ cup sugar with water in a saucepan and bring to a boil over high heat. Don't stir, but just whirl the pan around to make sure it bubbles evenly. Watch it closely. When it turns light amber, divide it evenly among 6 custard cups. While warm, take the cups up and twirl them around in your hands so the coating slopes up the sides.

Beat eggs and egg yolks with remaining sugar until light yellow. Add the cream mixture through a sieve as you whip. Stir in Grand Marnier and pour through a sieve into the cups.

Place the cups in a large baking pan and add hot water to the depth of half an inch. Bake 45 minutes, or until a knife inserted in the center comes out almost clean. Take the cups out of the water bath and let cool to room temperature. Cover with plastic wrap and refrigerate.

To serve, run a knife around the custards, then with a sharp tap unmold each onto a plate. The syrup at the bottom of the cup will make a sauce.

Cold Brandy Soufflé with Candied Ginger

1 tablespoon unflavored gelatin
1/3 cup brandy
4 eggs, separated
1 teaspoon vanilla
1/2 cup sugar
1/2 cup heavy cream
1/4 cup crystallized ginger, finely minced

SERVES 6

THIS TRIUMPH SHOULD be made with very fine cognac, and if you can't find crystallized or candied ginger, you could use ginger preserved in syrup.

Dissolve gelatin in brandy about 5 minutes, then place in the top of a double boiler with simmering water underneath, stirring until the gelatin dissolves. Beat egg yolks until thick, adding the hot brandy in a thin stream while mixing. Stir in vanilla and place the mixture in the refrigerator for about 10 minutes.

Beat egg whites until they form soft peaks. Gradually add sugar, 1 tablespoon at a time, beating until the mixture is very thick and shiny. Whisk one-third of this into the egg yolk mixture, then fold the rest in carefully. Whip the cream until it holds a peak and carefully fold this in with the ginger. Divide among 6 dessert cups, cover with plastic wrap, and chill an hour or more before serving.

"Food of the Gods"

1 cup almond macaroon
    crumbs
2 tablespoons rum, plus extra
    for dipping strawberries
1 egg yolk
2 tablespoons sugar
1 cup heavy cream
1 pint strawberries
Powdered sugar

SERVES 6

"FOOD OF THE GODS" is how this is usually translated from Wiener Gotterspeise, *and even if my German comes in toto from Lotte Leyna singing Kurt Weill, and the songs of Mahler, I suspect this means how the Viennese wish, God-like, to dine away their days. I always thought the gods were somehow beyond appetite, and it was only we humans who sat at table, but at any rate this is the heaven of Vienna—no doubt about it.*

Place crumbs in a bowl. Beat 2 tablespoons rum with egg yolk and sugar and stir into the crumbs. Whip cream stiff and fold into the macaroon mixture. Rinse a 3-cup mold with cold water and scoop the macaroon mixture into it, leveling off the top. Cover with foil and freeze 2 hours.

To serve, unmold onto a serving plate (if necessary, dip the mold into a bowl of hot water momentarily to loosen). Dip strawberries in rum, roll in powdered sugar, and place around the dessert.

If you like, the mold may be made a day or so ahead, though it should be taken out of the freezer and left to sit in the refrigerator an hour or so before presentation.

Cloud Bombe

2 eggs, separated, at room
  temperature
Pinch of cream of tartar
½ cup sugar, plus 2 tablespoons
½ teaspoon vanilla
1 cup heavy cream
2 tablespoons kirsch
⅔ cup milk, heated
Raspberries or halved strawberries (optional)

SERVES 6

WE GET SO MANY *fine ice creams these days in the market I've not included any here, for it's difficult to find any recipe that couldn't be store-bought. But you'd never be able to purchase this fine fantasy in a million years.*

Preheat oven to 250 degrees. Beat egg whites with cream of tartar until they hold a peak, then beat in ½ cup sugar, bit by bit, until you have a glossy meringue. Stir in vanilla. Line a baking sheet with baking parchment or brown paper and scoop the meringue into 3 piles. Smooth the piles until they are ½-inch thick—these should be separate and not flow into each other. Bake 1 hour and 15 minutes, then leave to cool with the oven door ajar. These can be made the day before, but if it is rainy you will want to keep them dry in a closed container.

Beat cream until it just holds soft peaks (it should not be stiff), then fold in 1 tablespoon of kirsch. Break the meringues up in about 1-inch pieces and fold them into the cream. Turn the mixture into a 1-quart mold or round dish and freeze. Beat egg yolks with 2 tablespoons of sugar until they are light colored, then beat in hot milk. Cook in the top of a double boiler over barely simmering water, stirring until the mixture thickens enough to coat the back of a spoon. Remove from heat and chill, covered, in the refrigerator. Stir in remaining kirsch and cover again.

To serve, unmold the bombe on a serving platter, using a handtowel which you have soaked in hot water then squeezed dry. Spoon the kirsch cream over the top. If you use them, sprinkle berries around the bombe and bring forth to table.

Easy Tarts and Tempting Cakes

ONE OF THE FIRST things I learned to cook was my mother's pie crust, which we—on my asking—went over and over together to get right. Her finest secret was that you have "to keep your hand in," and you do. This kind of simplicity seems to put some even very good cooks in a dither. So thinking on this, and about the glamour of restaurant and bakery tarts, I started to experiment. And if I can't recommend frozen pie shells, I celebrate two pastries probably better than you can imitate at home. These are frozen puff pastry and phyllo sheets. Once you get the simple hang of using either, you can create your own tarts, for I've hardly put more than the tip of an iceberg here. And for the very timid, I throw in a couple of recipes where you have only to press crumbs in, plus a few which achieve no crust at all, still absolutely delicious.

Remember those three-layer cakes, gooey fillings between, and frosting slathered thick over all? I give these up for good. No one wants them anyway after the first day, and they're dried out, so you almost have to have a party of teenage locusts in the house. My answer is that we should have smaller but choicer cakes. Cakes as attractive as tarts, and moist and rich enough to last through some private snacks, or even another dinner.

To Use Puff Pastry for a Tart

Thaw pastry according to package directions. Roll out on a floured board so you have a 10-inch square, then place the bottom of a 9-inch tart pan over it, and cut a circle an inch larger than the pan. Fit the pastry into the tart pan and refrigerate for 10 to 15 minutes (puff pastry should always be as cold as possible).

To make a precooked shell, prick the bottom well with a fork before refrigerating. Heat oven to 400 degrees. Place a square of foil over the pastry and gently press around the edges. Cut the points off with scissors and scatter a layer of dry beans over. Bake 15 minutes, then carefully remove the foil filled with beans. The pastry will have puffed up and will slightly stick to the foil. Again poke down with a fork and return to the oven 5 to 7 minutes, or until the pastry is crisp and light gold on the bottom. Remove from the oven and cool to room temperature. A precooked shell can be used in any tart recipe that calls for a filling of crème pâtisserie, a decorative topping of fruit, and a glaze.

Orange Cream Tart

2 large oranges
2 cups milk
4 egg yolks
⅔ cup sugar
2½ tablespoons flour
1 precooked puff pastry shell
  (see page 288)

SERVES 6

IN READING NED ROREM'S DIARIES several years ago, I was struck with his description of an orange cream tart he was disappointed not to find anymore in Paris, and I longed for it as he did in memory. I took a tip from my old friend Mapie, the Countess de Toulouse-Lautrec, as to the filling, but it took a while to experiment getting a cooked shell from puff pastry. It has become since one of my very favorites.

Peel oranges with a swivel vegetable peeler and place peel with milk in a small saucepan. Heat over low heat just until the milk starts to bubble around the edge, then remove and let cool a little. Whisk eggs, sugar, and flour in the top of a double boiler. Place over simmering water, strain the milk in, discarding the peel, and stir until it bubbles. Let cool to room temperature, then fit plastic wrap over and refrigerate.

With a small, sharp knife, remove all the white pith from oranges. Slice ¼ inch thick, remove seeds, and cut each slice in half. Spread pastry with orange cream and decorate the top with a swirl of orange slices.

Fernand Point's Tarte de Grand-mère

1 sheet frozen puff pastry
1 pound tart, tasty apples
½ cup sugar

SERVES 6

M. POINT'S GRANDMOTHER apparently turned out something similar to the famous Tarte Tatin, though that has regular pastry and is slathered in butter. Since all the flavoring here comes from the apples, you'll want ones that have perfume and flavor.

Thaw pastry according to package directions. Heat oven to 350 degrees. Unfold pastry, cut into a 9-inch circle, and discard the trimmings. Pierce the pastry all over with a fork. Refrigerate.

Peel and core apples and cut into ½-inch slices. Sprinkle half the sugar in the bottom of a 9-inch cake pan, then place apples decoratively over in a single layer. Chop the unused slices coarsely and sprinkle them over, then pour remaining sugar on top. Cover the apples with pastry. Bake 35 to 40 minutes, or until puffed up and crisply browned. Remove from the oven.

To serve, invert tart onto a baking dish and place under a preheated broiler. When the tops of the apples are caramelized, remove and cut into slices.

Rum Nut Tart

½ cup apricot jam
1 heaping cup pecans, plus
   extra for decoration
½ cup sugar
4 tablespoons butter
1 tablespoon rum, plus extra
   for glaze
½ teaspoon vanilla
2 eggs, separated
1 prepared puff pastry shell,
   uncooked (see page 288)
½ cup powdered sugar

SERVES 8

THIS EXTRAVAGANZA WILL DO YOU PROUD, for it is better, frankly, than most restaurant tarts.

Preheat oven to 375 degrees. Place jam in a saucepan and melt over low heat. Put pecans in a food processor and whirl until fine. Add sugar, butter, rum, vanilla, and egg yolks. Process until you have a paste. Whip egg whites stiff, but not dry, and fold them into the nut mixture.

Remove pastry shell from the refrigerator and brush a thin coat of apricot jam over the bottom. Pour in the nut mixture. Bake 30 to 35 minutes, or until puffed up and browned. Let cool 5 minutes, then brush with remaining jam. Combine powdered sugar with just enough rum to make a glaze and frost the tart with it. When it sets a bit, decorate with a ring of whole pecans.

Pear Almond Tart

3 large ripe pears
½ lemon
½ cup blanched almonds
1 tablespoon flour
⅓ cup plus 2 tablespoons sugar
5 tablespoons butter, at room temperature
1 egg
1 egg yolk
¼ teaspoon almond extract
2 tablespoons kirsch
1 prepared puff pastry shell, uncooked (see page 288)

SERVES 6

AN ADMIRABLE, handsome tart with lots of nuances of flavor and texture.

Peel pears, cut into quarters, and cut out the core. Drop into a bowl of water into which you have squeezed the lemon. Put almonds and flour in a food processor and whirl until chopped fine. Remove. Put ⅓ cup of sugar in the food processor with butter and process until well mixed, then add egg and yolk and mix well. Finally blend in the almonds, almond extract, and kirsch.

Place in the chilled pastry shell. Drain pears well and pat dry with paper towels. Place them in a wheel, rounded side up, with the points toward the center of the tart. Sprinkle with remaining sugar. Bake 30 to 35 minutes, or until golden. This pastry is best served warm.

Fruit Crumble Tart

1 prepared puff pastry shell,
   uncooked (see page 288)
3 to 4 apples, peaches, or
   pears
4 tablespoons butter
½ cup flour
½ cup walnuts, hazelnuts, or
   almonds
¾ cup sugar
¼ teaspoon cinnamon
Pinch of salt

SERVES 6

THE NAME SOUNDS RATHER HUMBLE, but it doesn't taste so. Also it is a most useful tart, capable of many variations of fruit and nut. Experiment and find your own favorite.

Preheat oven to 375 degrees. Peel fruit, core, and slice. Put the rest of the ingredients in a food processor and whirl until the nuts are well chopped. Layer fruit about two-thirds up the pastry and pour the crumble over. Bake 35 minutes, or until lightly browned on top. This is best served warm.

Alsatian Cherry Tart

1 prepared puff pastry shell,
    uncooked (see page 288)
1 pound Bing cherries
¾ cup sugar
Pinch of salt
2 tablespoons melted butter
2 eggs
3 tablespoons kirsch

SERVES 6

PITTING CHERRIES IS NO ONE'S IDEA OF FUN, though there are cherry pitters sold, or a few items around the house which will do. I first tried a partially unbent paper clip, which worked but was hard on the fingers after a minute or two. Then I got out an old, unused drawing pen—the kind you buy a nib for and fit into a wooden holder—which is perfect for the job. So I keep it in the drawer as a cherry pitter.

Preheat oven to 350 degrees. The pastry for this tart should be cut nearer to 1¼ inches larger than the pan rather than 1 inch. Stem cherries and stone them where the stems have been removed. Mix the rest of the ingredients together well. Place a single layer of cherries on the bottom of the crust and top with the mixture. Bake 30 to 35 minutes, or until puffed and golden. Let sit 30 minutes before serving.

Strawberry and Mascarpone Puff Pastry Tart

1 sheet frozen puff pastry
Sugar
1 pint strawberries
9 ounces mascarpone
¾ teaspoon vanilla
3 tablespoons light rum

SERVES 6

A KIND OF GLORIOUS STRAWBERRY SHORTCAKE, really, this makes a showstopper dessert. Its only drawback is that it grows soggy after sitting too long, but don't worry, for even four guests will probably scarf up the whole thing it's so good.

Thaw pastry in the refrigerator overnight. Preheat oven to 400 degrees. Unfold pastry carefully and, using the bottom of a 9-inch tart pan, cut a circle. Discard the trimmings. Prick all over with a fork and refrigerate it while the oven heats. Place pastry on a baking sheet and cook 20 minutes, or until puffed and golden brown. Remove from the oven and sprinkle while hot with a little sugar. Cool to room temperature and slice in half horizontally with a serrated knife.

Wash and trim berries and slice in half vertically. Sprinkle with ¼ cup sugar and toss. Refrigerate for an hour or so to gather juices. Beat cheese until light, then add 3 tablespoons sugar, vanilla, and rum. Cover with plastic wrap and reserve at room temperature.

Assemble at the last moment by spreading the bottom layer with cheese, then topping with berries and juice—let a few of the berries tumble around the pastry. Place the top lid on and serve.

My Warm Cherry Tarts

1 sheet frozen puff pastry
¾ cup sugar
½ cup walnuts or pecans
1 1-pound can sour pie
  cherries
1 tablespoon lemon juice
1 tablespoon cornstarch
2 tablespoons brandy
1 tablespoon kirsch
1 cup heavy cream

SERVES 4

THIS MAY SOUND a lot of bother, but it is really quite simple, and can be assembled for the table in minutes. It can be made with other fruit, as well, but since the pastry is sweet, it is best done with slightly tart fruits such as rhubarb or plums or raspberries, rather than something like apples.

Thaw pastry according to package directions. Put ½ cup of sugar and nuts in a food processor and whirl until finely ground. Press half the mixture into the pastry, rolling it out by about half an inch, then turn pastry over and press the rest into the other side, rolling out by about another half an inch. Cut 4 5-inch rounds out of the pastry, using something like the top of a coffee can for a guide. (The scraps can be baked and eaten like cookies, or if you are serving 6 you can cut the pastry into rectangles—though you will need more cherry sauce.)

Place rounds between sheets of wax paper and refrigerate 10 minutes or more. Preheat oven to 400 degrees and bake on a pastry sheet 15 minutes, or until puffed crisp and golden. Remove and cool to room temperature. These can be made ahead and stored in an airtight container overnight.

For the cherry sauce, drain the juice from the cherries into a saucepan. Bring it to a boil with remaining sugar and add lemon juice. Stir together cornstarch and brandy and add it, cooking over medium heat until the mixture thickens and is clear. (Some cherries have more juice than others, and you may need to stir in more cornstarch mixed in a little water to achieve a sauce about the consistency of heavy cream.) Add cherries and simmer over low heat several minutes. Cool to room temperature and stir in kirsch. This, also, may be made hours ahead, covered, and refrigerated.

To continue, bring cherries almost to a boil. Whip cream until it has thickened slightly—it doesn't need to hold a peak. Place pastry crusts on a dessert plate, top with warm cherries, and then side with cream. Serve with a dessert spoon and fork.

To Use Phyllo for a Tart

Phyllo is the extraordinarily thin sheets of pastry Greek cooks use to make baklava and many other sweet or savory pastries. It also is similar to the sheets used for strudel. You will need 8 to 10 sheets of phyllo for a tart and about 4 tablespoons melted butter. If your phyllo is frozen, thaw according to package directions. Since you won't be using most of the sheets in the package, immediately seal them very well before refreezing—air getting to the phyllo turns it to unusable flakes.

Lay out the sheets in a stack. Using the bottom of an 8- or 9-inch tart pan as a measure, cut the sheets about an inch larger around than the pan. Discard the trimmings. Cover the phyllo with a towel so it doesn't dry out. Using a pastry brush (or just a small paint brush), coat the bottom and sides of the tart pan with butter. Brush each sheet with butter lightly but thoroughly. As you paint them, fit 1 sheet at a time into your tart pan, smoothing and tucking the edges in as you go. The ends of the rounds ought to stick up around the sides in a pretty ruffle.

Light Apple Tart

¼ cup sugar

1 1-inch piece vanilla bean (or
  ¼ teaspoon cinnamon)

2 medium-size apples (Golden
  Delicious, if nothing more
  interesting)

1 prepared phyllo crust (see
  page 297)

2 tablespoons unsalted butter,
  melted

SERVES 4 TO 6

SO SIMPLE TO PREPARE, this needs no excuse at all to serve at table. In fact, for me it is a kind of "signature" dish— one that turned out the first time just right, with no more guide than that it would be a fine idea. It is impressive, delectable, and light enough to follow any rich spread for company.

Preheat oven to 350 degrees. Put sugar in a small bowl. Cut the vanilla bean lengthwise and scrape out the seeds with the point of a knife, then mix into the sugar with your hands. If using cinnamon, you only need to stir once or twice. Peel and core apples and slice them ¼ inch thick. Toss these into the sugar.

Lay apples on the pastry in overlapping, concentric rings, with the curved edges outward. Drizzle butter over and bake 30 minutes, or until the apples are done and the top and sides are lightly browned. Serve hot or at room temperature.

Walnut and Lemon Tart

1 cup walnuts
1 prepared phyllo crust (see page 297)
2 tablespoons unsalted butter, melted
1 cup sugar
2 eggs
Grated rind of a lemon
Juice of ½ lemon

SERVES 6

THIS IS THE NEXT TART, after Light Apple (page 298), I tried with first success. It is my final answer to the "too, too much-ness" of southern pecan pie, absurdly easy to prepare and turn out for the amount of congratulation.

Preheat oven to 350 degrees. Sprinkle nuts over the crust. Mix butter with sugar, eggs, lemon rind, and lemon juice. Pour over the nuts and bake 30 minutes, or until puffed and golden.

Serve warm or at room temperature.

Plum and Almond Tart

¾ cup blanched almonds
⅓ cup sugar
1 egg
2 tablespoons unsalted butter,
   melted
1 teaspoon vanilla
¼ teaspoon almond extract
1 teaspoon grated lemon rind
1 prepared phyllo crust (see
   page 297)
18 to 20 plums
½ cup currant jelly
1 tablespoon brandy

SERVES 6

THIS LOOKS AS ELEGANT as any restaurant tart, and tastes a good deal better than many. Since they are always tasty I prefer fresh purple Italian prunes in season, but you can use any not-too-large plum the pits come out of without tearing the fruit up, and if it tastes good on its own.

Preheat oven to 350 degrees. Grind almonds with sugar in a food processor. They should be quite fine, but don't process too much or you'll have a paste on your hands. Add egg, butter, vanilla, almond extract, and lemon rind and process just until mixed. Spread this on the bottom of the crust.

Slice plums in half and remove the pits. Lay in concentric circles, cut side down, over the almond mixture. Bake an hour, or until the almond mixture has puffed up around the plums and has turned lightly golden. Remove and let tart cool a little. Put jelly and brandy in a small pan and stir until it melts. Brush this over the top of the tart. Serve warm or at room temperature.

Rhubarb Tart

4 to 5 stalks rhubarb
1 prepared phyllo crust (*see
page 297*)
1½ cups sugar
3 tablespoons flour
¼ teaspoon freshly grated
nutmeg
2 eggs
2 tablespoons unsalted butter,
melted
Powdered sugar

SERVES 6

*THIS IS AN ADAPTATION of my favorite rhubarb pie, and
tastes just as good, but is definitely prettier—as any good tart
should be.*

Preheat oven to 350 degrees. Wash and trim rhubarb
and cut into ½-inch pieces—it's best to pick out rhubarb
all the same size here. Place on the pastry in concentric
circles. Put sugar, flour, nutmeg, eggs, and butter in a
bowl and mix until creamy. Pour over the fruit and bake
40 to 45 minutes, or until lightly browned on top. Remove from the oven and let rest 10 minutes. Sprinkle
lightly with powdered sugar pushed through a sieve.
   Serve warm or at room temperature.

Ricotta Tart

½ pound fresh whole milk
  ricotta
¼ cup sugar
3 eggs
1 teaspoon lemon juice
½ teaspoon grated lemon rind
2 to 3 tablespoons anisette
Pinch of salt
1 prepared phyllo crust (see
  page 297)
Fresh fruit or berries

SERVES 6 TO 8

A LOVELY RECIPE from a friend of a friend. Avoid the grainy packaged stuff usually found in the market and make with creamy, fresh ricotta. Not too sweet, tasting delicately of anise, it is a delicious treat to serve.

Preheat oven to 350 degrees. Put cheese and sugar in the bowl of a mixer and beat it on medium speed at least 10 minutes, or until the sugar is dissolved. Add 1 egg at a time, mixing to incorporate after each. Beat in lemon juice and lemon rind, then add anisette and salt. Fill phyllo crust and bake 30 to 35 minutes, or until puffed up and golden. Let sit at least 15 minutes before serving, or serve at room temperature. Accompany with fruit or berries—sliced peaches or raspberries being the best.

Grape Tart with Cookie Crust

1 cup flour
1 cup sugar
⅓ cup pecans (or other nuts)
1 teaspoon baking powder
6 tablespoons unsalted butter
2 tablespoons heavy cream
½ pound seedless green
  grapes (or any berry)
⅔ cup white wine
2 tablespoons lemon juice
¼ teaspoon grated lemon rind
1 tablespoon cornstarch

SERVES 6

THIS IS A MOST USEFUL TART I developed years ago to take advantage of a crop of wild blackberries, then later with grapes when berries are out of season. It is particularly lovely to use half green and half purple grapes, or with grapes and raspberries.

Preheat oven to 325 degrees. Put flour, ½ cup of sugar, nuts, and baking powder in a food processor. Whirl with an on/off pulse until the nuts are finely ground. Cut butter into pieces and add, pulsing again until the butter is incorporated, then pulse with cream until you have a moist dough. Put all but ½ cup of the mixture in a 9-inch tart pan, or if you happen to have a 10-inch pan it can all be used. (The extra can be discarded or rolled out into cookies and baked at the same time as the crust.) First press a ¼-inch thickness of the mixture into the fluted edges, then press down smoothly over the bottom. Bake 20 minutes, or until golden and crusty. Remove and let cool to room temperature. The crust can be made well ahead and kept at room temperature.

Slice grapes in half and place cut side down in concentric circles over the crust—you should have enough to completely cover it. Put wine, lemon juice, remaining sugar, lemon rind, and cornstarch in a small saucepan and cook over medium-high heat, stirring until thick and clear. This takes only 3 to 4 minutes. Let cool to room temperature, then glaze the top of the tart with it. (You won't need all of it for a 9-inch tart.)

Lemon-Cheesecake Tart

1½ cups vanilla wafer crumbs
4 tablespoons melted butter
¾ cup sugar
8 ounces cream cheese, at
    room temperature
2 tablespoons flour
2 eggs, separated
¼ cup lemon juice
1 teaspoon grated lemon rind

SERVES 6 TO 8

EVERYONE ADMIRES CHEESECAKE, but one can serve an army, or else it lasts a long time tempting you in the refrigerator. This is the perfect solution.

Preheat oven to 325 degrees. Make crumbs in a food processor, measure, and discard any extra. Return crumbs to the food processor. Add butter and ¼ cup of sugar and process until well mixed. Butter a 9-inch tart pan (a 10-inch tart pan will also work with this recipe). Put 1 cup of the mixture into the tart pan and press a ¼-inch thickness of it into the fluted edges, then press down smoothly over the bottom. Use more crumbs if needed, but don't make the crust overly thick, and you'll also want to reserve ¼ cup to top the tart later.

Place cheese in a mixing bowl and beat smooth. Gradually add the remaining sugar and beat at medium speed 5 minutes. Add flour, egg yolks, lemon juice, and lemon rind and beat smooth. Beat egg whites until they hold soft peaks, then fold them into the cheese mixture. Pour this into the tart shell and smooth the top.

Bake 40 to 45 minutes, or until set and the top is lightly golden. Remove to a rack, sprinkle with the reserved crumbs, and let cool to room temperature. Cover the tart with foil or plastic wrap and refrigerate several hours before slicing.

Banana Cream Tart

1½ cups graham cracker
   crumbs
¾ cup sugar
6 tablespoons butter, melted
4 egg yolks
Pinch of salt
2½ tablespoons flour
2 cups milk, heated
1 teaspoon vanilla
3 medium-size bananas

SERVES 6

THIS TASTES LIKE old-fashioned banana cream pie, but it looks prettier.

Preheat oven to 350 degrees. Combine crumbs, ¼ cup of sugar, and butter. Lightly butter a 9-inch tart pan, or you can use a 10-inch tart pan if you have one. Reserve ¼ cup of the crumbs and press the rest first around the edges to a ¼-inch thickness, then smoothly over the bottom. If the crust is more than ¼ inch thick, discard the rest. Place in the oven and bake 10 minutes, then remove and cool to room temperature.

Beat egg yolks, remaining sugar, salt, and flour in a small bowl. Whisk in some of the milk. When the mixture is smooth, add the rest of the milk and stir well. Place in the top of a double boiler and stir over simmering water until the cream thickens. Don't let it come to a boil. Cool to room temperature and stir in vanilla.

Peel bananas and cut into slices a little less than ¼ inch thick. Pour half the custard into the crust and smooth it. Cover with a layer of banana slices evenly spaced. Smooth over the rest of the custard and cover with another layer of bananas. Sprinkle the reserved crumbs over and chill at least an hour before serving.

Apricot or Plum Flan

1½ pounds apricots or plums
⅓ plus ¼ cup sugar
¼ cup dry Madeira
1 tablespoon lemon juice
2 eggs
1 tablespoons flour
⅔ cup light cream
Freshly grated nutmeg
1 teaspoon vanilla
Powdered sugar

SERVES 4 TO 6

A DELICIOUS WAY TO USE either fruit when they are at the market, but not quite fine enough to eat out of hand—all too usual these days.

Preheat oven to 375 degrees. Slice apricots or plums in half and remove the seeds. Some plums are remarkably tenacious with their pits, but with patience you can pry them out with a small, sharp knife, though it's best just to get freestones. Place cut side down in a baking dish large enough to hold them in one layer. Sprinkle with ⅓ cup sugar, Madeira, and lemon juice. Bake about 30 minutes, basting twice—the apricots will look cooked, and the plums should have started to split their skins. Remove and let cool 5 minutes or so.

Lift fruit out of the pan with a slotted spoon and place in a 9-inch round cake pan. Beat eggs with ¼ cup sugar and flour, then beat in cream, a few scrapes of nutmeg, and vanilla. Pour over fruit. Turn heat down to 350 degrees and bake another 20 minutes, or until the custard is set. Dust with powdered sugar. Serve warm, with the cooking juices from the fruit as a sauce.

Fresh Fig and Raspberry Clafouti

1 pound ripe fresh figs
½ cup raspberries
¼ cup blanched almonds
2 tablespoons flour
¾ cup milk
½ cup sugar
2 large eggs
1 tablespoon brandy or kirsch
Pinch of salt
2 tablespoons butter

SERVES 4 TO 6

A CLAFOUTI IS A LIMOUSIN DISH usually made with cherries and baked in a sort of pancake batter. This is much more elegant, with a more delicate batter and dazzling fruits. If you can't get fresh figs, I find the dark purple Italian plums work almost as well. As the dessert should be warm, you can assemble the dish ahead, except for the final sprinkle of sugar, and then pop it in the oven to cook while you serve the rest of the meal.

Preheat oven to 375 degrees. Stem figs and cut in half from top to bottom. Arrange in a buttered glass or ceramic pie dish so they make concentric circles. Scatter raspberries around them. Put almonds and flour in a food processor and whirl until finely ground. Add milk, ⅓ cup of sugar, eggs, brandy, and salt. Process for a minute, then pour over the fruit. Dot with butter cut into small pieces, and sprinkle with remaining sugar.

Bake 30 to 35 minutes, or until the top is puffed, crusty, and slightly golden. Serve warm.

Thomas Keller's Warm Chocolate "Tarts"

4 ounces bittersweet or semi-sweet chocolate

1½ ounces unsweetened chocolate

10 tablespoons unsalted butter

½ cup plus 2 tablespoons sugar

½ cup plus 2 teaspoons flour

1½ tablespoons unsweetened cocoa

¾ teaspoon baking powder

3 large eggs

SERVES 6

CHEF KELLER OF NEW YORK'S RAKEL *has invented one of the best chocolate desserts of all time with this recipe, uncovered by food writer Richard Sax. It is simplicity itself to cook these "tarts" with a warm cakelike exterior and a melting chocolate center, after you've cleared the dinner plates. Keller serves them with poached pears, and a cold pear puree, but that's gilding a very fine lily indeed. I like to keep them in the freezer for a quick dessert any time.*

Lightly butter six 1-cup soufflé dishes or custard cups. Melt both chocolates with butter in the top of a double boiler set over simmering water. Stir in sugar until it dissolves. Scrape into the bowl of a mixer. Add flour, cocoa, baking powder, and eggs. Beat 7 to 8 minutes, or until it thickens almost to a mousselike consistency. Divide among dishes, cover with foil, and freeze at least 3 hours.

To continue, preheat oven to 375 degrees. Remove covering from the dishes and bake 11 to 13 minutes. (Keller says 11, but I use perhaps heavier glass dishes, and it takes me 13.) It's easy to tell when they are done: First the edges set, then the center shows moist and shiny, and then just a minute after that they are cooked. Don't overbake. Cool 10 minutes, then invert onto dessert plates. Serve immediately with vanilla ice cream.

Chocolate-Raspberry Cake

3 ounces unsweetened baking
  chocolate
¼ cup water
12 tablespoons unsalted butter
3 eggs, separated
¼ cup flour
½ cup sugar
3 tablespoons strained raspberry jam
1 teaspoon vanilla
1 10-ounce package frozen
  raspberries in syrup,
  thawed
1 cup heavy cream
¼ cup powdered sugar

SERVES 6

NOWADAYS EVERY RESTAURANT HAS its "flourless" chocolate cake, but this one from Linda Pearl has been kicking around since the sixties—and no wonder! It's one of those recipes you can't not give out. It's worth looking up a mold for, even if you're not going to make an aspic ring or molded Jello salad. Since they're not used much any more, it's easy to find one at a flea market for pennies, though they are to be had in the hardware store, I suppose.

Preheat oven to 375 degrees. Melt chocolate, water, and butter in the top of a double boiler set over simmering water. Remove and let cool 5 minutes. Beat in 1 egg yolk at a time, then stir in flour, sugar, jam, and vanilla. Beat egg whites until just stiff and fold them into the chocolate mixture.

Butter an 8-inch ring mold (the kind your mother used to make Jello or aspic rings in) with a 4-inch center hole and pour batter into it. Place in another pan, a 9-inch cake pan is best, and pour boiling water through the center hole until it comes halfway up the sides. Bake 50 to 60 minutes, or until springy and shrinking from the edge of the mold. Cool 5 minutes, then turn out onto a serving platter.

Meanwhile, put raspberries through a ricer into a bowl, or whirl in a food processor and force through a sieve to remove the seeds. Chill.

At serving time, whip cream and add powdered sugar, then fill the center of the cake with it. Drizzle some of the raspberry *coulis* over the top and serve the rest separately in a bowl.

Apricot–Cream Cheese Cake

1 8-ounce package cream
  cheese, at room temperature
4 tablespoons unsalted butter,
  at room temperature
½ cup sugar
1 large egg
½ teaspoon vanilla
1 cup flour
½ teaspoon baking powder
½ teaspoon baking soda
Pinch of salt
2 tablespoons milk
½ cup apricot preserves
1 cup powdered sugar
1 tablespoon kirsch (or milk)
16 whole pecans

SERVES 6 TO 8

ONE OF MY FAVORITE cakes of all—rich, moist, very suave—and the icing is incredible! I once had a guest say, "This is one of the best cakes I've ever had from a bakery, where do you get it?"

Preheat oven to 350 degrees. Put half the cheese and butter in the bowl of a mixer and beat until light and fluffy. Add sugar bit by bit, beating continuously, then beat in egg and vanilla. Sift flour with baking powder, soda, and salt. Beat it in along with milk.

Butter and flour an 8-inch cake pan, shaking out excess flour. Spread half the batter in the bottom of the cake pan. Spread preserves over, up to about a quarter of an inch from the sides. Drop the rest of the batter by a spoon evenly over the preserves, then spread it carefully over with a spatula or knife. The preserves should all be well covered. Bake 25 to 30 minutes or until springy to the touch. Cool on a cake rack to room temperature. Remove from the pan.

To make the frosting, beat the remaining cream cheese until light. Sift the powdered sugar and beat it in gradually, then add kirsch. Spread over the top and sides of the cake. Decorate the rim with a round of nuts.

Pineapple–Macadamia Nut Cake

4 tablespoons butter, at room
    temperature
½ cup sugar
1 large egg
½ teaspoon vanilla
1 cup flour
½ teaspoon baking powder
½ teaspoon baking soda
Pinch of salt
½ cup sour cream
1 8-ounce can pineapple rings
⅔ cup macadamia nuts
    (preferably unsalted)
¾ cup powdered sugar

SERVES 6 TO 8

THIS IS BASED ON A CAKE I used to get from a mail-order company every Christmas, just for myself alone. Theirs was done with candied pineapple, but in testing I found market pineapple had almost no flavor but corn syrup, and I also found making pineapple glacé a bore. So I tried the stuff just as it comes from the can, and—lo and behold—it was much better than the mail order! It is so rich and moist it will last several days, covered, at room temperature.

Preheat oven to 350 degrees. Cream butter until light, then add sugar bit by bit as you beat. Beat in egg, then vanilla. Sift flour with baking powder, soda and salt and stir it in alternately with the sour cream. Take out 3 rings of pineapple (reserving the rest and the juice) and cut into ¼-inch wedges. Fold them by hand into the batter. If the nuts are salted, put them in a sieve and run under water, then drain on paper towels. While still on the towels, take a small knife and cut each whole nut into quarters—macadamias are very pesky nuts to chop, as they roll like marbles. Fold them by hand into the batter. Butter and flour an 8-inch round cake pan, shake out excess flour, and smooth the batter into the pan.

    Bake 30 minutes, or until springy and a toothpick inserted toward the middle comes out clean. Let cool and remove from the pan. Stir powdered sugar with just enough of the pineapple juice to make a glaze, then frost the top of the cake, letting it drizzle down the sides. Cut the remaining rings of pineapple into ½-inch wedges, pat dry with paper towels, and decorate the rim of the cake with a round of them.

Brandied Cherry Cake

½ cup butter
3 large egg yolks
¾ cup sugar
¾ teaspoon baking soda
½ cup buttermilk
1 cup flour, plus extra for
    coating cherries
1 teaspoon vanilla
⅔ cup brandied cherries, in
    their brandy
½ cup pecans, coarsely
    chopped
24 brandied cherries for the
    top
¾ cup powdered sugar
12 whole pecans for the top

SERVES 6 TO 8

I'VE NEVER UNDERSTOOD why fresh sour cherries are no longer in the market, keeping us from getting cherry pies like I knew in my youth. Some enterprising Wisconsin growers, however, are now drying them, sugaring them lightly, and marketing them like raisins. Eating them out of hand is a joy, but I also like to buy a quantity and place them in a jar with a little sugar and enough brandy to cover, and within a week you have brandied cherries in the refrigerator. They are superb in cakes or cookies where you would ordinarily use raisins or prunes. Hunt them out, or ask your market. The store I get them in can hardly keep them on the shelf, because the employees snack on them all day.

Preheat oven to 325 degrees. Melt butter in a small saucepan and let cool 5 minutes. Beat egg yolks with sugar until light and thick. Dissolve soda in buttermilk and add it alternately with flour. Stir in vanilla and 1 tablespoon of brandy from the cherries. Drain cherries and pat dry with paper towels. Place in a bowl and stir in a little flour to coat. Put in a sieve and shake to rid them of excess flour (this coating keeps them from sinking to the bottom of the cake during baking), then mix along with pecans into batter by hand. Butter and flour a 9-inch cake pan, tapping out the excess flour. Smooth the batter in and bake 30 to 35 minutes, or until golden on top and a toothpick inserted in the center tests clean. Cool on a rack.

While the cake bakes, put a couple dozen of the largest cherries in a small saucepan with enough of their brandy to cover. Bring just to a boil, cover the pan, remove from the heat, and let sit to plump up. Remove cake from the pan and place on a sheet of wax paper. Mix powdered sugar with just enough brandy from the cherries to make a glaze, then ice the top of the cake, letting it drizzle down the sides. Decorate with drained plumped cherries and whole pecans.

Lemon-Almond Cake

1 cup blanched almonds plus
   12 for decoration
1 cup sugar
1 cup unsalted butter, at
   room temperature
4 large eggs
1 tablespoon grated lemon
   rind
1 cup flour
1 teaspoon baking powder
Pinch of salt
½ cup lemon juice
2 cups powdered sugar

SERVES 8

I HAVE TRIED A LOT of lemon cakes, but this rich, moist confection is tops in my estimation.

Preheat oven to 350 degrees. Put the almonds and sugar in a food processor and whirl until very fine. Cream butter until fluffy, then beat in the almond mixture until light. Add 1 egg at a time, beating after each addition. Stir in lemon rind. Sift flour with baking powder and salt and add alternately with ¼ cup of lemon juice, blending well in between.

Pour batter into a buttered and floured 9-inch cake pan and bake 40 minutes, or until springy on top and a toothpick inserted in the center comes out clean. Let cake cool about 10 minutes, then turn it out and cool to room temperature.

To make the glaze, put the remaining lemon juice in a small bowl and sift the sugar over it gradually, whisking smooth as you go. Pour this glaze over the top of the cake, smoothing it well and letting it drizzle down the sides. Place a ring of almonds around the edge of the cake.

Walnut-Orange Rum Cake

¾ cup butter, at room
  temperature
1¾ cups sugar
3 large eggs
1 cup sifted flour
1½ teaspoons baking powder
½ teaspoon cinnamon
¼ teaspoon nutmeg
¼ cup milk
1 teaspoon grated orange rind
1 cup walnuts, finely chopped
⅓ cup orange juice
¼ cup rum

SERVES 10 TO 12

WHAT I CALL "BOOZE CAKES" have become popular these last few years, and no wonder, for they are as rich as all-get-out and can last for a week or more, getting better and better. This is one I've cooked for years with enjoyment from friends and relatives and neighbors.

Preheat oven to 350 degrees. Cream butter and ¾ cup of sugar until light and fluffy. Add 1 egg at a time, beating after each addition. Sift flour, baking powder, and spices together. Beat them into the mixture alternately with milk. Stir in orange rind and nuts. Butter and flour an 8-x-8-inch square pan and spread the batter in.

Bake 40 to 45 minutes, or until the top of the cake is springy. While it bakes, combine the remaining sugar and orange juice in a saucepan. Bring to a boil, reduce heat, and simmer 5 to 6 minutes, then stir in the rum.

Remove cake from the oven and let rest a few minutes, then prick all over with a toothpick. Pour the syrup over the warm cake until it is all absorbed. Serve warm or at room temperature.

Ginger-Pear Cake

1½ cups sugar
3 cups water
1 tablespoon lemon juice
3 large pears
½ cup blanched almonds
¼ cup flour
1 teaspoon baking powder
½ teaspoon ground ginger
2 tablespoons sliced
   crystallized ginger
2 large eggs
5 tablespoons butter, melted

SERVES 6

MORE PEARS THAN CAKE, really. This is not only delicious, but it is also very easily put together with a few flicks of a food processor.

Preheat oven to 325 degrees. Put ¾ cup of sugar in a large saucepan with water and lemon juice. Set it over medium-high heat and let come to a boil. Meanwhile peel and stem the pears, cut in half, and scoop out the seeds, dropping them into the sugar syrup as you go so they won't darken. Cook pears until just tender when a small, sharp knife is slipped in them. The time will depend on the ripeness of the pears—and fairly hard winter pears are excellent here. When done, drain the pears and place cut side down and small ends to the center in a buttered 9-inch cake pan.

Put almonds, flour, baking powder, and ground ginger in a food processor and whirl until fine. Add the crystallized ginger and process with an on/off motion until the ginger is minced. Scoop out the mixture into a bowl. Add eggs and remaining sugar to the food processor. Mix well, then add butter and mix again. Add the flour mixture and process just until the flour disappears. Pour this batter over the pears, making sure they are well coated.

Bake about 40 minutes, or until golden brown and slightly crusty on top. Remove and let cool at least 10 minutes. This cake is best served warm, with whipped cream, but room temperature is just fine.

Pistachio Cake

A LOVELY GREENY CAKE with a breathtaking flavor. Serve with plain whipped cream, or even pistachio ice cream.

1 8-ounce package cream
  cheese, at room temperature
4 tablespoons unsalted butter,
  at room temperature
½ cup sugar
1 cup shelled, unsalted
  pistachios
1 large egg
1 cup flour
½ teaspoon baking powder
½ teaspoon baking soda
Pinch of salt
½ cup milk
1 cup powdered sugar
1 tablespoon kirsch

SERVES 6 TO 8

Preheat oven to 350 degrees. Put half the cheese and butter in the bowl of a mixer and beat until light and fluffy. Put sugar with ¾ cup of nuts in a food processor and whirl with an on/off motion until the nuts are finely chopped—they don't have to be ground, but make sure there aren't any large pieces. Add this to the cheese-butter mixture, stirring well. Add egg and beat until it is incorporated. Sift flour with baking powder, soda, and salt. Add it to the mixture alternately with milk.

Butter and flour an 8-inch cake pan, tapping out the excess flour. Pour the batter into the pan and smooth well. Bake 30 minutes, or until golden brown and a toothpick inserted in the middle comes out clean. Let cool to room temperature.

Run a knife around the cake and unmold it onto a sheet of wax paper. Beat remaining cheese until light. Sift powdered sugar over it and beat until smooth. Mix in kirsch. Ice the cake with this, top and sides. Chop remaining nuts coarsely and sprinkle evenly over the top. With a spatula lift the cake off paper onto a serving plate.

Toffee Cake

1 cup flour
1 cup light brown sugar,
    packed down
5 tablespoons butter
½ cup buttermilk
1 large egg
½ teaspoon baking soda
½ teaspoon vanilla
3 1.2-ounce Heath Bars (or 4
    ounces homemade toffee)
¼ cup slivered almonds,
    lightly toasted

SERVES 8

THIS CAKE IS FOR THOSE who like rich, scrumptious crunchabilities.

Preheat oven to 350 degrees. Put flour and brown sugar in a food processor and whirl with on/off motion until any large pieces in the sugar are broken up. Slice off 4 tablespoons of butter into the mixture and process until it looks like coarse meal. Measure out ½ cup of this to a bowl and reserve. Pour buttermilk into a cup measure and stir in egg, soda, and vanilla. Add to the food processor and process for 1 minute. Don't worry if the butter is still in tiny pieces. Butter and flour a 9-inch cake pan, tapping out excess flour. Pour the mixture into the pan.

Break up toffee with your hands, then chop with nuts until all the large pieces are broken. Add this, the reserved mixture, and remaining butter to the cleaned bowl of the food processor and pulse a few times to make a very coarse mixture (just don't have any ¼-inch pieces of toffee left.) Sprinkle this over the cake.

Bake 30 to 35 minutes, or until cake is golden brown and springy to a touch. Remove from the oven, let cool 10 minutes, then slice and serve. It's best warm, but also fine at room temperature.

Bordeaux Torte

3 egg whites, at room temperature
½ cup sugar
½ teaspoon vanilla
1 package Pepperidge Farm Bordeaux Cookies
¾ cup coarsely chopped walnuts
1 teaspoon baking powder
1 cup heavy cream, whipped

SERVES 6

I GOT THIS RECIPE from a southern cook who used a package of Nabisco Chocolate Wafers, and though of an intriguing consistency, both crisp and moist-chewy, it had a rather blah flavor. To remedy this, I thought to substitute one of Pepperidge Farm's most delicious productions. The result, I think you'll agree, is not only one of the easiest desserts imaginable, but also one that you could serve the most discriminating diner. I do think, however, Pepperidge Farm ought to give me a commission.

Preheat oven to 325 degrees. Butter an 8-inch cake pan (or pie plate). Beat egg whites until they make soft peaks, then add sugar bit by bit as you whip, until you have a stiff meringue. Beat in vanilla. Break cookies up with your hands into about ½-inch pieces. Place in a bowl with nuts and baking powder and stir to mix. Fold gently into the meringue. Smooth mixture in the prepared pan.

Bake the torte for 35 minutes, then remove from the oven and let cool to room temperature. Serve with whipped cream, or if you wish with a custard sauce made with the 3 yolks, 1¼ cups hot milk, ¼ cup sugar, and ½ teaspoon vanilla.

Chocolate–Grand Marnier Torte

1¼ cups blanched almonds

8 ounces semisweet chocolate

¼ pound butter, at room temperature, plus more for greasing pan

1 cup sugar

3 large eggs

3 large oranges (peel only)

¼ cup very fine, freshly made bread crumbs (see page 325)

2 tablespoons Grand Marnier

⅓ cup heavy cream

SERVES 8 TO 10

THIS IS QUITE A PRODUCTION, but your guests will deem you worthy of the best confectioners, and your chocoholic friends will snatch what's left.

Preheat oven to 375 degrees. Butter the bottom and sides of an 8-inch cake pan. Cut out a circle of wax paper using the bottom of the pan as a guide. Fit it in the bottom and butter it also. Finely grind nuts in a blender or food processor—a blender does a better job, but you can do it with a processor. Simply put the nuts through a sieve, then grind what won't go through. They should be as fine as possible. Melt half the chocolate in a double boiler over hot, but not boiling, water. Cream butter until light and fluffy and add ⅔ cup of sugar gradually while beating. Add 1 egg at a time, then stir in melted chocolate. Grate the zest of 1 orange and stir it in with nuts and bread crumbs.

Pour batter in the pan, smooth the top, and bake 25 minutes. Let cool 30 minutes. Run a spatula around the edge and turn cake out upside down. Peel paper off and drizzle 1 tablespoon Grand Marnier over.

While the cake bakes, peel strips from remaining oranges with a swivel vegetable peeler. Cut into strips as fine as a toothpick. Drop into a pan of boiling water and simmer 10 minutes. Drain, run under cold water, and pat dry with paper towels. Add remaining sugar to the saucepan with ¼ cup water and bring to a boil. Cook over medium-high heat until the syrup registers 230 degrees on a candy thermometer, or until it spins a thread when you drop a small amount into a cup of cold water. Drop in orange peel and let sit 30 minutes.

To make the icing, melt remaining chocolate in the top of the double boiler. Stir smooth. Remove from the heat and stir in cream. Discard the hot water and fill the bottom of the double boiler with ice water. Stir until slightly thickened, then stir in remaining Grand Marnier. Ice the cake with this, smoothing over the top and running a spatula around the sides to form an even covering. Drain the candied orange peel and sprinkle over the cake. Refrigerate until the icing is quite firm.

White Chocolate–Almond Cake

½ cup slivered almonds
4 tablespoons unsalted butter,
    at room temperature
½ cup sugar
1 large egg
1 cup flour
½ teaspoon baking powder
½ teaspoon baking soda
Pinch of salt
½ cup sour cream
½ teaspoon almond extract
6 ounces white chocolate
3 tablespoons cream

SERVES 6 TO 8

IT TOOK ME A WHILE to get this one just right, but the abandoned trials were worth it. I have a neighbor who even liked those! I once asked Marion Cunningham what she did with all her baking tests, and she said she had neighbors with lots of kids she gave them to, but that she had begun to notice they were putting on a little weight she felt guilty about—and even the dog was fat.

Preheat oven to 350 degrees. Butter and flour an 8-inch cake pan, tapping out excess flour. Place almonds in a baking dish and put in the oven while it heats. When they are lightly toasted, remove—they should not brown, but only take on an ivory color. Beat butter until fluffy, add sugar bit by bit, and then beat in egg. Sift flour with baking powder, soda, and salt. Add it alternately with sour cream. Stir in almond extract.

Cut 4 ounces of white chocolate into pieces about the size of a peanut. Stir into the batter along with the cooled nuts. Place in prepared cake pan and smooth top. Bake 30 to 35 minutes, or until the top of the cake is golden and springy (the toothpick test will not work here because of the melted chocolate). Remove from oven and let cool to room temperature. Run a knife around the cake and remove from the pan to a sheet of wax paper.

Cut up remaining chocolate and melt in the top of a double boiler over hot water, along with the cream. Stir until melted and smooth, then drizzle with a large spoon in ribbons over the top and sides of the cake.

Aunt Marie's Rum Cake

3 large eggs
1¾ cups sugar
3 tablespoons lemon juice
1 teaspoon grated lemon peel
1 cup flour
1½ teaspoons baking powder
Pinch of salt
2 teaspoons vanilla
½ cup dark rum
2 tablespoons plain gelatin
2 cups milk
3 egg yolks
1 cup heavy cream
12 to 16 pecans

SERVES 10 TO 12

THIS IS AN HEIRLOOM RECIPE which has passed through a friend's family for four generations, and one can well imagine why. It is easy, delicious, and makes a festive presentation. The original recipe did not sprinkle rum on the cake, but I like it a little rummier. It also included maraschino cherries in place of the whole nuts on top of the cake, but pretty as they are, I find them inedible.

Preheat oven to 350 degrees. Coat a springform pan with vegetable spray or butter or oil. (The usual springform pan is 9 to 9½ inches wide and 3 inches high. This cake is made for a larger pan, so if you have only the regular one, simply discard ½ cup of the cake mixture before you bake it, and then use as much of the topping as will fit.)

Beat the whole eggs well, then gradually add 1 cup of sugar. Beat until thick and light colored. Add lemon juice and lemon peel. Sift flour with baking powder and salt and beat it in. Stir in vanilla. Scrape the mixture into the pan and bake 20 to 25 minutes, or until the cake has started to shrink from the edges of the pan and a toothpick inserted in the center comes out clean. Let sit 5 minutes, then sprinkle with half the rum. Cool the cake completely.

While cake cools, soften gelatin in ¼ cup water. Heat the milk in a saucepan, then stir in gelatin until it melts thoroughly. Stir in remaining sugar and let the mixture heat without coming to a boil. Beat egg yolks well and pour the milk mixture into them gradually. Pour through a sieve into a bowl, then stir in the rest of the rum. Refrigerate until it becomes syrupy—about an hour.

Whip cream stiff and fold into the chilled gelatin cream. Pour over the cake and refrigerate until it begins to set well. Make a ring of nuts around the edge of the cake, then coarsely chop a few more nuts to sprinkle the middle of it well. Cover with plastic wrap and refrigerate for an hour or more. The cake can be made the evening before, if you wish. To serve, unpin the edge of the pan and transfer the cake to a platter.

Tiramisu

Sponge Cake
2 large eggs, separated
½ cup sugar
2 tablespoons boiling water
1 tablespoon lemon juice
½ cup presifted cake flour
¾ teaspoon baking powder
Pinch of salt

Tiramisu
2 large egg yolks
½ cup sugar
1 pound mascarpone
1 teaspoon vanilla
4 tablespoons light rum
2 tablespoons heavy cream
½ cup freshly made espresso
   (or instant)

Topping
¼ cup unsweetened cocoa

SERVES 8 TO 10

IF YOU CAN FIND a good, light loaf cake in a bakery, this is one of the simplest and most beguiling desserts of all time. Tiramisu has swept the city restaurants by storm the last few years, though it is so new you won't find it in traditional Italian cookbooks. Some places use ladyfingers instead of cake, and some use coffee liqueur or brandy instead of rum, but whatever fillip or garnish, they all have coffee-soaked cake and melting cheese filling. Tiramisu seems to mean "pick me up," and rumor has it that it originated in the brothels of Venice as a kind of restorative, though no one mentions whether for the customers or the ladies. It certainly isn't light on calories, but your guests will call for seconds anyway.

To make the cake: Preheat oven to 350 degrees. Cut out wax paper to fit the bottom of a 9-x-5-inch loaf pan. Beat egg yolks until very light, then add sugar gradually, continuing to beat. Beat in water, then lemon juice. Sift flour again with baking powder and salt and add gradually. In another bowl, beat egg whites until stiff, but not dry, then fold gently into the yolk mixture. Pour into the pan and bake 25 to 30 minutes, or until a toothpick inserted in the center comes out clean. Cool the cake.

To make the Tiramisu: Whip egg yolks with ¼ cup of sugar until light and pale colored (this is important). Add mascarpone, vanilla, 2 tablespoons of rum, and cream and beat to mix well. Do not overbeat or the cheese will turn to butter. Stir remaining sugar and rum into hot coffee.

To assemble: Remove cake from the pan and cut with a serrated knife into 3 layers. Sprinkle layers with the rum-coffee mixture. Place the bottom layer back in the loaf pan and spread half the cheese mixture over. Top with the middle layer, then spread the rest of the cheese mixture over and add the top layer. Cover with wax paper or plastic wrap and set another loaf pan on top to lightly weight it down. Refrigerate several hours, then unmold and sift cocoa over. Serve in slices.

Hazelnut and Raspberry Meringue Cake

¾ cup hazelnuts
5 large egg whites, at room temperature
1¼ cups sugar
½ teaspoon vanilla
1 cup heavy cream
1 8-ounce package fresh raspberries
Powdered sugar

SERVES 8

THIS IS A GLORIOUS Austrian sweet, and unlike most of their tortes, it is quite easy to prepare. It is most definitely a cake for important occasions.

Preheat oven to 300 degrees. Bake nuts in a shallow pan 10 minutes, then remove and cool to room temperature. Put them in a food processor and whirl with the metal blade until finely chopped. Turn heat up to 350 degrees.

Line 2 9-inch round cake pans with circles of baking parchment (not wax paper). Beat egg whites stiff, then add sugar, bit by bit, as you continue to beat. The mixture should be very stiff and glossy. Fold in the nuts. Divide the mixture between pans, and swirl the top of one with a fork. Bake 35 to 40 minutes. Let cool to room temperature.

Whip cream until it holds a peak and add raspberries and sugar to taste—not too much, for the meringues are sweet. Remove meringues from the pans. Lay the unswirled one on a serving plate and spread raspberry cream over, then top with the swirled meringue. Sift a little more powdered sugar over the top. The cake can be assembled 1 or 2 hours ahead.

Chocolatissimo

10 tablespoons unsalted butter
½ cup sugar
12 ounces semisweet chocolate
1 tablespoon brandy
4 large eggs, separated, at
    room temperature
1 teaspoon vanilla
Pinch of salt
Powdered sugar

SERVES 8 (OR 4 AND 1
CHOCOHOLIC)

I FIND THIS every way superior to "Chocolate Decadance," which is so dense as to be often indigestible. This has a little less chocolate, and the whites are beaten as if for a soufflé, rendering a cake with a lightly crisp crust and an almost puddinglike center. I vote it perhaps the best chocolate dessert ever.

Make the cake a day ahead. Preheat oven to 425 degrees. Place butter and ¼ cup of sugar in a saucepan set over low heat. Stir until sugar dissolves, then add chocolate and let it melt. Stir until smooth, remove from heat, and stir in brandy. In a bowl, beat egg yolks until quite thick and pale, then stir in chocolate and vanilla. In another bowl, beat whites with salt until they hold soft peaks, then add the remaining sugar bit by bit. Fold one-third of the whites into chocolate mixture, then gently fold in the rest.

Butter a 9-inch springform pan with 2½-inch sides. Add some sugar to the pan and swirl to coat completely, then tap out any excess. Pour the mixture into the pan and bake 15 minutes, or until the top forms a crust but the center of the cake is still undercooked. Remove and let sit at room temperature overnight. Run a knife around the edge of the cake, then remove the sides of the springform. Put powdered sugar in a sieve and with your hands press through to sprinkle evenly over the top.

In Praise of Ingredients

Anchovies   Any way you look at it, recipes calling for a whole can of anchovies are suspect, and to buy one can for only two or three fillets makes for waste. A good solution is to keep a tube of anchovy paste in the refrigerator to spark a pasta sauce or give a hint of mystery to a salad dressing, if not, as their manufacturer intends, to be squeezed out in wiggles on canapes. You shouldn't have to visit a gourmet shop for this, either, as fine supermarkets carry anchovy paste these days.

Beef stock   Though good stock is the basis of the most exquisite sauces, hardly anyone keeps a stockpot on except restaurants. For home use, I usually open canned beef bouillon, which, if not ideal, is better than bouillon cubes. Don't be ashamed of it—I doubt even Julia Child always makes stock.

Bread crumbs   I find packaged bread crumbs akin to sawdust, and good fresh crumbs can make all the difference in a dish. It may be very little things which make a fine cook, but one is the secret of keeping a loaf of sliced homestyle bread in the freezer. Pepperidge Farm makes a particularly good one. These slices thaw in minutes, to be trimmed of crust and whirled in a food processor for superb crumbs. If a recipe calls for fine crumbs, you can dry these out in a very slow oven (they shouldn't brown) and then process again.

Butter   I would rather have a little butter than a lot of any substitute. Recently I was on an airplane that served up a sealed packet of something that had over a dozen unknown ingredients I can't imagine anyone ingesting. I haven't been overly fussy about calling for unsalted butter here, except in recipes that don't need any salt at all, but unsalted sweet butter is usually a better buy since it seems to be more delicate in flavor.

Capers About shopping for capers, I can say only there are two sizes: the BB's you see in ordinary stores, and those the size of a pea found in Italian and Greek markets. I tend to buy the giants since around the corner I can buy a bottle three times the size at a third the cost of supermarket varieties, but either are an essential to a fine refrigerator. I like their taste, their salty tart quality like a cliffside on the Mediterranean. Those who live by that sea use capers (possibly the world's best pickle) in moderation, as a last-minute garnish, or to spark the flavor of a bland sauce. Try chopping capers with garlic and parsley, and a smidge of grated lemon rind if you have it, to add in the final stir of a stew, and see why they are worth stocking for keeps.

Cheeses There is a joke in California about a town so backward they stock Velveeta on the Gourmet Shelf, and certainly we have progressed so much the last decade there is perhaps a book to be written about native cheeses alone. Still, most consumers have to be told that cheese should be at room temperature for tasting. Most British and French homes have a cool cupboard for storage—a benefit for any cheese not overripe. But if we do not have this amenity, we can at least take a cheese out of cold storage an hour or two before serving. Most recipes here calling for Parmesan can also be made with Romano or Asiago—either of which is better if you can't get the real Parmigiano-Reggiano. Buy any of these in chunks and grate fresh for every use, for even fine cheese dries out and loses flavor if pregrated and packaged. With a good grater it takes about 30 seconds to grate a cup of cheese. Many recipes here call for goat cheese (or chèvre), a relatively new experience for most Americans. Though there are now quite a few domestic goat cheeses of superior quality, the tip-top of the line remains French Montrachet, if you can find it. For cooking purposes make sure to buy a plain one, which will look like a creamy log, rather than the fancied-up varieties flavored with herbs, garlic, cracked pepper, and more.

Chicken stock Since I usually cut up my own chickens, I like to use the giblets (except the liver) and backs to make a stock. You simply put them in a pot (or better yet, a pressure cooker, which takes a fraction of the time) with a sliced onion and carrot and celery stalk, a tuft of parsley, clove of garlic, a good pinch of whole peppercorns, and either some basil, thyme, or summer savory (fresh or dried). Add water to cover, and simmer for a couple of hours (thirty minutes in a pressure cooker). I salt lightly toward the end, for sometimes you wish to reduce a stock. Strained and refrigerated until the fat can be lifted off the top, this can be frozen for further use. Also, I keep a bottle of Spice Islands Chicken Stock Base in the refrigerator, which is preferable to bouillon cubes, for times only a small amount of stock is needed.

Crème fraîche This is easily made at home by adding a tablespoon of buttermilk to a one-cup carton of heavy cream. The carton should then be closed and set in a warmish place (say, over the pilot light of your oven) until it thickens—a process that will take six hours or more. When thick, it can then be refrigerated, and it will last about a week. This is not to say you have exactly the crème fraîche you get in France, but it is as close as we can come.

Croûtes When a recipe here reads "toast" that is exactly what it means. Croûtes, on the other hand, are made from trimmed slices of homestyle white bread, brushed with either melted butter or olive oil, then toasted in a dry frying pan over medium-low heat until golden brown on both sides, then left to crisp a little in a low oven.

Garlic The best way to peel a clove of garlic is to lay it on the counter, then smack it deftly with the flat of a kitchen knife. The outer husk then peels off easily. I'm not a fan of garlic presses, which can extract some harsh oil which knifing never seems to do. It takes only a minute to mince.

Green peppercorns Unlike kiwi fruit and other culinary fads, these will surely remain a great culinary addition to our heritage. Theirs is a *fragrance* of hotness only—almost addictive as a last-minute addition to many a sauce. Those bottled in brine last best in the refrigerator.

Ham Good ham is becoming a luxury item these days, and by good ham I don't mean slices packaged in plastic, tinned ham, hams pumped up with water, or boneless hams. For very best flavor they should have a bone in. If you have a small family, these can be cut into pieces and frozen for future enjoyment.

Kirsch Many of the desserts here use this elect essence of cherries which can make the soul of a dish. Never bother with domestic kirsch, which has hardly any fragrance—always buy a French or German brand.

Lettuces The French term *mesclun*, for an assortment of tiny, tangy greens, is not to be found in earlier cookbooks. Even the precise Elizabeth David shirks it as something untranslatable, certainly not to be found in London's Soho. Now found nestled in bins at good supermarkets, legend has it that Alice Waters, for her new restaurant Chez Panisse, planted a garden of herbs and lettuces, and for the first time gave iceberg lettuce a run for the money in this country. An assortment of meaty arugula, crisp frisée, shreds of radicchio for color and bite, and young lettuces such as curly-leaf red or green, Bibb, red romaine, green Oak-leaf, bronze lettuce, and even tiny mustard—*mesclun* really redefines the term "green salad." Those without enterprising growers nearby might make a mix of their own with watercress, endive, and butterhead lettuce.

Madeira The best Madeira is dry Sercial, if you can find it. It's more expensive, but worth every drop. There are other brands of Madeira, of varying quality, but always make sure the label states that it is dry, for a sweetish one can really screw up a sauce.

Mayonnaise One of the best things in the world is a homemade mayonnaise, with a fine olive oil poured in, drop by drop, while you whisk. However, these days we are being warned more and more about raw eggs in preparations, and the risk of salmonella. To be on the safe side, purchase a good commercial mayonnaise—never use the sweetish products called "salad dressing" as a substitute for honest stuff.

Mushrooms Long gone are the days when any recipe would call automatically for canned button mushrooms. Fresh are found even in corner markets now. Unless gritty, they should never be washed, only brushed with a damp paper towel, and if possible buy them with the caps closed and with no browning at the cut stem. More and more we also get cultivated field mushrooms, and the ones I have used here are the most common: shiitake and oyster mushrooms, the first with a fine meaty flavor, and the other with a delicate elusive quality. Always cut off and discard the stems of shiitake mushrooms, as they are woody and inedible.

Nutmeg I've always suggested here you use freshly grated nutmeg. Unless you buy grated nutmeg in very small containers and use it up within a month or two, it loses flavor quickly.

Oils We now have a lot of choices in olive oils, from the greeny, cold-pressed oils, with a lot of fruity olive flavor, to more delicate honey-colored ones when you don't want to be that assertive. For cooking, or for simple vinaigrettes, you often don't want a cold-pressed oil. Remember also that the smaller the container, the more expensive the oil will come out to be. If you use a fair amount, buy it in a gallon tin at an Italian or Greek shop, and store in a cool place—it only gets rancid if too warm. Also in this book I have suggested here and there either a walnut or hazelnut oil—both to be found in gourmet shops, and both delicious to experiment with in fine salads. (I have a friend who swears by walnut oil in popping corn.)

Olives Specialty and ethnic markets have an array of different olives that makes one long to sample and compare. Sometimes one wants the dry, wrinkled, oil-cured Italian olives, and then again plump brine-cured Greek olives are the choice. My favorite Italian market makes their own huge, garlicky green olives which I like just to munch on straight from the refrigerator. The oil-cured Italian and Greek Kalamata are usually to be had everywhere, but when you can find other varieties, you might want to treat your guests to an olive-tasting cocktail party, sometime, to discover unknown subtleties and new textures.

Paprika Most Americans have a bottle of dusty paprika on the herb shelf, only used to give a blush to the top of a bland dish. Throw it out, I say, and get a tin of real Hungarian paprika (perhaps both sweet and hot) and use it for flavor!

Pine nuts These are also labeled pignoli or piñon nuts. They are most often marketed in small packets which have stayed too long on the shelf, and have an off-flavor. Pine nuts are harvested in the fall, and then is the time to get them sweet, in bulk, at your nearest health food store. They can then be frozen for future use in many a pleasant way. Try browning them lightly in butter, then toss with cooked rice, for a simple dish you and your family will want again and again.

Roasted peppers Most cookbooks tell you to roast peppers on a long fork over an open flame, until charred black all over, to remove the skins. This is fine, but tedious if you have more than one or two to prepare. For those with electric stoves it is usually suggested the peppers be done under a broiler, turning now and again, to make them come out evenly. This is also a bother—and sometimes a scorcher. On a hint from another cook, I recently tried broiling them sliced in half, which makes the whole process easier. Simply cut them vertically, leaving the seeds in, place cut side down on a sheet of foil, and then broil about three inches under the heat source. When blackened, slip the peppers into a plastic or paper bag and let steam fifteen minutes or so. Remove the seeds and scrape the skin off with a small knife—if necessary, brush any tenacious scraps off under a running faucet. The peppers are then ready to be used in any recipe calling for them.

Sesame seeds In most recipes these are called for "lightly toasted." To do this, put the seeds in a small, dry frying pan set over medium-low heat. Shake and stir the pan until they are lightly golden—this brings out their flavor admirably. Instead of garlic, sometime sprinkle sesame seeds over buttered French bread, before wrapping in foil and warming, or try tossing some with cooked rice for flavor and texture.

Shallots Without fuss, I have called for a shallot here, in recipes, as if they didn't differ quite a bit in size—some even double. Most of the time more or less won't make much difference, but if you want to be finicky I'd say one minced shallot equals about a tablespoon. They may seem expensive, but if you keep a supply on hand to experiment with in your favorite recipes, along with the garlic and/or onion, you'll find why they are becoming more and more popular in this country.

Tomato paste Like anchovy paste, it's good to know you have a tube in the refrigerator, when you want only a tablespoon or two in a recipe. As a plus these are usually imported from Italy, labeled "Double Concentrate," and have a superior flavor to domestic canned pastes.

Sun-dried tomatoes Bottled in savory oil, imported from Italy, these are a very expensive delicacy (though you usually use them in small quantities). However, I find plain dried tomatoes even in supermarkets these days, at about half the price. These can be made into about the same product, by tossing 1½ cups dried tomatoes with a tablespoon red wine vinegar, 2 tablespoons water or red wine, a teaspoon salt, a pinch of cayenne or a dash of Tabasco, about ¼ teaspoon dried thyme, and a bay leaf. Cover the container and shake it until the tomatoes are coated. Let stand overnight, turning the container a couple of times, until all the liquid is absorbed. Add olive oil to cover, and keep the container refrigerated for a week or so. Taste them, and if still not softened, warm slowly in the oil and refrigerate again. Anytime you use them you should use some of the tasty oil as well.

Although I've never done so, I've read that cherry tomatoes are easy to dry at home, by putting them cut side up on a greased cookie sheet, placing in a hot oven, then turning the heat off. Next day they should be done. Larger split Italian plum tomatoes are said to be done the same way in a two hundred-degree oven for about eight hours.

Vanilla Always buy real vanilla extract rather than artificial, and if you can find vanilla beans, keep one or two on hand, sealed in a jar. Their chaste but tropic aroma can perfume a whole apartment. To substitute a little scrape of the inside of the bean for extract can make the difference between fine and exquisite. The British always keep a canister of sugar with a vanilla bean nestled in it to perfume. The sugar is then used as usual in cakes and other sweets. This is also a fine way to stretch what is rather an expensive delicacy, since one bean can be used for rather a long time, with successive sugars until it dries out.

Vinaigrette I've never quite understood all those bottled dressings in the market, with the Lord knows what in them for preservation, and "flavor enhancers" which make rather an assault on the tastebuds. How long does it take to shake together a ½ cup good olive oil with 2 tablespoons wine vinegar, a ½ teaspoon Dijon-style mustard, salt and pepper, either some onion pulp or a smashed clove of garlic, and whatever herb you please? It also tastes better. Always, though, go easy on the vinegar, as a true vinaigrette is never sharp but always teases the palate.

Vinegars Like olive oils these days, there stands a great array of fine vinegars in the market. I always keep on hand a good red wine vinegar, white wine vinegar with tarragon, sherry vinegar, raspberry vinegar, and a balsamic vinegar for use. You can go all the gamut from blueberry to hot garlic, but that's like having too many gadgets in the kitchen.

Notes on Wine

by John Hartman

As WINE CONSUMPTION increases in America, we are receiving a much more varied selection of wines from abroad. If you're not familiar with these, seek out a good wine merchant and enjoy the experiment of tasting foreign vintages. For example, I very much enjoy Arnold Tudal's 1984 Napa Valley Cabernet Sauvignon which sells for $18.00. I would ask the merchant, What do you have that's ready to drink, as good or better, and from abroad?

Another example of how your merchant may be of value—years ago I stopped at a pricey wine shop in San Francisco and asked, What do you have for dessert wines? I was shown from a Château d'Yquem at $155.00 all the way to a Chenin Blanc at $8.95. I said, Chenin Blanc—that's a dry wine! The merchant gently replied, Sir this one has been made sweet. I left the shop with the Chenin Blanc and it was enjoyed by all with dessert.

ADDITIONAL ADVICE:

• If it's a special occasion and you can't decide which wine to choose, champagne is the answer. But never serve a cheap champagne (in 1990, less than $10.00).

• Serve only wines or beers that you've tasted and enjoy—ignore fad and fashion.

• Your refrigerator is not the place to store wine.

Wine matures best in a dark, cool (forty to fifty degrees Fahrenheit) and vibration-free place.

• Uncork full-bodied, mature, red or white wines one to two hours before serving and keep in a cool place (they deserve this honor).

• If you tell your wine merchant that you want the best Cabernet Sauvignon that he has, to serve to-night, and he points *only* to his most expensive wines, distrust him. Also, if his whole range of wines is suggested, remember at least a quarter of his stock should be laid down for time to come, not drunk that night.

• One of the rules of fine dining (and a sensible one, too) is that the progress of courses ought to be accompanied by a progression of wines: light to full bodied. For instance, you would not ordinarily choose a first course best with a red wine, followed by a main dish best with white. Any menu should be thought out, either with this in mind or with the same wine served throughout.

VARIETAL WINE NAMES:

• *Dry white wines* include Chablis, Chenin Blanc, Sauvignon Blanc, Columbard, or Johannisberg Riesling.

• *Fruity white wines* include Gewürztraminer, White Zinfandel, Fumé Blanc, Cabernet Blanc, Grenache Rosé, Rosé of Cabernet Sauvignon, or Gamay Beaujolais.

• *Full-bodied white wines* include Chardonnay or Pinot Blanc.

• *Medium-bodied red wines* include Merlot, Petit Sirah, Carignane, or Grignolino.

• *Full-bodied, mature* (over five years bottle age) *red*

wines include Cabernet Sauvignon, Pinot Noir, Sirah, Barbera, Aleatico, Zinfandel, or a Bordeaux-style blend.

(John Hartman is a gourmet, superb cook, and an award-winning home wine maker.)

Index

sauce, catfish with, 86
sauce, pork loin with, 125

noodles, puffed, leeks with, 194
nut(s):
avocados with pistachios, 23
see also almond(s); hazelnut(s); pecans; pine nuts; pistachio(s); walnut(s)
nutmeg, 330

oils, 330
olive(s), 330–31
onions and zucchini à la grecque, 53
olive(s), black:
baked feta cheese with red peppers and basil, 34
blue cheese, cauliflower, and watercress, 26
caponata in red pepper shells, 24
fresh tuna with tapenade, 80
and orange salad with red onion rings, 54
sauce, broccoli with, 179
olives, green:
caponata in red pepper shells, 24
chicken with pine nuts and, 150
onion(s):
Cassis, swordfish with, 82
flan (Queen Mary), 248
green, orzo with parsley and, 199
and zucchini à la grecque, 53
onions, red:
rings, orange and olive salad with, 54
sweet-sour, 198
orange(s):
cream tart, 289
custards orangerie, 282
marinated in pomegranate juice, 265

and olive salad with red onion rings, 54
pork chops with, 129
walnut rum cake, 314
orzo with green onions and parsley, 199
oysters:
fish fillets ubriacati, 76
fried with crab, 56
on the half shell, 55

paprika, 331
and sage cream, pork chops with, 131
shrimps Waldorf, 96
Parmesan, 326–27
asparagus and prosciutto, 19
asparagus with two cheeses, 18
Bookbinder potatoes, 233
braised fennel, 193
cauliflower with browned butter and, 187
celery, and mushroom salad, 29
cream, Brussels sprouts in, 182
gratin of fennel, 246
green beans, 169
Italian turkey scallops, 160
mushrooms stuffed with pine nuts, 196
my mother's creamed potatoes, 235
pesto, 95
pork cutlets milanaise, 123
Queen Mary (onion flan), 248
salad with sautéed shiitake mushrooms, 60
scalloped scallops, 92
shrimp crostini, 64
Simpson's jellied cheese, 31
stuffed artichokes, 16
zucchini-stuffed baked potatoes, 232
see also sformati
Parmigiano-Reggiano, 326–27
parsley:
chicken sauté with *fines herbes*, 146

orzo with green onions and, 199
sage, rosemary, and thyme roast chicken, 142
shallot butter, fried potatoes with, 222
pâté:
chicken liver, 35
de foie gras, shiitake mushrooms with, 197
smoked salmon, with radishes, 62
peach(es):
fruit crumble tart, 293
Melba, 268
meringues, 266
ricotta tart with, 302
pear(s):
almond tart, 292
baked in red wine, 269
in butter sauce, 267
with chestnut cream, poached, 270
fruit crumble tart, 293
ginger cake, 315
peas:
braised with cucumbers, 201
garden, 200
with prosciutto, fresh, 57
sformato with lettuce and, 251
snow, with tree oyster mushrooms, 202
pecans:
apricot cream cheese cake, 310
brandied cherry cake, 312
chicken breasts with Madeira and, 156
grape tart with cookie crust, 303
my warm cherry tarts, 296
rum nut tart, 291
pepper(s), red:
baked feta cheese with basil and, 34
butter, lamb chops with, 119
butter, potatoes in, 228
gratin, 241